D083663

THE FIRST TRIAL

Where Do I Sit?
What Do I Say?

IN A NUTSHELL

SECOND EDITION

By

STEVEN H. GOLDBERG

Professor of Law
Pace University School of Law

TRACY WALTERS McCORMACK

Director of Advocacy
University of Texas School of Law

WEST®

A Thomson Reuters business

Mat #13349126

COPYRIGHT © 1982 WEST PUBLISHING CO.
© 2009 Thomson/Reuters
610 Opperman Drive
St. Paul, MN 55123
1–800–313–9378

Printed in the United States of America

ISBN: 978–0–314–21159–0

TEXT IS PRINTED ON 10% POST CONSUMER RECYCLED PAPER

For Julia

— SHG

To my family and teachers.
Thanks for sharing your knowledge,
passion and wisdom.

— TWM

*

PREFACE TO THE FIRST EDITION

---

*I needed this book for my first trial
and couldn't find it!*

Just before my first trial, I would have killed for a short book that told me enough about trial to help me figure out where to sit, what to say when the judge said, "Mr. Goldberg, you may inquire," and how to tell the jury that I was finished talking. I found books in the library that told me more than I wanted—not needed, wanted—to know about being a trial lawyer. Most of the books had answers that I did not quite understand, to questions that I had not even thought of, about subjects in which I had no immediate interest. I found books that told me about investigation, tricks of discovery, socio-psychological jury selections, and the like. I could not find one little book that had lots about where to sit, who to talk to, and how to say it without looking foolish. Following my forefathers (at that time there were hardly any foremothers) at the bar, I learned where to sit and what to say as I was sitting and saying at my first trial, without the foggiest notion of whether it was proper, let alone effective. By the time I had three or four trials behind me, I began to think of the questions and appreciate the answers in most of those books on the library shelves, forgetting the mayhem I was prepared to commit to obtain the little book about "Where do I sit?" and "What do

I say?" Those burning questions of my inexperience faded from memory—until I taught my first semester of Trial Advocacy.

It was not until the middle of that first semester of discussion about sophisticated fact analysis and subtle trial persuasion that a student had the good sense to interrupt my discourse with a simple question. It was followed by a flood of simple questions—questions that rang a faint but familiar chord: Where do I sit? What do I say when . . .? Who marks the exhibits? Do I have to go to the bench for that? Why can't I draw the diagram myself? Where do I stand when I talk to the jury? The questions and the anxious looks made me remember what I had been willing to do before my first trial for a book with the answers to the simple questions.

This little book is a primer for beginning students of trial advocacy and those few unfortunate graduates without a law school forum in which to mess up their first trial. It contains rules and reasons that anyone can apply to the conduct of that first trial. The rules will help, but the reasons are the most important. It is a simple book of limited value. The simplicity is both the value and the limitation.

There is not a single new idea between these covers. The techniques discussed have been discovered, tested, and well preserved by generations of successful trial advocates. If you take the time to remember the rules and understand the reasons, you will approach your first trial feeling confident that you can proceed from one end of it to the other without looking or feeling inadequate. That's it for the value.

The dictionary says that a primer is a short introductory book. This book is so introductory that it will not be of any value after your first trial—certainly not after your third. That's the limitation. You must understand it in order to get the maximum value from this book. This book teaches technique, not art. Technique will get you through your first trial or two. It you want to go further you must learn the art of trial advocacy.

If you master the techniques in this primer and achieve that feeling of adequacy about your first trial, you will suffer under a bit of an illusion—an illusion that will make you feel good for the present, but will hurt you in the future if you do not remember that it is only an illusion. You will feel a whole lot better that you are. The art of trial advocacy, as practiced by the most accomplished trial artists, is very subtle. Unfortunately, those who have merely mastered the techniques needed for the appearance of adequacy in a courtroom are few in number. The result is that the latter are often mistaken for the former. Do not be fooled by your feeling of adequacy. You will not be a trial advocate just because you know where to sit, how to question a witness, how to address the court when making an objection, and how to get around the courtroom without falling on your face; anymore that you could claim to be an artist because you had learned how to hold a brush, mix the oils, and apply them to the canvas in a variety of strokes.

The rules you are about to learn will make you a technician, not an artist. They will not make you a winner, although they may save you from being the creator of your own losses. While not everyone has the creativity it takes to be a trial advocate, no one possesses enough creativity to be a trial advocate without first learning to be a trial technician. Everyone has the talent needed to apply every rule and understand every reason stated in the primer. Once you have done that, you will be prepared to do two things: (1) get around the courtroom during your first trial, and (2) determine whether you have talent to go on to a second trial.

Because techniques are the foundations of an art, there are two important aspects of this book. The first is perspective. It tells you how to view the second, the techniques. There will be a great temptation to skip the perspective and get right to the techniques. If you do, you will miss most of the value. How you look at something is at least as important as what you are looking at. Further, the reason for employing a technique is more important than the particular technique. The reason may serve you when the technique will not. If the situation in court is different from the situation for which the technique was developed, the reason for the technique will help you to devise your own technique for the new situation.

If this primer helps you in surviving your first trial, you, with me, owe a debt to Dean Robert A. Stein of the University of Minnesota, whose encouragement made a teacher of this lawyer; and to Margaret Osborn Keet, a fine Little Rock lawyer, whose suggestions and editing made a book of these trial notes.

STEVEN H. GOLDBERG

Little Rock, Arkansas
April, 1982

*

PREFACE TO THE SECOND EDITION

Tracy was luckier than Steve, by the time she came through law school the first classes in Trial Advocacy were being taught and national mock trial competitions gave students the chance to work with real trial lawyers to develop skills. Tracy had been taught where to sit, stand, how to make an opening statement and closing argument, how to argue objections and motions. She knew most of "what" to do, but not always "why" she was doing it. Her knowledge was also limited to mock cases and pretend judges, instead of real cases and juries. So she, too, followed the lead of the trial lawyers ahead of her. Fortunately, trials were a steady part of her diet. She got to go to trial often and had lots of variety in the type and magnitude of the cases she tried. In many ways her generation of lawyer had it easier than today's young trial lawyers, they had enough trials in which they could develop and hone their craft through experience. And they had great trial lawyers ahead of us that we could watch and ask.

Trials are not as plentiful today, so learning what to do and why you are doing it requires more effort. Now that Tracy is teaching, she tries to combine both the "what" and the "why" so that students can make more informed choices in their advocacy.

Tracy says the "what" is the easier part; it is the "why" that seems harder to find and is more helpful when found. So today we offer suggestions on how students can practice trial skills outside the courtroom. We look at the social sciences to borrow concepts that might help in our endeavor to persuade. In some ways it is harder to try cases now than it was 30 years ago. Judges and certainly juries are more diverse than ever in our history. Technology has radically changed the way people learn, transmit, and discover information. Generational differences can be more significant because of these cultural and technological changes. Attention spans are shorter and the ability to listen to a purely auditory message is more limited. All of this makes the trial lawyer's job more challenging.

So here you are, either beginning Trial Advocacy in law school or preparing for your first trial in practice. No matter what your age or years of experience your first trial is an extraordinary experience. It is daunting and exhilarating all at once. This book is meant to help you mesh both the "what" and the "why" so that you can get through your first few trials. We have tried to keep it simple and concrete enough to be a basic guide. Once you complete your first few trials you can continue exploring and learning how to be a better trial lawyer. You have to walk before you run. Clarence Darrow and every trial lawyer before and after had to try that scary first case. Your clients will be better served because you have learned how to try a case. Your discovery will be more efficient and effective, your settlements, mediations and arbitrations will be better because you know how to try cases. Clients deserve lawyers with a full compliment of tools to help solve their problems. Society deserves a judicial system with lawyers that have fundamental confidence in it and the knowledge to use and improve it. Trying cases is hard work; be proud of what you do and the role of lawyer in our world. Work hard at your craft even if you use the entire skill set rarely; watch and learn as often as you can. Read new materials and think about how you can use them to be a better communicator, persuader, and lawyer.

You will get the most from this book if you can read it straight through to get the big picture. The earlier before your Trial Advocacy course or your trial you can read the book the better. Whenever you read it, focus on the fundamental concepts of trial and keep what you do simple. This book is meant to help you take your "pre-trial" file of facts and turn it into a trial story. It gives you an approach to your first trial (and the ones following it) from organization of your notebook through closing argument. This is also a book to re-read before your fifth or your twentieth trial. It never hurts to refocus on your role as the director of the trial that is about to unfold before your juror audience.

In this edition, we have dealt with the changes in the law since the first edition written more than a quarter-century ago. To some extent, it proves the old adage that the more things change the more they stay the same. Technology is dramatically different than it was when the first edition was written, yet preparing to be a trial lawyer is much the same. The essential concerns of presenting your case to your jury are also the same. Lawyers, judges and jurors may look different than they did in 1981, but the fundamentals of persuasion are much the same. We hope you will find this primer useful to you whether you are getting ready for Trial Advocacy, preparing your first trial, or getting ready for your twentieth.

STEVEN H. GOLDBERG
White Plains, New York

TRACY WALTERS MCCORMACK
Austin, Texas

November, 2008

OUTLINE

THE FIRST TRIAL

TRIAL

Where Do I Sit?
What Do I Say?

IN A NUTSHELL

SECOND EDITION

*

PART I

PERSPECTIVE

Most of us had a better understanding of what a trial is all about before we entered law school than we do after a year or two of legal education. Before law school, most of us thought that trial was high drama, performed by giants, with the victory going to the most skilled. Some of us went to law school to become a courtroom giant. Others, thinking it an injustice that the skill of the lawyer might overcome the "truth" of what really happened, went to law school to change the system.

In the first year of law school, the giant seekers were disappointed and the truth seekers comforted by the revelation that the legal profession presides over a dispute resolution system bottomed upon the proposition that the "truth will out." Another two or three years of sweat over appellate opinions taught us that the legal system seeks "truth" through the mechanism of the trial. Armed with that understanding, we approach our first trial secure in the knowledge that if our client's cause is just, and if we have prepared the facts and the law, we will win.

We knew more about it when we thought it was drama.

1

"The truth will out"—the basic assumption of our legal system—is an absolute prerequisite to its survival. It is as important for contemporary society to believe that trial results reflect the truth as it was for past societies to have faith in the hot knife on the tongue, the ducking stool, or the joust as mechanisms for truth telling. Although the legal profession has a stake in the society's continuing faith that "truth" drives trial results, the trial lawyer cannot afford to indulge the myth. The lawyer who approaches the trial believing that only the "real truth" is needed to prevail will land on the same thing as the knight who, because the cause is just, approaches the joust without cinching the saddle.

The techniques of trial are not easily appreciated from the lawyer's perspective. They often seem trivial or fatuous in light of the understanding that everything will, after all, work out in the end. It is common to understand that once the lawyer's skills in investigation and discovery are exercised and all of the facts are in, nothing remains but for the witnesses to be sworn and testify, and for the jury to reach its decision. Trials, unfortunately, are not so simple. Some witnesses lie; some truthful witnesses appear to be lying; some lying witnesses appear to be telling the truth; some witnesses forget; some witnesses are not heard; some jurors do not listen; some lawyers make mistakes; some witnesses make mistakes; some judges make mistakes.

Only the jury is always right—whether it is or not.

Trial Is Theater

Trial is the presentation of an idea (why your client should win), to an audience (the jury), through the medium of performers. Because lawyers have a stake in the system, we do not like to say "trial is theater." We prefer to explain that a witness' demeanor is important, rather than to admit that it might be central and that a jury verdict can be as much the result of how the audience liked the play as it can be the result of a jury "compelled by the truth." "Trial is theater" raises the spectre of "pretend," with the implication that creativity, costuming, pace, and rehearsal may carry the day despite a contrary "truth."

But the courtroom is a theater and the trial is a play, even if the performers are called "witnesses.". "Truth"—what really happened—has no independent significance, because the jurors never see it happen. They hear about it, but the trial/play is what they see happen. The jurors' decision is going to be about what they see before them—the courtroom drama. We do not mean to suggest, and you should not adopt, the cynical view that the truth that you and your opponent have developed from investigation and discovery is irrelevant to the outcome. The "truth" you found is as relevant to the trial as a script is to the play. But as we all know, many a good script has been scuttled by a lousy production. The most important technique for a trial lawyer is to view the trial from the perspective of the director of a stage play. No theater director would miss understanding that the only "truth" is what the audience perceives. Too many lawyers, unfortunately, forget that it is what the jury sees, not what the lawyer knows, that counts. If lawyers viewed the trial from the perspective of a director, they would understand that a good script will not sell itself.

A few examples will make the point.

The lawyer will ask a witness, "Just tell us what happened, Mrs. Webb," and expect the narrative response to have an impact upon the jurors because it is the truth. (The lawyer's occasional interruption of, "and then," will prove that the lawyer is awake even if the jury is not.) The director knows that the long dissertation, alone, will hide the important details in a fog of undifferentiated facts.

Only a lawyer believing that "real events" have more to do with a jury verdict than the theater of the trial will cross examine a lying witness with the question: "Tell the jury how you can explain that, Mr. Benton?" The question will be accompanied by the lawyer's look of smugness that can arise only from a certain knowledge of the "real truth," and absolute faith that the "real truth" has been successfully conveyed to the jurors by the look on the lawyer's face. The director knows that the lawyer is going to get a response that puts the lying witness center stage to retell the direct examination in perfect detail, explaining why the testimony is believable, consistent, and inevitable.

The lawyer's failure to read stipulations to the jury, or have them before the jury in any other way, must come from that same crazy notion that something other than what the jury knows—the "real truth"—will decide the case. The director knows that the audience begins the play knowing nothing, and that all it will know at the end is what the director presents.

Lawyers often act as if they believe that the jurors will believe the "truth" when it is put before them, no matter how unpersuasively. Directors know that how something is presented is at least as important as what is presented. If you doubt the directors' wisdom, wait until your first unsuccessful impeachment of a lying witness. It will go something like this.

During direct testimony, the witness testifies that "the car was going twenty-five miles per hour." (During discovery, the witness had testified under oath to the "truth" that "the car was going forty.")

Now it is your turn to cross-examine. With that little gleam in your eye that tells the jury that you've caught the witness in a lie, you ask: "Do I understand you to say that the car was going only twenty-five miles per hour?"

"That's right," says the witness, "twenty-five miles per hour. Might have been twenty seven or eight, but not faster."

Now, because you have not properly indexed the deposition so that you can locate the damning contradiction, you hem and haw while you page through the deposition in desperate search for the "truth." People are starting to fidget in the jury box and at the counsel table, so you ask a couple of inane questions about what the witness was doing and where the witness was standing—all the time looking for that damning answer. You will find it immediately after the witness has made a reasonable explanation for the contradiction. The earlier statement, when you finally locate it, that the car was going "at least forty" is one explanation too late for you to bring it to the jurors' attention with any impact. The jury believes the witness' direct testimony because the "truth" is not what happened; it is how it was presented.

The director's perspective—that the trial is theater—is more useful for an understanding of what is going on with the jury than the lawyer's perspective—that the jury verdict is a reflection of the "truth." You need look no further than to the demeanor instruction that every judge gives to every jury at the end of every trial. With insignificant differences in the wording, judges tell jurors that they are the sole judges of the credibility of the witnesses, and that they *may* consider the witness' demeanor along with the other evidence in judging credibility.

The instruction reflects the lawyer's perspective that the words are the reflection of the truth, and that the manner of presentation is a separate, minor part of the equation, of which the jurors might take separate and conscious note. The instruction assumes that the jurors first consider all of the evidence that has been collected, collated, stapled, spindled, mutilated, and finally presented; and then accept or reject it upon a separate conscious appraisal of the witness' demeanor.

Although the instruction accurately reflects both the law and the lawyer's perspective, it has nothing to do with what the jurors do. Any director can tell you that judges are telling jurors that they *may* do what they inevitably and subconsciously have done before the instruction was even given—*and what they would do even if the judge said they could not.* The witness' manner not only affects whether the testimony is believed; it determines whether it was even heard. When was the last time you tuned out someone that you did not like, or found yourself in a mental haze during a monotonous monologue?

Everything that follows in this primer focuses on the jury trial as theater. If you have completed the pretrial work, cannot reach settlement, and are about to go to trial, how do you get the jury to accept your "truth?" You should evaluate everything you read here, or in other trial books, for that matter, from the perspective of the director trying to sell an idea to an audience. If you do not think a suggested technique will help persuade the jury, do not accept it unless there is some very compelling non-theater reason for doing so. If you think a suggested technique will help in persuading the jury, do not abandon it without legal compulsion.

The Lawyer's Part

"Director" is the lawyer's part. Besides accurately describing the bulk of the lawyer's work, the job description provides a useful clue to solving the mystery of pretrial fear, stage fright, and nerves. Most beginning lawyers have difficulty persuading themselves to approach the trial as a play when considering trial techniques and tactics of presentation, but they quickly exhibit the actor's anxieties when contemplating their own parts in the trial: "How do I look? How do I sound? Am I developing credibility with the jurors?" You're not an actor, you're the director. The director's perspective will help to soothe your personal anxieties while helping you to understand the lawyer's part in the trial.

The director is at the center of the play, but is not center stage. The director works with the script, but is not responsible for writing it. It is the director's play, but the director is not the ultimate winner or loser. The witness-actors are center stage. The litigants are the writers. The client is the ultimate winner or loser. The director only takes the litigant's script to smooth out the rough edges. Although the director works with the available actors and actresses, arranges for stage blocking and props, rehearses the play, and at the performance stands by to make sure that everything goes as prepared, the director's main work is behind the scenes.

If you adopt the director's perspective, you will be concerned with the presentation of the client's play, rather than the personal "acting" success of the lawyer's part. If your brain is asking, "Is the jury hearing my witness? Is that testimony clear?", there is no time or space for your ego to waste your time with, "How do I look? and "How do I sound?" If your ego is not heated up, your palms will not sweat and your knees will not knock.

Legal theater is different from legitimate theater in two respects, both of which have an effect on the lawyer's part. The director is always on stage in the legal theater. Even though the lawyer has no substantive dialogue in the trial/play, the lawyer's presence on stage has an effect upon the jurors. Secondly, legal theater is competitive. Although the lawyer is primarily concerned with the presentation of the client's play, there is an opponent with the same view, and each lawyer must be concerned with the other.

Presence is the most important quality in the lawyer's part. Presence is both attitude and technique—and both can be learned. Presence is what we admire in others, want for ourselves, and look for in trial lawyers. It is a word that describes something most of us recognize, but are hard-pressed to define. Words like "assertive," "forceful," and "aggressive" are often used as synonyms, but they are not necessarily the same as presence. Presence is really the appearance of being comfortable with what you are doing.

"Appearance" is the important word, because presence is something we identify in others from the "outside," without any real knowledge of how the person feels "inside." We admire presence because we assume that what we see on the outside reflects how the person feels on the inside. It is presence, not style that allows the lawyer to make a positive impression on the jury. The respect that the lawyer needs from the jury comes from the presence the lawyer exhibits in addressing the jury, addressing the court, interrogating witnesses, sitting in the chair, listening to others, handling exhibits, walking back to the counsel table, and all other activity that takes place on the courtroom stage.

The techniques of courtroom presence (explored in later sections) are designed to give you the appearance of comfort in the courtroom regardless of the actual level of your anxiety. It is worth noting, however, that while you can learn to appear comfortable when you are not, it is a lot easier when you are.

That feeling of comfort that makes comfort something natural comes more easily if you adopt the director's perspective.

Ask a lawyer whose courtroom the client's case is being tried in, and the lawyer will tell you a judge's name. If you have ever been around a director during rehearsal or performance, you have heard something like: "Don't put that on my stage." "What are you doing on my stage?" "I never want to see you on my stage again." Of course, the stage belongs to the theater owner or, if rented, the

producer of the play. But you will never find concepts of property law standing in the way of the
director's certain knowledge that it is the director's
stage. Although the owner or the producer has the
power and the opportunity to tell the director what
can or cannot be done on the stage, the director's
possessive attitude about the platform on which the
players walk makes that stage the director's.

The director's possessive attitude, that idea of
control, is useful for the lawyer's approach to the
courtroom. Granted, the lawyer's view that the
courtroom belongs to the judge is right in law, the
lawyer cannot suffer that possession in fact. Courtrooms, and the judges sitting in them, exist solely
as tools and servants to the resolution of society's
disputes. Their only function and justification is to
assist lawyers in presenting the client's cause to the
jurors. Courtrooms belong to litigants, and to their
representatives, the lawyers. They belong to judges
no more than the stage belongs to the theater
owner or the producer. If you realize that the courtroom exists for you, and that your part is to control
what goes on in it, you will feel more comfortable in
it. Once you have learned that the courtroom is
yours, what you can do in that courtroom is up to
you. Once you have decided to do something in that
courtroom, you do not need to apologize to anyone
for doing it. Even when you are wrong, you are
wrong on your own turf. While you might wish to
apologize to someone if you have unintentionally
offended, you should never feel or act apologetic

about doing what is necessary in the courtroom—it is yours.

The only restrictions upon your activity in your courtroom are imposed by the judge's interpretation of the rules of legal theater, and the fact that there is at least one other lawyer with an equal claim to the stage. For those of you still bothered by the idea that trial is theater, it is the competition and the restrictions that make the art form an acceptable method for resolving disputes fairly, in a fashion approximating the truth.

The competition between the advocates, unchecked by rules of ethics, evidence, and procedure, would make the adversary system no different from a back alley brawl. In fact, some trials in some jurisdictions seem to be more like a back alley brawl than any other recognizable institution.

The competition of the trial does not determine the lawyer's part, but it does describe an inner attitude that may prove useful. So, before you become completely wrapped up in the facts, the search for the truth, or the theater of your presentation, remember that there is another lawyer who wants the stage, wants to win, and is looking for an edge—not an unfair edge, just an edge.

The last thing to be said about the lawyer's part has to do with those rules of ethics, evidence, and procedure. They are the restrictions upon the lawyer's unfettered control of the courtroom stage. The power of the judge in the courtroom derives directly from these rules. The lawyer who goes to trial without knowing what is fair, what can be presented to the jury, and how to get it there, will never be comfortable in the courtroom because the judge will own it every time the judge steps in to rule against the lawyer. The rules of ethics, evidence, and procedure are the only things more basic to your first trial than the perspectives and techniques in this primer. In the long run, the rules are the guarantee of the lawyer conduct that serves to validate the dispute resolution system. While the hot knife and the joust had God to validate the efficacy of the system, our adversary search for the truth has only the honor of lawyers to guarantee the system. The rules define the limits of the lawyer's part, and are listed in the order of their importance: ethics, evidence, and procedure. If you deviate from proper procedure, the judge will correct you in a way that will cause you minimal embarrassment, and probably allow you to complete the task. If you do not understand the rules of evidence, your opponent may, with the assistance of the judge, be able to stop you from presenting your very best "truth" to the jury. But if you violate an ethical rule, the judge may embarrass you beyond what your client's case can withstand. Worse, your opponent will wait for an opportunity to hang you out to dry, and pass the word that you are the least thing alive—a lawyer whose honor can be purchased with a twenty thousand dollar fender bender.

The rules for trial define the lawyer's critical part in society's continued faith in the adversary system. No perspective is more important as you begin to think about your first trial. If we lose the perspective, we will lose the system.

The Other Players

No director would ever open a play without knowing all the other players and their parts. Some of what follows is repeated throughout this primer, but a quick look up front at the cast is important.

You should know all of the court personnel and how they might affect your trial. You should treat every person with the same respect that you treat the judge. It is good manners and shows respect for the judicial system. If manners and respect don't persuade you, consider practicality. Many of the people with whom you will deal have direct access to the judge and will share their opinions about you with the judge. You may also need the help of any one of these people in your first and subsequent trials and few people are eager to help the arrogant young lawyer that treated them like they were "just the clerk."

CLERK of either the entire court or a particular judge is the official recipient of all documents that become the court file. The clerk makes sure that all pleadings and filings are accessible to the court and handles any filings that come up during the case. Remember, if it is not in the file, it did not happen. The only record that goes up on appeal is the one the clerk sends.

BAILIFF is usually the judge's right hand person. In some jurisdiction this might be the judge's clerk.

Pay less attention to the title and more to the function. In some courthouses the bailiff may have been around a lot longer than the judge and will know more about juries and trials than any book can teach you. The bailiff is the only person that has direct access to and communication with the jury during a trial. The bailiff is the go-between for the judge and jury. The bailiff is usually the person that summons witnesses placed under the rule, hands exhibits to the jury and arranges the seating charts of the venire panel for voir dire. A bailiff that likes you is a friend indeed. The bailiff is typically a great source for answers to your questions about how the judge runs the courtroom. An advance visit with the bailiff can make you look as if this is at least your third trial instead of your first.

COURT REPORTER takes down all that is said in the courtroom. A proper trial transcript is critical to a successful appeal. A proper trial transcript requires understanding the court reporter's job and limitations. A few rules may help. Court reporters can only transcribe what they can hear. Whether it is you, a witness, a venire panel member in the back of a courtroom, a bench or chambers conference, the court reporter has to be able to hear, so make everyone speak up. Wait for your court reporter to join you at the bench, in chambers or for an offer of proof. If you don't, a whispered conference at the bench will just read ''bench conference'' in the transcript. The offer and critical ruling will not exist in the record. No offer and no ruling: no appeal. The court reporter can only transcribe one person at a time, so don't interrupt a witness, opposing counsel or anyone else. It takes two hands to transcribe, so if you have asked the court reporter to mark an exhibit, you can't keep talking as well. Remember the record when pointing to exhibits. "This", "that", "over there", nodding, shrugging shoulders all make sense in the courtroom at the time, but not on a cold transcript. If you are not specific and do not identify there will be nothing to appeal. The easier you make your court reporter's job the better your transcript will be, the fewer looks of exasperation the judge or jurors will see, the more competent and polite you will appear and the faster that court reporter might get to you that rush transcript you want of the prior days testimony!

VENIRE PANEL is the potential jury for your case. Six, twelve, or however many will be your jury will come from that panel. They are citizens of your community that lead lives outside the courtroom and have somewhere else to be other than in jury service. They are serious about the justice system and for most of them this is their only insight into how it works. The opinion they take away from the jury selection process will color what they think about lawyers, judges and the justice system as a whole. They are not witnesses to be cross examined, they are not the enemy; they are people. (More about them in the chapter on jury selection.)

YOUR CLIENT is the reason for the case. Clients are the stars of the show whether they testify or not. It is their passion that brings the disputes to the big stage and requires all the other members of the cast. They are their cases, not yours. You may be the director, but you are not the lead and the events did not happen to you, they happened to your clients. Your clients still decide whether to settle or plead during trial even when you think the jury will definitely find in the client's favor. The consequences of the trial will be visited on them, not you. You will go back to your office and will live to try another case. They have put their confidence and trust in you. They have hired you to help them present the best possible version of the truth of their cases. Your clients will be scrutinized from the moment they leave your office doors until the last juror files out of the courthouse. They are on trial during every ride or walk to the courthouse, every bathroom break, every lunch, every minute of the trial.

THE OTHER SIDE'S CLIENTS usually feels exactly the same as your clients. They believe their truth is the only real truth and that the jury will find in their favor.

THE LAWYERS ON THE OTHER SIDE believe their clients the way you believe yours. Never forget that the adversary system works because both lawyers advocate the best case for their clients. Because it is not possible for both sides to be one hundred percent correct, we have judges and juries. It takes both passion and objectivity to be a good trial lawyer. The ability to see your case through another set of eyes helps you not only prepare a better case, but to know when to "hold 'em" and when to "fold 'em." Regardless of your relationship with your opponent during pretrial or discovery, once in the courtroom you treat opponents with courtesy and respect. The jury has no knowledge of what transpired before they arrived and so won't understand why there is so much hostility between the lawyers. Have patience when your opponent lacks the behavior of an appropriate lawyer. It will show and your client's case will benefit if you are smart enough not to respond in kind.

THE JURY, depending upon the trial and the jurisdiction will be the first six or twelve members of the venire panel not struck in the selection process. They are not "chosen;" they were just not struck. They become the deciders, the ultimate critics of the drama that is about to unfold solely for their benefit. They are like students that will be given a final exam at the end of the case, except that they cannot ask questions, take notes, do outside research, or even talk to each other about what they are seeing and hearing until it is over. They are likely not to know anything about the subject matter when they sit down in the jury box. They have to listen to the information through witnesses in a question and answer format. Some of the information is useful, some is not. Much of the information is not what they want to know. And just when they think they have a clear picture of what has happened, the other side cross examines and raises new questions. The exam they take at the end will have questions presented in arcane language and will contain very few instructions about how to really answer the questions. They carry with them all the pressure of trying to make a right and just decision for the people sitting at the counsel tables. It is a tough exam on which they will try to do their very best. The better the information they get from your play, the better chance you will like the ending. Like it or not, reality will be the answers the jurors provide to the exam they are taking.

WITNESSES, from a cynical perspective, are people who happened to be at the wrong place at the wrong time. They saw, heard or know something that needs to be relayed to the jurors. If witnesses don't have something to relate, they might have been useful to you in some fashion, but they don't make it to the stage. Witnesses come in two flavors, the ones you get to choose and the ones you don't. The latter category, unfortunately, is the one into which most witnesses fall. That makes your choice among them so important. Every director looks at the ensemble and tries to complement it or shore up its weaknesses. You want to do the same with the witnesses that you get to choose. Most of your witnesses are likely to be less familiar with courts than you are, even when it is your first trial. The jurors will look at each witness as a source of information. It is your job to help "direct" your witnesses to give their information in an interesting and understandable way so that the jurors will believe and use the information to support a verdict in your favor.

CHAPTER 1

THE STAGE: WHERE DO I SIT?

The courtroom is a stage under the constant
scrutiny of the jury. The lawyer who knows it well
does well. The lawyer who is comfortable with it
receives comfort from it. The lawyer who does not
consider how to manage it and walk upon it depends upon luck to insure that the jurors hear
witnesses, see the exhibits, and understand the
case. We begin our consideration of trial techniques
with the courtroom stage because it is common to
everything that the lawyer does at trial, common to
everything, planned or accidental, that the jurors
learn about the case, and common to the first
concern of almost every beginning lawyer: "My
God, where do I sit?"

You do not know whether you are supposed to sit
at the right table or the left table. What is more,
you are a whole lot more concerned about the
answer to that question than you are about what
you are going to say in your opening statement.
After all, a less than lucid opening statement could
be tolerated, and in time, mitigated by the evidence.
But what are you to do when your opponent objects
that you are in the wrong seat, and the judge orders
you removed forthwith? We can picture the bailiff
picking us up by the scruff of the neck to deposit us,

floundering and humiliated, into our proper place. A couple of weeks of concerted work on the problem drove us to the final source of all research—the boss. The answer was good for the chair and table problem, and for a whole lot more.

"Go over to the courthouse," said the boss, "and find out."

We would like to think that your concern for the courtroom/stage stems from your director's eye view of the trial, and from your interest in how best to stage manage your witnesses, your props, and your case. Whatever your motive, be it personal fear or professional competence, the first rule for considering the courtroom/stage is: "Go over to the courthouse and find out." Do you practice in a jurisdiction where you sit at the table of your choice if you get there first, and the one that is left if you don't; or where the plaintiff always sits at the table closest to the jury and the defendant furthest away? See what is there, how it is used, and think about your trial/play. Watch how the judge conducts a trial. How does the judge tend to handle objections, requests to approach the bench, jury selection? Think about the logistics. Is there a good place to display exhibits? Is there a way to play a video taped deposition if need be? How are the jurors responding to the lawyers and the witnesses? Just walking into the trial, can you understand what the case is about, what the witnesses are saying? If not, why not? What kind of nonverbal cues are you picking up about the clients, lawyers, witnesses, jurors? Watching a trial especially when you have one coming up can be an invaluable learning experience. You can learn from good lawyers and bad. It is as important to see what works as well as what doesn't, what alienates a judge or jury. Focused watching is never wasted time, so do as much of it as you can.

If possible go to the courtroom where your case will be tried, at a time when your judge is presiding. In addition to the rules of ethics, evidence, and procedure, every courtroom is governed by rules of local custom. Sometimes local rules are posted on the Court's website, sometimes they are hardly written, numbered, or indexed. Your library skills may not be of any help. The local custom, nevertheless, will dictate how you may manage the courtroom/stage. Local custom will determine where you must be when interrogating witnesses, how you mark exhibits, how much freedom you have to move about the courtroom, and occasionally, where you sit. The local custom may be that of the jurisdiction, the court district, the courthouse, or even the particular court. The rigidity with which the local rules or customs are enforced will vary from judge to judge. When you preview the courtroom/stage, the more specific you can be the better. At a minimum, go to see the courtroom, whether it is being used or not, and talk to someone who has tried a case before your judge. Much of the mystery of your first trial and your personal apprehension can be reduced by knowing the characteristics of the courtroom and the habits of the judge. If you cannot find a lawyer who has practiced before that judge, these are perfect questions for the Judge's bailiff.

When you get to the courtroom, if you look at it through lawyer's eyes, you will see a bench, a couple of tables, a bunch of chairs, and an area behind the bar where the audience sits if it is a famous case, and where witnesses wait to be called if it is not. The director will see a very different sort of stage for a very restricted kind of theater. The director will see that the audience does not sit behind the bar, but is located in twelve chairs on the stage.

You must see the problem the director sees. The jurors are in a position to see everything that is happening, but what the lawyers want to happen is more heard than seen. While trial is heavily oral, good theater is heavily visual. People prefer to learn through their eyes, not their ears. Although movement, props, and pictures are allowed at trial, the law has determined that the trial's reflection of the truth will be mostly oral. The director will see that the oral trial will become very boring for a visually oriented jury/audience. Your understanding of the stage the jurors can see is important, because you must be prepared to do everything that you can to combat juror boredom.

If you do not combat juror boredom, the jurors may indulge in a little self-help—like sleeping. More frequently, jurors will combat the boredom by listening with their eyes. Even though you and your opponent may give them little to look at, the jurors' eyes will remain their dominant information collector. You may consider what the jurors see to be of little importance, compared to the testimony that they are supposed to be listening to, but the jurors will not. Because jurors hear with their eyes, you ought to keep the following assumptions in mind as you look at the courtroom/stage and consider your trial/play:

1. The manner of presentation is as important as the substance presented.

2. The courtroom is a stage that the jurors can see when no one is speaking.

3. Evidence that can be seen has more impact— good or bad—than evidence that can be only heard.

4. If you capture the jurors' eyes, you capture their minds.

While law school teaches us to focus on words, the words by themselves do not convey the heart of any message. All of us rely far more on the nonverbal than the verbal when processing a message and deciding whether to believe it. We pay attention to what we see in the messenger's demeanor, the pitch and rate of speech more than the actual words. Suppose you ask a friend, "How they are doing?" and get a standard reply of "I'm fine". If the person is sobbing or saying it through clenched teeth, we know to discount the actual language and trust what our eyes and gut tells us. We make assessments about people and situations based on what we see all the time for good and bad. Our trial system is based in large part on the human ability to detect deception, sincerity, and the range of human emotions. Appellate courts defer to trial court findings on credibility precisely because they were not there to see and experience what happened in the courtroom. This is not to say that language is not important, rather, it is to emphasize that trials are not decided on the papers. We bring in a jury of our peers who will make decisions based on all of what they see and experience in the courtroom. So how will they form impressions of us? Since jurors can't base their impressions on reality—they don't know who we or our clients really are, or what really happened—they base it on their perceptions. Their impressions and perceptions will come from what they see of us, what we say, how the judge treats us, and how we treat others. So what do we want them to see? That we are confident, prepared, honest, fair, sincere. Why? Because we hope that it translates into credibility for us and our client's case. There are numerous books written on communication skills, nonverbal communication, and the psychology of persuasion that in the future will help you become expert in non-verbal communication. In this primer, we raise the issue and focus on a few simple rules to help you in that first trial.

The number one rule is to be your most persuasive self. While we would all love to be like the great trial lawyers of history, we cannot be anyone other than ourselves in the courtroom. Even though the twelve jurors do not know us, they know when we are not being ourselves. You will be your most persuasive self when you are conscious of your body movement, of how you are treating everyone in the courtroom, and when you recognize that your every action is being watched by someone, even when you are not talking. Remember that the twelve some ones who are watching are jurors who have put their lives on hold to help decide a matter that might be the most important matter in your client's life. They and your client deserve the best preparation. If you prepare with an eye to what those jurors will want to know in order to decide the case in your client's favor, you will feel the confidence that will help you be your most persuasive self.

Preparation is entirely within your control if you will spend the time and effort to do it. This primer teaches you how to prepare for your first trial, step by step. The central task of a lawyer—and what all jurors expect—is that the lawyer be honest and fair in representing the client's cause. If you have been vigilant in preparing your client's case to be fairly presented to the jurors, you may not be perfect or smooth, but you will be credible. You cannot be "experienced" at your first trial, but you can be competent. Focus first on being your most persuasive self, that self that has convinced someone to do you a favor, go out on a date, or hire you for a job— the persuasive self that did all of those things without notes or cue cards!

Eye contact between presenter and juror is the single most important technique of persuasion. Unfortunately, it seems to escape the attention of beginning lawyers. Whether it is because we refuse to look at the courtroom as a stage, or because we do not understand the importance of the eye; we read opening statements with our heads down, allow our witnesses to talk to the lawyer rather than the jurors, rarely look to see what the jurors are watching, and finish up by reading most of our closing argument. If you carry only one idea to your first trial, understand the dominance of the human eye as the brain's information source. People know, intuitively, that the human soul lies right behind the eye. We will believe someone who looks us right in the eye, and lies, in preference to someone who cannot look at us while telling the truth. A speech, even about us, puts us to sleep if the speaker stares off into space. We listen, however, to a speaker whose eyes compel us, even if the recitation is of a telephone book.

Most experienced trial lawyers prepare with conscious consideration to stage management, and to what the jurors see, while most beginning trial lawyers give no consideration to stage management, even though being on stage is a source of their anxieties. As you look at the courtroom, remember that you are not involved in a kind of private ceremony for truth between you and your witnesses. The jurors' presence is not an incidental part of the drama. The trial is a courtroom drama for the sole benefit of the jurors. Watch them and remember that they are watching your play.

Interrogation of witnesses, handling of exhibits, and addressing the jury present the most common stage management problems. Most of us spend an enormous amount of time considering what we will ask, offer in evidence or present in argument, and little time considering how it is done. And so it should be. You cannot afford to think about stage movement and procedure during trial. You need your awareness for more immediate concerns. The how of stage movement and the "by the numbers" portions of your presentation ought to be second nature. The problem, of course; it is not second nature until you have given it some consideration and practiced a little. Just as a director blocks the play before it is presented, the lawyer's preparation should consider the physical aspects of the trial beforehand, leaving the lawyer free during trial to attack the important substance of the trial/play without worrying about "Where do I sit?"

There are two rules of stage movement that every director knows and that every trial lawyer would do well to adopt. 1) Movement with a purpose can create emphasis. 2) Aimless or nervous movement is distracting.

The director does not allow actors to move aimlessly around a stage because the audience's eyes, and therefore, their focus, will follow them wherever they go. If the audience is following movement it probably isn't listening to the actor's lines. The same is true for the trial lawyer addressing the jury. If you pace aimlessly while speaking, the jury will be focused on your movement not your content. On the other hand, specific movement with a purpose, from one part of the stage to another, can create visual emphasis and can give power to the actor's line as well as to the lawyer's argument.

Interrogation of Witnesses

The interrogation of witnesses is usually conducted from behind a lectern or from a seated position at the counsel table. This is almost always a matter of local custom, subject to significant difference from judge to judge. Most of us picture the examiner, at least the cross examiner, standing near the witness in a threatening posture. Few courtrooms afford counsel the freedom to move around at will during interrogation, and even fewer allow a cross examiner to physically intimidate a witness. If, when you enter the courtroom, you see a lectern facing the witness box, you can bet that you are expected to interrogate from behind it. If there is no lectern, look for a microphone on the counsel table. Court reporters have increased their use of recordings and architects have become more sensitive to the need for courtroom sound systems. If there are a number of microphones around the courtroom, and if you are not behind one of them when interrogating a witness, you are probably in the wrong place. If you are in a courtroom where the local custom allows freedom of movement, or where you have persuaded the judge to allow you to move around so long as you do not abuse the privilege, there are two simple techniques for stage managing your interrogations.

Try to get off stage during direct examination. The witnesses are the principal players in the courtroom drama. Imagine the courtroom is dark except for the use of a spotlight. During direct examination you are presenting your play for the jurors' consideration, your spotlight would be on the witnesses as they testify. The more that the jurors focus upon your players; the more likely they are to be influenced by the lines your players deliver. While you, as the examiner, are an important catalyst to the effective direct examination, the witness has the major speaking part. Once the witness is on the stand, there is little that you can do to influence the substance or the personal manner of the witness; therefore, this is not your time in the spotlight. You can, however, influence two matters of importance. You can make sure that the witness speaks loudly enough to be heard, and you can force the witness to look at the jurors when speaking. With your most important witnesses, or with the most important portion of a witness' testimony, interrogate from someplace to which the witness cannot talk without looking at the jurors and without speaking up. By standing where the jurors are between you and the witness, you allow the witness to speak to the jurors without forcing the witness to do something that does not come naturally. Most of us speak to those who are speaking to us. It is unnatural for a witness to look at you while you are asking a question, and then look away and answer that question to someone else. In some courtrooms you will not be able to interrogate your witnesses from a place behind the jurors. It is important for you to discuss this with your witnesses so that they will speak to the jurors when answering your questions, even if they must look away from you to do it. You may assure them that, although it seems unnatural and phony to them, it will not seem so to the jurors to whom they speak. But remember the advantage of emphasis by placing yourself so that the jurors are between you and the witness, at least some of the time. If you are stuck behind a lectern, and the lectern is on wheels, consider asking the judge before court convenes whether you might move the lectern to a spot close to the last juror in the front row. While this will not put the all of the jurors between you and the witness, it will make it much more natural for the witness to look at the jurors when testifying. If you are forced to sit at counsel table occasionally remind your witness with something like, "Tell the jurors what it was like when you saw the headlights coming directly at you".

Take over center stage during cross examination. Cross examination is usually a time for diminishing the impact that a witness and that witness' testimony have on the jurors. Now the spotlight is on you. The witness is the opponent's player, and the witness' dialogue is part of the opponent's play—not yours. All of the reasons which compel you to get off stage during your witness' direct compel you to get your opponent's witnesses off stage during cross. You can do that best by taking center stage yourself. The techniques for cross examining most witnesses (Chapter 9) encourage you to "testify" and to "control" the length of the witness' response. By closing the space between you and the witness, you can discourage explanatory answers by the force of your physical presence. Be careful. You cannot get right up on a witness and be obviously intimidating without receiving an objection from your opponent, an admonition from the court, and a black mark, for unfairness, from the jurors. Remember that even if you are in a jurisdiction where you cannot physically move during cross you still want the spotlight focused on you. Your voice, your energy, and your eye contact with the jurors are all ways to steal center stage, even if you can't move. With some obvious exceptions for those times when it is to your advantage to have the jurors focus on the witness, you want them to focus on you during cross examination, and to ignore the witness. Move up as close to the witness as the judge and propriety will allow.

Where do I sit (stand)?

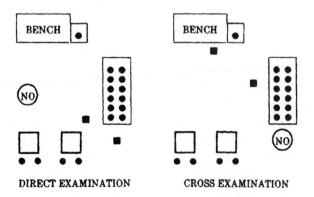

DIRECT EXAMINATION   CROSS EXAMINATION

Presenting Exhibits "By the Numbers"

Exhibits and diagrams present unique visual opportunities in an otherwise heavily oral environment. They also present substantial stage management problems. If you do not conquer the stage management problems, you will lose the opportunities. Because juror attention is heightened when visual evidence is suggested, you may lose ground if you cannot handle exhibits and diagrams effectively. Your failing will occur at the worst possible time—when the jurors are sure to be awake and paying attention. Most first time trial lawyers pay no attention to the "by the numbers" ritual for handling exhibits. The result is that long pauses, unscheduled interruptions, and confusing foundation interrogation transform a visual opportunity into a ritual of juror boredom. Presenting exhibits should be like performing the compulsory skating exercises in the Olympics. They should be your chance to shine, to show that you are the prepared, confident lawyer that jurors want to see. Practice really can make perfect, so make your office a courtroom and do it "by the numbers" until you can own the stage with your exhibits.

Whether an exhibit will be helpful, when it should be used, and how to weave it into the remainder of the interrogation is discussed in Chapter 5. Assuming that you have decided to use an exhibit, and that you have made a reasonable judgment about when to offer the exhibit, this is how you ought to stage manage its admission into evidence "by the numbers."

Start with identifying the proper evidentiary rule and foundation for the exhibit. Make sure that you have thought through any potential objections to the evidence and how you will cure them. The rules of evidence lag behind technological advances, so make sure that when you are dealing with electronic and digital evidence you have looked at recent cases addressing any concerns about the admissibility of the evidence. Think about whether you can lay the proper foundation for an e-mail, digital photographs or computerized animations. Secondly, think about how you are going to display the evidence to the jury. While you probably don't want to use your computer during your first trial, many courts have document cameras and screens available. If you are using a document camera, practice with it beforehand. Practice placing an exhibit on it and zooming in or out for emphasis, enlarging it to the right size for the jurors to see. Document cameras are an effective and amazing tool. They allow you to display virtually any piece of physical evidence to a jury, with no additional effort; but you must know how to work the camera. If you do not practice, it is easy to make jurors seasick with the motion of zooming in and out. The jurors' attention will go elsewhere, such as to your jewelry, watch or nail polish (all no-no's for trial), instead of to the exhibit.

Are you using blow ups, multiple copies or even juror notebooks? Evidence that jurors can see, touch, and examine can be very powerful when properly displayed. But because it carries power, when and how it gets displayed can either heighten or destroy the moment. Don't let it work against you because you stumble through the presentation. Always have your original exhibits and copies ready to go. Once you start the "by the numbers" dance, you want it to be smooth and fluid. This is one part of the trial you can practice and where your preparation can pay off in a smooth performance. You can gain credibility with the judge, opposing counsel, and jurors when you can lay a proper, smooth foundation and handle exhibits with ease.

Mark the exhibit for identification. All evidence or prospective evidence must be identified for the people involved in the trial and for any appellate court that may have to review the record on appeal. Oral evidence is identified by the simple step of having the witness testify to name and address. Physical evidence, because it can endure or be lost, and can be reviewed only by looking at it, must be marked. Because it may be reviewed in conjunction with a written transcript, it must be marked in a way that will distinguish it from all other pieces of proposed physical evidence and it should always be referred to by that marking during a lawyer's interrogation. There are as many variations on identification marks as there are markers. Check the local custom. As a general rule, an item of proposed evidence is marked with the party designation, for example, "Plaintiff's," and is followed by a number or letter, for example, "1." The plaintiff's first proposed exhibit, then, would be marked:

```
Plaintiff's
Exhibit
1
_____
```

It is referred to as, "Plaintiff's Exhibit Number One, *for identification*," until the court has accepted it as evidence. Once it has been accepted, the "for identification," may be dropped, and the exhibit is referred to as, "Plaintiff's Exhibit Number One." In some jurisdictions, the plaintiff's exhibits are numbered and the defendant's lettered. It matters little which method is used so long as the item and the offeror can be identified clearly.

In many jurisdictions, exhibits are pre-marked, either at a pretrial hearing or just before the trial. The advantage to that system is explored in the later discussion of the use of exhibits. Most of what follows after the marking is probably advisable even in those jurisdictions where pretrial activity makes it optional. If you are marking at trial, you will either begin the interrogation of a witness, or interrupt your interrogation, by asking the court's permission to have the clerk mark an exhibit:

"Your honor, May I have the clerk mark an item for identification?"

By asking the court, even if the local custom does not require it, you demonstrate the courtesy and respect for the court that the jurors expect of you.

You give the court an opportunity to tell you that local custom calls for you to show the item to opposing counsel before, not after marking. Although most jurisdictions are to the contrary, you will avoid embarrassment if you happen to be in a place where you show first and mark second. Most importantly, you call the jurors' attention to a rare and alluring kind of information—something that they will get to look at. If you have more than one item to show to the witness, you might consider having them marked at one time—unless it will take so long that the jurors will lose the flow of the testimony: "Your honor, I have three items that I would like to show to the witness. May I have the clerk mark them for identification?" If the court says, "Yes," nods in your direction, or otherwise assents, you may proceed with the marking process.

Take the exhibit to the clerk—or court reporter, in some jurisdictions—for marking. Whoever marks exhibits is likely to be across the courtroom from where you stand or sit to interrogate witnesses. Do not use the trip to the marker as an opportunity to carry the exhibit in a way that allows the jurors to see it before the judge admits it into evidence. Not only is it unethical to show something to the jury that will not—may not—be admitted, you are likely to look foolish when your opponent takes the opportunity to comment on your ethics: "Your honor, counsel knows better than to try to unfairly influence the jury. Would you please instruct counsel not to display to the jury exhibits which have not been admitted?" If you are trying to sneak something to the jury that will never be admitted, you may pay a price beyond the gain and damage your ethical reputation as well.

Be certain that the item is marked in sequence. You are involved in a process outside the hearing of the jury when you have the clerk mark an item, and you should conclude it as promptly and quietly as you can so that you might continue your presentation. Do not count on the clerk to know what number is next in sequence. Tell the clerk how you want the item marked. Some jurisdictions require either the clerk or the lawyer to announce the general description and the marking of the item so that court and counsel can keep their exhibit list current: "Your honor, I have marked a document as Plaintiff's Exhibit Number one, for identification." Other jurisdictions allow counsel to accomplish the announcement by identification during the interrogation of the witness. If you have taken more than one item to be marked, be sure that you ask the clerk to mark them in the order in which you expect to ask the witness to identify them. It will make everyone's bookkeeping easier, especially yours, and you must keep track of the status of your own evidence. If you have three or four items that form a natural group, and that you want the jury to know "go together," ask the clerk to mark them with the same number, and a sub-designation letter to differentiate them. For example, a box containing three glassine envelopes full of green leafy matter might be marked as "State's Exhibit Number One," for identification, with the three envelopes receiving the designations, #1a, #1b, and #1c. When the items end up in the jury room (some jurisdictions will not allow marijuana in the jury room), the jurors will remember that they "go together" even though you are not there to tell them. A last word about marking: do not ask questions of a witness in order to fill space while the clerk or the court reporter marks the exhibits. No one will listen, and if the court reporter is doing the marking, you will have no record.

You must show the marked item to opposing counsel, even if opposing counsel has seen it before or has a copy. This is not a mere formality. Counsel has a right to see the actual proposed exhibit that will be offered to the jury. (The first time that you do not look at an exhibit because you have a copy will be the time that something has changed to your detriment.) If you go promptly to counsel with the exhibit, you maintain control of the pace of the interrogation of the witness. If you do not take the exhibit to counsel, you are likely to have your interrogation interrupted right smack in a spot where you hope to have an impact on the jurors: "Excuse me, your honor; counsel has not given me an opportunity to see the exhibit." You never want to look as if you are trying to pull anything over on anyone. If you do not show your exhibit to counsel before you proceed, you are likely to have the judge tell you to do it. Do not allow your well planned presentation to stumble over small discourtesies.

Take the exhibit to the witness for identification and authentication. In some jurisdictions, you are required to secure the court's permission before approaching the witness. Although the rule developed as a method to control cross examiners who wished to close in on a witness for intimidation, it is applied to direct examiners in the most formal courtrooms. You ought to ask the court's permission to approach the witness even if it is not required. Too much courtesy rarely looks bad: "Your honor, may I show the exhibit to the witness?" If you expect to go up to the witness more than once, you will want to find a way to avoid asking each time you approach the witness box: "Your honor, I have a number of exhibits to discuss with this witness, may I go to the witness box when I want the witness to identify one or another of them?"

Do not stand between the witness and the jury. Someone once told every law student that there was a technical foundation for every exhibit, and although it would be a boring technicality for the jurors, it had to be completed. As a result, ten out of twelve of you will walk up to the witness and position yourself directly between the witness and the jurors with your back to the jurors. Besides being discourteous to the jurors, they will be able to see neither the witness nor the exhibit. Take a position near the witness that allows you to see the witness and the jurors, the jurors to see you and the witness, and the witness to see you and the jurors. If the exhibit is one that the jurors ought not see until the foundation has been completed and the evidence accepted, employ some technique for preserving the integrity of the offer other than placing yourself between the witness and the jurors. If it is a photograph, you might take care that both you and the witness keep the back of the photograph towards the jurors. If it is a particularly inflammatory piece of evidence you might employ a file folder or some other container to protect the exhibit from the curious eyes of the jurors. The important point is "curious eyes." When you take an exhibit to a witness, you begin a process in which the jurors have inordinate interest. Do not shut them out from the process. Use it to build their anticipation.

Stage the foundation interrogation. The law school emphasis on evidentiary foundations and legal hurdles for admission of evidence explains both the back to the jurors posture and the whispered, secret meeting, legal mumbo-jumbo approach to laying a foundation. It is true that you must cover every aspect of the foundation. It is not true that it must look like some secret and unintelligible conspiracy between the lawyer and the witness. Even in the most restrictive courtroom, where the judge almost ties the lawyer to the chair, an exhibit gives you an excuse to get up to the witness, or get the witness out of the witness box to a diagram, or to vary the visual monotony in some other way. The foundational requirements for the admission of an exhibit—identification and authentication—and the procedural magic words required to tell court, counsel and the record what you are doing provide a framework for putting some sparkle into your case. You ought to view the laying of a foundation as an opportunity rather than a burden.

If the witness does not have an opportunity to identify the item, the jurors will not know what it is. Even if the admissibility of an exhibit has been stipulated, take the opportunity to have the witness look at it and identify it for the jurors: "Mr. Mahoney, I'm handing you what has been marked for identification as Defendant's Exhibit Number Two, can you tell us what it is?" If there is a contest over the admission of the exhibit, and it is a sensitive item, you might warn the witness not to make a prejudicial answer: "Mr. Mahoney, I'm showing you what has been marked, Defendant's Exhibit Number Two, for identification. Without telling us what it says, can you tell us what kind of a document it is?" The witness' identification of the item is the first knowledge that the jurors have of the exhibit. Be sure it is done with style.

If the witness does not authenticate the item, the jurors will have no reason to rely on it. Most authentication of exhibits is to insure that the item is what it purports to be. If the exhibit is of any importance to you, it is probably important that the jurors be convinced of its validity. Even if there is no quarrel about how the witness knows that the exhibit or what the witness has identified it to be, let the jurors know how the witness knows: "How do you know that State's Exhibit Number Two for identification is the knife found in the defendant's car?"

Tell the court and jurors, again, what you are presenting. Beginning lawyers have a silly habit of doing everything up to the offering of evidence, and then forgetting to get the evidence admitted. Aside from the terrible hole that might leave in your case, it is a terrible waste of an opportunity for you to stage an important part of your case. After you have completed your foundation, take a step back from the witness to a position in front of the jury, and without turning your back on the jury, address the court with a request for admission that tells the jurors how the exhibit fits into your case: "Your honor, the State offers the knife taken from the defendant's car for admission into evidence as State's Exhibit Number Two." (Notice that the previously necessary modifier, "for identification" is no longer necessary when the item is offered and admitted.) Do not proceed until you have an explicit ruling from the court that will be reflected in the written record. A nod, a grunt, a question, or "any objection?" is not the equivalent of admission. Until the court says, "State's Exhibit Number Two is received," or something similar, the exhibit has not been admitted, and the jurors do not know that the judge "approves" of your evidence.

The jurors must hear, touch, or see the exhibit. "Publish" is the technical term for getting the exhibit to the jurors. Although it is an awkward phrase for use in front of the jury, and you should find a substitute, it is a concept that you must remember. You have spent some time offering the exhibit and raising the jurors' anticipation, do not leave them wondering what the exhibit is like "up close" while you proceed to other things. Technology now offers numerous options for "publishing" your exhibit. The document camera allows for the quick posting of the exhibit on a screen, but it is not always effective. Documents are sometimes still too small to be read, or jurors want to read all of or more of the text than you want to emphasize. The real issue with any screen publication, as any director can tell you, is that it is impossible to emphasize two ideas simultaneously. If there are two separate ideas on stage at once, one will be lost, and you cannot predict which one. Whether you are displaying the exhibits on a screen, a blow up, or passing the original through the jury, the jurors have to decide whether to focus on the witness or on the exhibit. There are two ways to avoid the difficulty. The first is to anticipate the problem and presume that the court will allow the pause if you choose to pass the exhibit to the jurors immediately: "Your honor, may we take a moment so that the jurors can have an opportunity to look at the knife before I continue with Mr. Mahoney?" If you believe it is critical that the jurors see the exhibit before continuation, rather than after the testimony, let the court know: "Your honor, I believe that the jurors will have a better appreciation of Mr. Mahoney's testimony if they have an opportunity to view the knife before I proceed with further questions?" This may work on critical exhibits, but do not expect the court to slow down proceedings for routine documents, photographs, letters, etc. If the court is not going to allow the pause, this method of asking will warn you off before you are committed to passing the exhibit to the jury immediately.

If the court tells you that you may pass the exhibit to the jurors, but that you ought to continue questioning, you must weigh the need for an immediate view against the undesirability of divided attention. If you decide against dividing the jurors' attention, suggest to the court that you will pass the exhibit at the end of the interrogation: "Your honor, if I may, I would like to withhold the exhibit until after I have finished questioning Mr. Mahoney, and have the jurors view it then. I don't want to deprive any of the jurors of the full force of Mr. Mahoney's testimony." Most judges will allow you to wait. The cross examiner then has the problem of asking questions while the jurors are occupied with the exhibit. When that becomes apparent, the court might relent, and allow you to pause immediately to pass the exhibit. If you are the cross examiner, ask the judge to delay your interrogation if the judge has forced the jurors to see the exhibit after the direct examination is completed. If the court tells you to get on with it, anyway, shuffle your papers or ask questions of no importance to your case. Few judges will put you in that position, but you must be prepared to handle the situation if it arises. Some exhibits can be published more effectively and expeditiously without going to the jury: "Your honor, in the interest of time, may I ask the witness to read the letter to the jury?" Some exhibits may be more dramatically published by the demonstration of some fear if the item is put into the hands of the jury: "In the interest of safety, your honor, may the witness hold the butcher knife up so that the jurors can get a good look at it without the risk of jurors accidentally cutting themselves?" If you are displaying documents simultaneously with your testimony then weave the testimony into the exhibit to get the full effect of imprinting (Chapter 5). Build effective pauses into the testimony so that jurors can focus on the exhibit and the testimony. Consider highlighting the language in documents that you want the jurors to read and focusing the document camera on that portion (or call outs if you are determined to use Power Point). Try to gauge eye contact with the witness before you move on to important testimony.

Retrieve the exhibit after the last juror has seen it. If the exhibit is worth marking, offering, and showing, it is probably worth preserving for future use. When the last juror has seen the exhibit, retrieve it, offer it to the judge, and if the judge does not want to see it, deposit it with the clerk. When you want to use the exhibit with another witness, everything goes more smoothly if you do not have to spend five minutes tracking it down. Even if you have no further use for the exhibit with further witnesses, you will want it available for use in your closing argument. In some jurisdictions, only the bailiff can hand exhibits to or retrieve them from the jury.

Staging the Use of a Diagram

Diagrams are special exhibits from a stage management perspective. Most of the rules of the handling of exhibits apply to diagrams. Because a diagram is usually an aid to testimony rather than a substitute for it, and because most diagrams are on constant display throughout the trial, there are special stage management problems not normally encountered with other exhibits.

Timing is important. Present the diagram as early in the witness' testimony as is natural to discuss the detail of the diagram. The introduction of a diagram during a witness' testimony presents an unusual and continuing visual dimension to what the witness has to say. Because it attracts the attention of the jurors and will be a magnet for the witness' eyes as well as the jurors', it is important to introduce it at a time and place that will complement rather than detract from the witness' testimony. Although identification and authentication of the diagram are necessary for meeting evidentiary requirements of admission, they are more for the jurors' understanding of the case. The earlier in the testimony the jurors understand where the event took place; the easier it will be for them to appreciate the witness' testimony. If the witness through whom the diagram is offered is also an occurrence witness, the diagram will enhance the testimony as well as that of following witnesses. If the witness gives the occurrence testimony without the aid of the diagram, the diagram will appear to be an afterthought.

Place the diagram where the jury can see it, but not where it will be an unconscious focal point when it is not being used. If a diagram is worth the trouble, it is something that is likely to remain on an easel within the view of the jury throughout the trial. This is a good place to remember that less is often more. If you fall into the trap of using an electronic display for a good diagram or visual, you lose some permanency. Computer displays or document cameras are good for shorter evidentiary displays that don't need to stay up throughout the trial or even through a witness' testimony. Think back to what elementary school classrooms look like. They are filled with visuals that support the subject being taught all around the classroom. Whether it is primary colors, bats, periodic charts or skeletons and charts of the bones in the body, the lesson is being reinforced through control of the visual playing field.

Placement of the diagram is critical, and in most courtrooms, difficult. Ideally, the diagram should be easily visible to the jurors, the judge, and your opponent—not to mention the witness. Few courtrooms are built to make that accommodation. In choosing a place for your diagram, and in determining the size in the first instance, sacrifice the jurors' view last. You should try to find a place that allows the witness to move easily to the diagram and point to various aspects of it within close view of the jury. Be sure that neither you nor the witness is in a position that forces you to put your back to the jurors while pointing to or writing upon the diagram. Because the court will be interested in the diagram, and may have to make some rulings with respect to it, you will probably be obliged to select a place that will allow the judge to see the diagram too. Use of a lightweight easel will help you move the diagram to different locations for witness use and for addressing the jury. For example, you may elect to place the diagram just to the side of the witness box during testimony—allowing easy access for the witness, but squarely in front of the jurors during closing argument.

The final consideration in the placement of the diagram should be your understanding that its visual impact means that witnesses are likely to refer to it while testifying, even if the reference to the diagram adds nothing to the testimony. This distracts the jurors' attention away from your witness to the diagram. It breaks the eye contact between your witness and the jury. If you place the diagram in a position where it cannot be seen easily from the witness box and the witness must leave the box when referring to it, you will avoid having a witness who talks to diagrams instead of to jurors. If distraction is a problem or if a visual belongs to your opponent and does not help your case, then politely take it down. After the witness has testified on direct for example and before you begin your cross, ask the court for permission to move the exhibit so that you may begin your cross examination. You can always just place it resting near counsel table, but with its back to the jury. Just remember that in all courtroom maneuvering you can't have it both ways. Don't expect the judge to allow you to leave your exhibits up and take the other side's down.

In some situations, it will be helpful to make the witness' access to the diagram inconvenient enough so that the witness must leave the witness box to refer to the diagram. This breaks the visual pattern and tells the jurors that it is time to listen to something important. It will insure that your diagram will focus rather than divert the jurors' attention. Because you have this double barreled device of a visual aid plus stage movement to draw juror attention you ought to use it sparingly and plan your witness' testimony so that you reap all of the available benefit. Among other things, you must be sure to avoid the up and down, jack-in-the-box, approach that sees your witness at the diagram ten times during the interrogation or looking over at the diagram because the point would be better made if the witness was at the diagram. Depending upon whether you want the witness to refer to the diagram or mark on it (and in view of your faith in the witness' ability to stand in front of the jury and talk without the protective wall of the witness box) you may find it useful to go to the diagram with the witness. Be certain that neither of you is blocking the jurors' view of the diagram. If the witness is referring to the diagram, it is helpful to give the witness a small pointer. The pointer makes the demonstration more precise and it provides something to occupy the witness's hands. While it might go against the grain, an every day ruler is probably a better choice than a slick, telescoping pointer, or worse, a laser pointer. Keep it simple.

The first step in the use of a diagram is to have the witness identify everything of importance to your case—even if there is a legend on the diagram that explains symbols. The jurors will not read the legend from the jury box. Do not ask occurrence questions that require the witness to refer to the diagram until everything on the diagram has been explained. If you evoke occurrence testimony before explaining the diagram, the jurors will miss "what happened." They will be trying to figure out what the diagram depicts rather than listening to the testimony. If the witness describes the diagram first, the oral testimony will become attached to the visual diagram that remains in front of the jury after the witness is gone. When you have completed that portion of the witness' testimony that makes use of the diagram, invite the witness back to the witness stand. If you were forced, while working with the diagram, to put it in a position where it competes with the witness for the jurors' attention, move it back. If your opponent is using a diagram and has placed it where you cannot see it, ask permission of the court to move to a place from which you can see the testimony that is being offered.

Remember that the diagram is a powerful tool for focusing juror attention and pinning oral testimony to a visual reminder. Save it for your important points and always have the witness go over to the diagram and make a specific reference (not a wave of the hand) to the relevant part of the diagram. Some exhibits will be admitted into evidence and go back to the jury room while others will be admitted only as demonstrative aids. Be sure to keep track of the category into which the various exhibits fall.

Addressing the Jury

Addressing the jury is the one trial function that puts the attorney center stage—at least physically. Addressing the jury involves stage management and stage presence. Because you are the main thing to be managed, the two ideas merge. Most of the techniques for stage managing while the lawyer addresses the jury exist to increase stage presence. If you learn and follow the techniques you may not feel comfortable, but you will appear comfortable and that is what stage presence is all about.

Do not address the jury from behind a lectern unless the court insists, or unless holding on is the only way you can stay on your feet. The lectern is a barrier between you and the jury in an environment that already has more barriers than you need. Moreover, there is a special hidden danger in this particular piece of furniture. The lectern has a place for extensive notes. Extensive notes are an invitation for the nervous lawyer to read. The nervous lawyer's reading is an invitation for the jurors to go to sleep. There is no way to overemphasize the restriction that the lectern places upon your ability to persuade a jury. Both the lectern, and the notes you place upon it, are crutches which not only hold you up, but also keep you from going anyplace.

The rules of ethics, and to some extent the rules of persuasion, prohibit you from explicitly asserting your personal belief in your client's position. Nevertheless, nothing is more important than the jurors' perception that you are not merely selling a bill of goods, but in fact, believe in your client's cause. The lectern gives you something behind which to hide your nervousness, but at the same time, it hides the communication of your belief in your client's cause. When was the last time you were persuaded by someone reading something to you? If reading were an effective method of persuasion, we would encourage witnesses to do it. On the contrary, we ask witnesses who might legitimately use notes to do it as little as possible. Let the jury see you. There is persuasive value in the implicit openness of an advocate presented without barrier or crutch. Your being thrust in front of the jury without extensive notes or without something to hide behind forces you to speak with the conviction that your client's cause deserves.

Once you are out from behind the lectern, you must appear solid. Don't look nervous. "Easy for you to say," you say. There is a simple technique that will mask your nervousness even if it does not actually stop the butterflies in your stomach or the weakness in your knees: Do not move unless you have someplace to go. There is nothing wrong with movement—except when it betrays nervousness. If you pace back and forth before the jury in a pattern that becomes noticeable, you are taking the jurors' attention away from what you are saying and putting it on what you are doing. You want what you are doing to put the jurors' attention on what you are saying. It is a useful technique to talk directly to the jurors. That can be facilitated by standing in front of some jurors some of the time and other jurors at other times. The important difference between pacing in front of the jury and the purposeful movement from one set of jurors to another is the message that the movement communicates. Don't move when you can't help it—move when it helps. You may find it effective to move away from the jury so that you have room to raise your voice. You may wish to move over to a diagram, or to pick up an exhibit, or to write on an artist's pad. You may wish to move up close to the jury to whisper an important point. (Be careful not to move too close. The jurors have a territorial interest in the jury box, and you might cause some squirming if you invade their space by putting your hand on the jury rail or otherwise leaning into jury territory.) Movement adds to your presentation if it is purposeful; otherwise, it detracts from your presentation.

Because many courts are using lecterns and microphones to facilitate courtroom sound and court reporting, you might find a lectern so obviously placed that it would be odd to address the jury without standing behind it. Ask the court before trial or at a break if you may move the lectern. Even courts that are very restrictive about movement during interrogation are likely to be more flexible when it comes to addressing the jury. If you are forced to stay near the lectern while addressing the jury, change it from a barrier to a prop. Stand to the side of it—holding on to the side if that is required to satisfy the court that you are using the lectern—and speak directly to the jury.

If you are forced or beguiled into using the lectern while addressing the jury, do not take extensive notes with you. If you do, no matter how well you know what you want to say, you will read the notes. You should consider, as a substitute for extensive notes, a page with five to ten words that reflect your outline or that will remind you of main ideas. Do not write little words on a little card and refer to it surreptitiously. It not only looks funny when you squint at the card, but you convey the impression that what you are doing is an oration rather than a straight forward discussion of obvious facts and conclusions. The suggestion to avoid notes is not because the jury takes off points if you cannot "memorize" a speech. The suggestion recognizes that you cannot look at the jury while you read and that you cannot persuade jurors that you don't look right in the eye. The five or ten words that you take to the lectern should be written in large capitals on a legal pad. The bigger the words the easier they are to read and the less they will draw your attention away from the jurors.

Courtroom Stage Presence

Courtroom stage presence is something that lawyers are continually admonished to exhibit and rarely taught how to achieve. It is what the lawyer wants to exhibit while addressing the jury. But it is more. Because the courtroom/stage is constantly under jury scrutiny—even when nothing is happening—and because you are always on that stage— even when you are not active—presence always matters. Presence affects juror respect for the lawyer, and indirectly, the client's case. Much of the difficulty with presence is that lawyers confuse it with style. This final consideration of the courtroom as a stage is concerned with presence of the kind you were concerned about when you were worried about "Where do I sit?" For those of you without sufficient faith to believe that total concentration on your client's case will translate into a useful stage presence born of true comfort, here is a laundry list of things to do that will give you the appearance of comfort in your environment regardless of the truth about your comfort level.

Always be courteous. Courtesy is the luxury of the comfortable. It is a subtle signal to the jury that you are in your element.

The most obvious courtroom courtesy is getting to your feet. When you are introduced to the jury, stand. Never address the court with your posterior in a chair. Even if you must interrupt something you are doing when the court says something to you, get to your feet to respond—even if it is merely to say, "Yes, your honor," or "Ready, your honor." By the number of lawyers who fail to demonstrate common technical courtesy towards the judge, you would think that jurors pay no attention to the relationship between counsel and bench. No matter what you or others may think of a particular judge, no one in the courtroom has more of the jurors' attention and respect than the judge. If your actions do not mirror the way the jurors feel about the judge, you are more than discourteous, you are a fool. Some of you will try your first case in front of a judge who is mean and who likes to pick on young lawyers. (There are precious few, but there are some.) Although it is beyond the scope of this primer to detail how you handle such a judge, the courtesy rule maintains. Do not confuse courtesy with a lack of firmness. Insist upon your rights and your position, but do it with courtesy. Even if the jury can see what the judge is doing, and does not like it, your courtesy will help, not hurt.

"May it please the court," are the first five words of every address to the jury. It is a request to proceed and is usually met with a nod from the bench.

"Your honor" are the first two words of every discussion with the court.

"Thank you, your honor" are the last four words of every exchange with the court or ruling by the court—particularly those that go against you. The "thank you" is not for the result, but for the consideration that went into the ruling. What's more, it may confuse the jury as to which side won the point. Most important, you cannot say "thank you, your honor" at the same time you are grimacing or in some other way telling the jury that you have been wounded.

"May I ... your honor" is the best way to move about the courtroom. Many courts do not require permission before going to the clerk, to the witness box, to a diagram or whatever. No lawyer ever went wrong asking and some have been embarrassed by their failure.

" 'May we approach the bench, your honor?" is a necessity before a sidebar conference. Aside from the courtesy, it is a warning to court, counsel, and court reporter that a matter of importance that cannot be shared with the jury is at hand. If the court reporter is not stationed near the bench, ask the reporter to join you when approaching the bench. No reporter—no record. No record—no appeal.

Waiting your turn is a courtesy that gives the jury the impression that you are comfortable in the courtroom. If speaking to the court over your opponent's voice or interrupting a witness when it is uncalled for does not strike you as rude and ineffective, remember the court reporter. The court reporter making the transcript can only hear and transcribe one voice at a time. The court reporter is the person who gets you the emergency appeal transcript, reads back cross examination questions if you ask, finds a piece of direct examination during a break so that you can use it on cross, and in some jurisdictions, marks exhibits. If you do not want to make a permanent enemy, do not do anything to make the court reporter's job harder. If you speak while your opponent is speaking, the court reporter may highlight your lack of presence to the jury: "Mr. Goldberg, I can't take this down if you keep interrupting Ms. McCormack—wait your turn." While you are thinking about the court reporter, remember that the court reporter's ears do not see. If your witness only nods, and does not say "yes" or "no," the court reporter may tell the jury that you do not understand courtrooms: "Counsel, please ask the witness to answer audibly so that I can get this down." Worse, the judge may say it.

Presence is partly the appearance of professionalism. "Professional" does not mean haughty, stuffy, or officious, any more than the admonition that trial is theater means that a lawyer should appear "theatrical." Professional means precise and knowledgeable. The appearance of professionalism is the combination of a number of small techniques, some of which follow.

Keep an organized counsel table. There are as many ways to organize a trial as there are lawyers. One of the advantages of the trial notebook (Chapter 3) over the multiple file approach is that it is almost impossible to make a mess with a trial notebook. Files, on the other hand, end up all over the table, causing an embarrassing thirty seconds of blank space while you grope for something.

Do not appear hesitant or tentative. This is the kind of advice that is usually met with: "That's a great platitude, but—uh—well, I mean, you know—

uh—how do you do it?'' The trick of instilling self-confidence is far beyond the scope of this primer, but the appearance is a simple technique. Keep your mouth shut tight until you have decided what to say. Once you have decided what to say, do not rethink it in mid-sentence. Say it straight out. It is better to be wrong but impressive than to be correct but hesitant.

Never say something just to fill space or because it seems like it is your turn. This admonition, along with the preceding and following, involves control over the one muscle that most lawyers have difficulty controlling—the one that shuts the mouth until the brain has an idea worth conveying. Nervousness drives us to fill silence. The knowledge that it is our turn to speak compels us to say words. If you do not have a specific idea to communicate—shut up. Purposeless noise is the one thing worse than silence.

Start questions with an idea not with a sound. In order to demonstrate continuity of thought, or a lack of formality, or a kind of rapport between questioner and witness, we start questions with: ''I see,'' ''all right,'' ''o.k.,'' ''now,'' ''and a,'' ''uh,'' or something worse. The problem is that it gets to be a pattern that may catch the jurors' attention and diminish your presence in their eyes. The false start, like the sound without an idea, comes from a fear of silence and is cured by working on the mechanism that times the mouth engagement with the brain activity.

Leave your toys at home—or at least bring silent ones. Extraneous noise that betrays nervousness and robs you of presence is best made with a click type pen or change in your pocket. Imaginative lawyers can do it with paper clips, folded paper, wooden pencils, and magic markers. Every lawyer must find an individually satisfactory answer to the question first posed by the great advocate, Cicero: "What do I do with my hands?" What you should not do, is give them something to play with in a fidgeting pattern while you are trying to keep the jurors' attention on a witness or on what you are saying. If you need something to hold onto make sure it has no moveable parts that your uncontrollable hands can snap, crackle, and pop.

Avoid "put on" physical speech. Phony nonchalance is a common facade for the nervous lawyer. The obviously disinterested lean back in the chair and the overdone shrug are examples of facade. It is like the tortured straight line that the practiced drunk can walk. The line is straight, but that is how you can tell the drunk is a drunk. Grimaces, head shakes, and other "signals" communicated while the opponent is doing something are both unethical and ineffective. Ask any juror.

Check the props before the show. It is embarrassing, and detracts from presence to drop diagrams, misplace items, and otherwise look like you do not know what you are doing. The time to locate and learn to handle an easel is prior to trial, rather than during the trial while the judge, jurors, witness, and spectators twiddle their thumbs. The only thing worse than fumbling your way through use of an easel is to be unable to use a diagram that you have thought about, paid for, and authenticated; because there is no easel upon which to place it or whiteboard to which it might be taped. You must check the courtroom before you begin, not only to see what is there, but to see how it works.

Some of the newer courtrooms throughout the country, and many metropolitan courtrooms of any vintage, come fully equipped. They have two counsel tables (or one large one), six chairs, a blackboard or whiteboard, an easel, an artist's pad, and more than one electrical outlet. You may even find a screen, computer consoles, document projectors and jurors with monitors in the jury box. Some courtrooms are high tech havens and others don't have a working electrical outlet. Never assume anything when you go to court. If you need something for the presentation of your case bring it yourself and make sure the court has anything else it requires. If you have recorded depositions you will need to play instead of live witnesses, make sure you have a monitor, player and other necessary equipment. (If you need the screen or the outlet for your first trial, your client may have bitten off more than you can chew.) There is no assurance that a courtroom will be equipped with more than tables and chairs, so if you intend to try as many as two cases you might consider investing in the trial lawyer's survival kit:

One light, collapsible easel for mounting,

One artist's pad and same sized mylar overlays. They are low tech, but still very effective

Four different colored grease pencils, markers and dry erase pens.

One ruler (15 inch will fit in your brief case)

Assorted tacks, clips, tape, rubber bands and white out.

One extension cord (for the second trial).

If the survival kit is beyond your means or desires, find out, before trial, whether the courtroom has the props that you will need—and learn to work them. When you have mastered working with the basics you might consider a document camera and projector. The document camera is like an overhead projector, but because it does not require transparencies it can display anything that can fit below the lens. Many courthouses have a document camera that can be reserved in advance. You can also share technology with other lawyers and defray the costs.

Present yourself in a manner that is not inconsistent with the jurors' view of a professional. This is often a sore subject with beginning lawyers, particularly young, beginning lawyers who believe their individual expression and comfort should extend to the courtroom and that the important business of justice ought not be concerned with counsel's appearance. It matters little whether that is right or wrong; what matters is how the jurors react to your appearance. While this general caution might be applied to hair length, body piercings, tattoos, and the like, for most lawyers it is about what you wear. While you ought not expect jurors to be aware of dress in the sense that they will take conscious note of it, you can safely assume that your opening statement will have less positive impact for your client's cause if you make it while wearing a beanie with a propeller on it. Remember that it is your client's cause and that you are not dressing for yourself. With some flexibility for your personal preferences within a range of acceptable choices, you are dressing for the jurors. There are no useful rules about what you ought to wear. There is one useful rule about what not to wear. Do not dress in a manner that is likely to offend the jurors. If you wear something that is totally outside of the average citizen's expectation, you run the risk of taking the juror's attention away from your client's cause and directing it at your surprising garb. If your appearance symbolizes a social statement directly in conflict with what a juror believes, you can expect to have difficulty getting that juror to accept you or your client's cause. Remember that you are not usually trying your case to your peers. The jurors (and some judges) often will be older adults who are far more traditional in what they consider proper courtroom attire for a lawyer than jurors born after the 1970's. You may have to consider, "what would my grandmother think was appropriate?"

Do not present something that you are not. Many young lawyers, concerned with how they will "come off" in front of the jury, make the familiar mistake of confusing presence with style. Having little knowledge of their own style, they try to emulate a lawyer they have seen and admired. The point is so important, it is worth repeating. Don't do it. You may profit from copying what another lawyer does. You cannot copy what another lawyer is. Presence is the appearance of being comfortable. You cannot be comfortable in someone else's skin. Do not sacrifice your presence by concentrating on someone else's style. Let your own style develop gradually and naturally.

It is important for you to put these ideas about presence and stage management in perspective. They have been discussed at some length, not because they are the most important consideration for trial, but because they force you to consider: "Who am I?" and "Where must I do this?" They have been discussed first so that once they are out of the way, you can proceed to learn, comfortable in some knowledge of your environment and your personal ability to handle it.

A final note about the handling of the courtroom/stage that will help you when all else fails. If you do not know, or cannot figure it out—ask the clerk or bailiff. The clerk of court, and more specifically, the deputy clerk of court assigned to the courtroom in which your case is to be tried, knows the answers to all of the most important questions that went unanswered in law school: "Is it okay if I move the blackboard so that I can use it in my opening?" "What time is the court likely to recess in the morning?" "If I'm third for Tuesday, am I really likely to try the case that day?"

We are professionally saddened by the necessary implication of one last admonition: Treat everyone at the courthouse with respect. Nobody is as arrogant as a young lawyer who does not know what to do, and does not want it to show. If you talk down to the clerk, you will talk down to the jurors. In that event, it will not matter if you know what you can do, the jurors will tell you. Judges talk as much about lawyers as lawyers talk about judges—a lot. Your reputation is your most valuable asset as a lawyer and it will follow you wherever you go. Reputation is almost impossible to change and is gained fairly quickly. Courthouses are small communities, the clerks, bailiffs, staff and judges all talk. What you do in one courtroom is known in the next sometimes before you even make it back to your office. It can spread across a state in short order. You want everyone at the courthouse to see what you want the jurors to see: that you are honest, sincere, fair, confident and credible. The easiest way to make sure that everyone sees those qualities is for you to be them all the time, to everyone, trial or not.

CHAPTER 2

THE SCRIPT: WHAT DO I SAY?

Consideration of the first trial, even for the most nervous among us, shifts from thoughts about sitting in the wrong chair to concern about saying the wrong words. We worry about having it sound right until we realize that the most important thing is the idea that our words represent. When that happens, we proceed to the mountains of information we have accumulated through investigation and discovery—no doubt with a theory of recovery or defense in mind—and sort it by witness. We identify each witness, catalogue what the witness has to say, arrange the sequence of the witness' oral testimony, arrange the witnesses in an acceptable order, and pronounce ourselves more or less ready to proceed. All too often, this approach misses a main point of a claim or defense, and the judge never allows the legally insufficient claim or defense to go to the jury. Just as often, this approach puts so much information before the jurors that they miss the main point for all the irrelevancies. When a lawyer misses a main point, be it a legal point necessary to get past the judge to get to the jury, or a persuasive point needed to convince the jury, it is usually from knowing too much about the parts of the case and not enough about the whole.

Making a case that will avoid a directed verdict, or establishing a defense that can be submitted to the jury, is a relatively simple process of finding the applicable law, listing the necessary elements to be proved, and identifying the portion of the available evidence relating to those elements. This simple task should be done ideally before you even finish discovery. The time to find out that you are missing a key piece of evidence or testimony is while you still have a chance to go get it. The earlier you look at the likely questions the jurors will be asked to answer in the verdict form and match them to the available evidence, the better prepared you will be. It cannot be done informally in your head. Although the task is simple, it is a mandatory minimum for success at trial. Do the analyses, graph the evidence with the legal elements and the available witnesses, and use a checklist to ensure that you have produced what you planned. We do not mean to suggest that getting a case past a directed verdict or a defense into the jury instructions is a simple matter. If you do not have the evidence, it is impossible. If you have analyzed the law or abstracted the elements improperly, you will lose. The rest of your law school education has given you the tools with which to construct the submissible case or defense. If you have the good sense to use those tools to diagram your analysis and locate the facts that provide the minimum required showing, you will be ready to consider the more difficult question: "How do I persuade the jury to accept my version?"

The diagram that matches the legal elements to the facts of the case will probably not provide you with the key to jury persuasion. Although the diagram provides a necessary and indispensible foundation, it offers little help in determining what to do with the rest of the information that you have accumulated. Further, it may not tell the jury why your client should win. At best, it demonstrates why your client should not lose as a matter of law.

Theater considerations will provide a better starting point than legal considerations in finding the persuasive key. Every good play has a single point that can be described in, at most, a few sentences. Rather than use the diagram of the legal minimum to answer the question, "What do I say?" review all of your information until you can verbalize one, two, or three sentences that, if they are accepted by the jurors, will cause them to vote in favor of your client. You cannot know the answer to, "What do I say?" unless you know the sentence or two that you would say in the jury room if you were taking part in the deliberations.

Many experienced trial lawyers begin consideration of the case by thinking about the closing argument. The closing argument is the trial lawyer's opportunity to tell the jurors why the lawyer's client should win—not what the facts are, not what the law is, but why the client should prevail. (Chapter 11) Just like the playwright who uses the single, simple theme of the play as a guide to the creation of characters and dialogue, the trial lawyer uses a single, simple theme as the touchstone against which every piece of available evidence is measured. The theme—the reason that your client should win—becomes the relevance standard for every pretrial and trial judgment the lawyer is called upon to make. As you approach the first trial, you are likely to have more witnesses, more information, and more legal theories for recovery or defense than you can use effectively. The first step in preparing your trial/play is to understand that you have more than you can use. The second step is to identify the excess. Focusing on the theme of your closing argument helps you to eliminate the excess and recognize the relevant.

Lawyers are paid for finding what counts, not for counting all that they find. This very simple point is the most difficult concept for the beginning trial lawyer. We are not sure if it is fear of leaving something out, failure of precise factual analysis in the first instance, or a belief that two good ideas are better than one, but most beginning trial lawyers put more before the jury than they should, and as a result, get less from the jury than the client deserves. At times, we fear, the lawyer, not sure which of two theories is best, presents both, leaving it to the jury to select one as a justification for finding for the lawyer's client. The law allows you to plead in the alternative, but even if the facts are consistent with a couple of compatible reasons that allow your client to prevail, you must pick one. More is not better when it comes to trial. Just because you have "discovered" information, does not mean that you need to use it all. You have to sift through all the e-mails, letters and documents, testimony and statements and decide which will be most persuasive to jurors who do not know anything about the case and must decide it based on what you and your opponent present.

Two good and saleable theories are half as good as one. The trial/play is a contest between your play and your opponent's. No matter what you think or what the judge tells the jurors about sophisticated methods of measuring and burdens, the jury is either going to be persuaded by your play or by that of your opponent. Imagine that the judge takes a break just after both sides have finished their opening statements and that you overhear a juror talking on the telephone. What will the juror say when asked what the case is about? What do you want the juror to say? You want that juror to repeat the theory of the case you presented in your opening statement. You certainly don't want the juror to repeat your opponent's theory, and it is hardly better if you hear the juror say, "I don't know." If you don't know why your client should win, if you can't pass the telephone test, how do you expect the jurors to sift through all of the evidence for you?

When you present two theories that the jury can use to find for your client, you have implied that you are not too sure about either one. Even if there is evidence to support both, even if both fit the law, even if the two are not necessarily inconsistent, which are the jurors to accept as the "truth" they believe it is their duty to discover? What conviction have you demonstrated in your presentation or in your argument that they might rely on? If you take the rational, evidence-sifting, instruction-following view of jury deliberations, you may not be so concerned about alternative theories. On the other hand, if you believe the trial is an event to which the jurors react like an audience reacts to a play your presentation must be consistent so that the jurors can develop an attitude about it. A simple example might persuade you.

You ask two children to help clean up a park. You gain their assistance by telling them that you will reward the one that picks up and throws away the most cans. An hour later, the two children appear before you. The first child claims to have picked up fifty-five cans. The second child claims to have picked up seventy-two cans, though it might have been only sixty-four. You do not believe that either child is a conscious liar. Why did you hesitate in rewarding child number two? There is a necessary ambivalence in the presentation of two, even compatible, explanations for an event. Ambivalence is the antithesis of persuasion.

The failure to develop the one reason that your client should prevail results also in the presentation of a longer play than the audience wants or needs. The single most difficult task for both the playwright and the trial lawyer is to bring the entire world to the stage in a small enough package so that it will not overwhelm, confuse, or bore the audience and jury. Every lawyer knows about the relevancy objection at trial. The most important relevancy objection is the one that you raise with yourself as you assess your case and discard all facts, theories, and witnesses that do not relate to your single theme. The test is not legal relevance. The test is persuasive relevance. If you present all that is legally relevant, you are certain to have a well rested jury. "ZZZZZZZZZZzzzzzzzzzzzzz."

The single idea that you develop, the theme of your play, will be the result of a little bit of law, a little bit of fact, and a dash or two of common sense. If you try to develop the theme by concentration on the law, you will think about the case from the lawyer's perspective, and in the lawyer's language. The theme that you construct through that process will be of little use in communicating to the jury or in developing a useful factual presentation. You ought to develop your theme—the reason your client should prevail—without reference to the law. We do not mean to suggest that you will not work the law back into your play, or that a legal basis for liability or defense is irrelevant to the case. It is just that the law is not a good perspective from which to begin consideration of your trial presentation. The reason that your client should prevail should be one that you can relate to twelve non-lawyers who, if they never heard the law, would nevertheless respond, "makes sense to me." Test your theory ahead of time. Ask non-lawyer friends, hair dressers, store clerks, taxicab drivers what they think of your case as you describe it in your two to three sentences. Notice what kind of response you get. What kind of questions do they ask; what information do they want to know? It is likely that your jurors may have those same questions or concerns. In many instances, this may tell you nothing more than to concentrate on facts, not law, and tell it in people talk, not lawyer language. Your client's total recovery of compensatory damages for the defendant's negligent failure to yield the right of way will probably sound better to a jury if described as money for the broken car, lost wages, and six weeks of pain with every breath as the broken ribs, suffered when the defendant's car sped into the intersection, slowly mended. In some cases the reason that your client should prevail will be more than the mere translation of the law into the common sense and the language of human experience. It may be that you have a precise legal defense. The reason that your client should win is not the legal defense, but the reason for the defense in the law. The jurors will not apply the defense in your client's behalf unless the reason for the defense is one that the jurors accept. The judge will give them the law of the defense; you must present the reason that makes the jurors want to apply it. The same may be true of a claim. Consider the widow who recovers life insurance proceeds from the insurance company that is resisting payment because the evidence shows that the dead husband committed suicide. While the evidence, invariably, weighs heavily in favor of the conclusion that the husband committed suicide, the widow often wins despite the weight of the evidence. If you believe that the widow wins because jurors feel sorry for widows and believe that insurance companies can afford to be taken, you will be as far off the mark as if you ascribe the result to careful weighing of the physical facts measured against rigorous application of the law. It is established that most jurors do not believe that they could kill themselves. They, therefore, do not believe that anyone else could. In some states there is a presumption of the "love of life." But the reason that the widow wins is not the law of the presumption; it is that even the unarticulated presumption exists in the mind of every juror. One reason the jury system works is that we all share in the human experience. We ask jurors of different backgrounds, ages, cultural and economic experiences to evaluate the experiences of other human beings. Your theme helps explain "why," in terms of human dynamics, your client should win. Jurors may not have any experience with the misappropriation of a trade secret, but they do know about theft, betrayal and greed. Those kinds of human experiences can help transform facts into a real understanding of why the defendants in your misappropriation of trade secrets case did what they did or why they deserve to be punished.

The firm choice of the single reason your client should win is most important in the case where there are a couple of reasonable possibilities. The most obvious example is the need to select between the reasonable doubt and self-defense defenses in a criminal case. While they are legally compatible, particularly in those jurisdictions that do not label self-defense an affirmative defense for burden-shifting, you are unlikely to persuade a jury to acquit because the state did not prove your client fired the shot beyond a reasonable doubt, but if the client did shoot, the state did not show beyond a reasonable doubt that it was not in self-defense. Even if you have a good case for each individually, there is no way that you can persuasively present both propositions to the same jury. A more subtle example presents the same problem for the civil lawyer. Your client was involved in an automobile collision and claims that it was caused by the other party. Your investigation and discovery produces evidence that the collision may have been the result of excessive speed, but also may have been the result of faulty brakes of which the driver had months of warning. Unless the facts are such that you must rely upon the combination to find any causation— that is, neither condition alone could have caused the accident—you must make a decision as to which reason you will use to persuade the jury to find in your client's favor. If you do not make that decision, and attempt to provide the jury with a choice, you imply that neither alone caused the collision, or that you are not as certain that either caused the collision as your opponent is that neither did. The ambivalence will be reflected in the witnesses and testimony that you choose to present. Further, if the evidence for one of the propositions is stronger than for the other—and it almost always is—you allow your opponent to raise doubts about your better theory by attacking the weaker. The jurors are unlikely to discriminate between the weaker theory, the target of the attack, and your stronger theory, but rather, will chalk up points for your opponent as a general proposition—"the attack weakened the case."

There is always time to add information or ideas back into your case. If you do not start with a very simple and consistent idea for your case, you can never again whittle it down, you will have no device to tell you what parts to cut off. Build your case up—don't cut it down. The core of your play, the idea that you want the audience to remember, the couple of sentences you would say in the jury room if the opportunity was yours, is the talisman around which you will build a successful case and make precise and consistent trial judgments. No idea in this primer is simpler. None is more important. Do not look at your information; think about the theme, and then proceed because you know the answer to: "What do I say?" Write the theme before you proceed. If you cannot write it down, you have not got it. If you have not got it, you cannot begin work on a single examination or argument.

PART II

PREPARATION

Preparation for the first trial begins the moment that you first decide to take the case, and continues until you say your first words in the courtroom. Preparation is the indispensable ingredient in trial success. It is impossible to overrate its importance. Virtually every writer, lecturer, and casual observer about trial stresses the importance of preparation. It is, therefore, astonishing how many lawyers never learned or just forgot. It is even more important for the beginning trial lawyer, because preparation leads to confidence, even if we just look more confident than we actually feel! This primer deals with the last part of trial preparation—preparation of the theater. Once you have gathered all of the facts available, interviewed all of the witnesses that will submit, considered all of the possible legal theories, and developed every scrap of information that investigation, discovery, and research can provide, you must begin the process of selection. You cannot present everything that you know about a case, and should not if you can. You already know that you begin the selection process by choosing one idea about why your client should prevail. This Part is about developing that idea into a play, the presentation of which will make the idea live.

The organization used for investigation and discovery is of little use in preparing for trial. Investigation and discovery are used to collect all information that could conceivably bear on the case. Trial preparation is the opposite exercise. It begins with reducing that pile of information to a useful amount, and proceeds by considering how it can be most persuasively presented. Trial preparation, nevertheless, needs organization. If you do not organize your trial preparation, you will duplicate effort, miss some things, and not know when you are ready for trial. Even though organization is such an obviously simple first step, it is often not done until the bulk of the trial preparation is completed. In fact, organization of the trial preparation into something useful for trial is often the last item completed before trial. If you do it that way, you will spend more time completing the organization, and at the same time, lose some of the efficiency that would have resulted if you had organized first.

Technology has changed the way many lawyers organize trial materials. There is now a lot of litigation support software that allows for the indexing and searching of depositions, discovery and exhibits. The software can be very useful and may be indispensable in a big case. But if your first trial is about a twenty gigabyte case, you are in over your head, your client is in trouble, and this primer will not be able to help you or your client. For your first trial you have enough to worry about without also trying to handle trial support or presentation software. Computers and trial technology are wonderful and you will have to learn to master them for later trials, but in your first trial you have enough to worry about without adding failed technology to the list. Courtrooms, especially on the state level, are just beginning to make the transition to being technology friendly. Older courtrooms lack even the basic electrical needs to sustain your laptop, especially if you were hoping for an outlet near counsel tables. There is usually no screen or it is poorly placed. Invariably your laptop will freeze when you are ready to pull up your PowerPoint or you will hit the wrong button. Most lawyers are still not comfortable in the pressure of trial to change the order of slides or to alter text or graphics if the court sustains an objection. Learning to be an effective trial lawyer using technology is a difficult skill that few have mastered. It takes practice to design graphics, slides, or animations that convey the essence of your message without overpowering the witness or lawyer. Frequently lawyers are using technology for technology's sake, not because it is good advocacy. For most, your first trial will not justify bringing along a dedicated technology person to deal with all of those issues, so leave the technology at home.

Just because you shouldn't run technology during your first trial doesn't mean that you shouldn't use it ahead of time. Using litigation support software during discovery can make trial preparation more effective and efficient. Distilling great slides and graphics to blow up exhibits that you can use during trial is invaluable. Knowing how to use a document camera if the courtroom can support one is an invaluable way to present evidence. Continue to develop a comfort level with technology so that you will in the future be able to perform basic functions even during the pressure of trial. Even then, always have back-ups and a low tech way of presenting the information just in case technology fails. Learn to know whether your audience is receptive to technology. At the end of the day whether you are using a computer, paper or blackboard, the jurors have to see and hear your message, believe it, and retain it in order to return a verdict in your favor.

Regardless of how the case file was organized during pre-trial, you must decide how you need it organized for trial. Traditionally, lawyers used one of two methods for organizing trial materials: the file folder method and the trial notebook method. The file folder method is the one you will see used most often, though you should find it the least efficient. Its popularity persists for reasons that have nothing to do with efficiency at trial. When matters come into law offices, the first act is to open a file. The file is often divided into sections: correspondence, reports, depositions, documents, etc. Trial preparation consists of rearranging the papers. The file then goes to court with the lawyer. Because the file exists, it becomes adopted as a method of trial preparation. Cases often involve many issues and sub-issues. To facilitate organization of the mass of paper, the manufacturers of legal file folders have developed the expando, the super-expando, the super-expando with flap, and the super-expando with flap and tie. Except for a one issue, one witness, one dollar lawsuit, the file folders are fine for filing in law offices, but not very good for organizing a trial. They are too inflexible, too inadaptable, too bulky, and too likely to require an assistant at trial with no duties other than the searching of the files.

Remember since you are the trial lawyer, the file has to be organized so that you can find what you need. You have to be able to find it when you are nervous, when the witness has said something you did not anticipate, when the judge asks you to show your supplemental pleadings or discovery responses immediately. The jury and judge will be looking only at you as you fumble through papers that threaten to tumble onto the floor, or got shuffled while you looked for something earlier. The good news is that organization is easy and like preparation helps you feel (appear) more confident.

CHAPTER 3

PREPARE THE PLAY IN A TRIAL NOTEBOOK

The trial notebook is the most efficient and flexible method for organizing a trial. A three-ring binder of the type school children use, with a change in the advertising from "Mickey Mouse" to "lawyer sedate," substitutes for all of the file folders. While the size of the binder ought to be related to the size of the case, even in small cases be sure that the binder rings are large enough to allow easy turning of pages. The colored divider tab (made of paper, not plastic) is the basis for a simple method of organization of material into meaningful trial sections. If you find sub-sectioning helpful, use the same color tab for the sub-sections. In addition, there are a few departures from the normal routine of keeping a notebook that should help you at trial.

Use only one side of a page in preparation so that the opposite page will be available for notes during trial. As the trial increases in size, you may choose to forego this procedure in favor of using both sides of the page for preparation, a separate pad for trial notes, and a less bulky notebook. If you use a separate pad for notes, be sure that it has been pre-punched so that you can place completed pages into the trial notebook. If you use the one-side method, right-handers might consider doing the preparation on the backside of the page. If you organize your notebook so that the preparation material is on the left as the notebook lays open, you can write notes on the right hand side without obscuring your preparation materials in the midst of the trial. When using the one-side method, put as much of your preparation as possible on lined paper so that the notes you make during the "heat" of trial are easily legible.

Use plastic document protectors to preserve documents that must remain in original condition while keeping them in order. If there are too many pictures and documents to make document protectors practical, use an expanding file folder or some other device for carrying originals. Depositions, the most common trial document, fit into the notebook. You can put the condensed deposition or summary in your notebook and keep the original full size version at counsel table in case it is needed for impeachment at trial or for introduction into evidence. Make sure that you get the deposition out and put it on your table before you begin the examination of the witness. Rummaging through a box can kill the drama of a good impeachment.

The major organizational advantages of the trial notebook are: (1) it forces you to pull your file apart and consider each document as you decide to move it, and (2) only the most determined disorganizer can make a mess at the counsel table with a trial notebook—the rings hold everything in. Your thinking and your case will appear organized, even if your brain knows better.

The goal of the trial notebook is to have everything you need at any given time behind an easily found tab without any additional searching. Regardless of which organizational procedure you choose, organize the trial notebook, or files, into sections that are relevant to the trial, rather than relevant to the case. A section for correspondence is basic when a client case file is opened, but it is unlikely to have topical relevance for the trial. If individual pieces of correspondence are relevant, it is within a specified topic, and the topic should determine the organization. The section designations should, above all, facilitate the efficient trial of your case. The examples and discussion in the remainder of this Chapter constitute one way to develop a trial notebook. Your way must fit your individual work habits, but the principles in the example should apply.

The single most important trial unit is the witness. The individual witness ought to be the basic organizational unit in your trial notebook. Choose a different colored tab or label for each witness. If there are more witnesses than colors, be sure that duplicate colors are separated vertically so that the tabs aid, rather than hinder, quick access to the information. You will probably find it useful to have subsections for each witness. Using the same colored tab, consider tabbing depositions, written statements, information about the witness from other sources, or special items, and, in the case of an expert witness, the witness' qualifications. Use the front of the individual witness' tab divider for information about the witness and for trial organization information. At a minimum, list the witness' name, address, phone numbers for cell, home and work, and leave a place to note whether a subpoena has been served. Although you may wish to add more trial coordination information, you should have at least a list of the exhibits that the witness must either identify or authenticate. Your notes of examination preparation are the most important part of the individual witness section and should be the first item in the section.

It is tempting to organize all trial material by informational topic, e.g., medical, or by trial function, e.g., direct examination. Do not substitute that kind of organization for organization by individual witness. The flow of the trial is by the witness. If you cannot resist the urge, incorporate some topical and trial function organization into the trial notebook without destroying the basic organization by witness. You may wish to put your case-in-chief witnesses in order of presentation. On the other hand, you might decide to put all medical witnesses, yours and theirs, next to each other in your trial notebook. You may find it helpful to put the opposition's major occurrence witness right next to yours in your notebook organization, so that you can get from one to the other quickly. Some lawyers prefer two smaller notebooks to one large, putting the opponent's witnesses (the lawyer's cross-examination material) in a separate notebook.

Evidentiary problems are closely related to witnesses. If you expect that evidence problems will be discussed at pretrial or *in limine*, prepare a separate section in your trial notebook with additional copies of necessary exhibits, testimony and legal authority. If you expect the problems to come intermittently during trial, an evidence subsection in each witness section will work best. This is helpful if you are working from more than one notebook and the court wants a bench discussion of an evidentiary problem. If you decide to have separate evidence subsections for individual witnesses you must still maintain a separate section in the trial notebook, or carry a separate pamphlet containing the evidence rules. If you have prepared a short one page trial brief or have a highlighted version of a case for the court and opposing counsel, include it here. There are numerous evidence handbooks available. Whichever you choose, be familiar with it so that you can find what you need quickly.

Four separate sections of the trial notebook represent different overall views of the trial. "Opening Statement" presents a place for factual overview. "Jury Instructions" encompasses the law of the case. "Closing Argument" houses that one idea that, when fleshed out, is the persuasive view of your trial. The "Ooops" section—some lawyers call it "Must Do" or "Lists"—is the place in the trial notebook where the lawyer ensures that all the trial "i's" have been dotted and "t's" have been crossed.

The "Ooops" section should contain your elements-evidence-witness graph for making your minimum case and an exhibit list. The exhibit list should be located in a part of the notebook that is easily accessible. Some lawyers keep it in a separate pad holder with a pad for ideas that come up during the course of the trial for use in closing argument. The list is to ensure that all exhibits you have offered have been admitted, and that those offered by your opponent that were not admitted do not end up in the jury room. List potential exhibits in the order that you intend to offer them. Provide a space for filling in the exhibit number assigned at trial, and one for noting admission or rejection. As a check on your handling of witnesses, you may choose to supplement your individual witness preparation notes by designating on the exhibit list the witnesses necessary to identify and authenticate exhibits. This is particularly useful if you have many links in the chain of custody for an exhibit. Be certain to designate spaces on the exhibit list for describing and tracking exhibits marked by your opponent. The exhibit list must be updated concurrently with events throughout the trial. It is a good idea to check your lists with the court reporter's to make sure you are in agreement.

Other matters of which first-trial lawyers need constant reminder ought to be written on the back of the "Ooops" divider. Typical reminder items include: exclusion of witnesses before opening statements; motions for judgment as a matter of law; presentation of suggested jury instructions; exceptions to instructions; and polling of the jury. These items reflect a combination of things which, if missed, constitute waiver, and things which, though not legally required, are desirable and often forgotten in the rush and confusion of trial. Other items may be applicable to your particular trial such as jury sequestration, *Denno* disclosures, or *Daubert* challenges to expert witness testimony. The important thing is that you have a list to serve as a reminder for legal and persuasive necessities throughout the trial.

The "Closing Argument" section of your trial notebook ought to be in two parts, one in the trial notebook and one outside. The first entry in this section should be the one idea that summarizes your play in one to three sentences. The remainder of the section will depend upon how you want to handle the closing argument. If you write at least two closing arguments, one before the trial and a modified one after the evidence, the first draft will go into your trial notebook after the organizational distribution of the material in your case file. You will consider props for your closing argument as you begin to prepare the case for trial. A list of those possibilities ought to be kept in the "Closing Argument" section, and kept current as ideas occur. An important part of the section, and one that we suggest you keep outside the notebook, is the pad of blank paper upon which you can jot closing argument ideas as they occur to you during the presentation of evidence. The one pad that should be in front of you during trial is the one on which you record notes for closing argument. If you use a pad holder, the exhibit list can be stored in the front pocket. Again, be sure that you pre-punch the pad so that you can quickly remove the notes during a break and put them into the "Closing Argument" section of your trial notebook. Unless you are very concerned with economy of paper, do not put more than one closing argument idea on a sheet. It will ease the integration of the notes into your closing argument. If the use of paper seems too wasteful, leave three or four lines between ideas so that you can turn the paper into cards when you begin to organize the final draft of the closing argument. If your trial lasts at least a couple of days, the "Closing Argument" section should grow from a page or two, to more than a dozen. When an idea occurs to you, do not try to think if you have considered it before, just jot it down on the closing argument idea pad, and worry about culling the paper later. This method for modifying the closing argument is as valuable during preparation as it is during trial. Among other things, it serves as a security blanket against that constant suspicion that your good idea will be forgotten by the time it is needed.

The "Opening Statement" section of your trial notebook ought to be very active during trial preparation. You may choose to leave it in the office when you go to court. The opening statement ought to be a factual recitation of the theory of your trial/play. It is the natural place for the collection, inspection, and selection of the facts of the case. Unlike the closing argument, which ought to serve as the initial preparation step, being supplemented throughout trial by ideas of presentation rather

than substance; the opening statement ought to
grow substantively during preparation and take its
final form as the last step of trial preparation. As
you prepare the witness, evidence, and exhibit portions of your trial notebook you will be engaged in a
fact-filtering process. Notes on that process ought
to go in your "Opening Statement" section. You
may also find it helpful to make copies of your
examination notes for the individual witnesses and
keep them together in that section (unless you are
of the extensive-examination-notes school, in which
case placing your notes in this section will not
result in the filtered version of the facts needed for
the opening statement). Ideas for presentation of
the opening statement and props to be used will
develop as you sift through the evidence. The closing argument idea pad works for opening statement
ideas too. If you keep a pad handy during preparation, much of your opening statement will be written piece-by-piece before you ever begin a formal
draft. Because there are no imponderables to affect
the opening statement, it is the one part of the tri-
al/play that can be fully prepared and rehearsed.
Subject to modification for your own memory techniques, you ought to build the opening statement
up to a word-for-word draft, and then break it back
down to ideas. The last steps in preparation should
be to review the material in the "Opening Statement" section and construct an idea outline of the
opening statement; create a complete draft from the
outline; read and practice the draft until the ideas,
not the words, are locked in; reduce the draft to a

paragraph-by-paragraph outline; practice from the outline; reduce the outline to a subject by subject outline; practice from the subject outline; and then leave the "Opening Statement" section of the trial notebook in the office when you go to court. If you take the word-for-word draft or the subject-for-subject outline to court, you will be tempted to have those notes in front of you, "just in case." Your memory will work for you if you know that memory is all you have available. If the notes are there, you lose the pressure to dredge things out of your memory. If the notes are there you will use them and diminish the impact of your opening statement.

The "Jury Instructions" section of the trial notebook will be used throughout both preparation and trial. The first entries will be of the law and research you do in preparing your jury instructions before trial. You should have those instructions ready for submission to the judge before jury selection begins. Keep a copy of your submittal and the underlying research so that you can discuss them intelligently with the court, and so that after trial, you may preserve them in your permanent jury instruction file. In addition, you should receive a copy of your opponent's submission. If the court gives instructions of its own, it is likely to provide a copy of those instructions to you. Before the jurors are instructed, you will know what you have requested, and what the court intends to give. A resolution sheet, to ensure the proper exceptions and preservation of the record, ought to be at the front of the "Jury Instructions" section. The resolution sheet shows what you requested, what you opposed of your opponent's requests, and what the court decided to give. Reference to that document during instructions, with an ear for the instructions actually given, will help preserve the record. Many jurisdictions require exceptions to jury instructions at the completion of the instructions in court. Because it is the end of the trial in most jurisdictions, or the last event before closing argument in others, the instructions are often given while the lawyers are inattentive or let down. The instruction resolution sheet provides a one-page reminder of the exceptions to be taken and the instructions to be requested to preserve the appeal points. The well-organized "Jury Instructions" section of the trial notebook gives quick access to the complete text of instructions.

The final section of the trial notebook is the first to be used at trial. The "Juror Information" section ought to contain all information available about the prospective jurors. In addition to the one-page juror information sheet filled out by each prospective juror in most jurisdictions, you will probably include a copy of the total prospective juror list, annotated with basic information (age, job, marital status, address, etc.) for quick comparison judgments during the selection process. If you have done a preliminary juror ranking, it should be placed in this section. Legal authority for alternative selection methods, if important to your case, should be readily available. At the front of the "Juror Information" section, you should place your jury box diagram, to be completed as the jury is seated.

You may find additional sections helpful in your trial notebook. Your case or personal predilections may dictate a different organization. The specific organization you choose and the particular items that you decide to include are not as important as the initial decision to organize in a manner that will facilitate the trial, rather than accept an organization dictated by the filing system used when the case first arrives. The exercise of thinking about the organizational procedure and system will force you to begin structuring your first trial, rather than merely reviewing material that has been collected. Concentration on organization will make the preparation of your trial/play more efficient, and therefore, more creative. Obviously this method means that many parts of a lawyer's file will never make it into the trial notebook. That is as it should be. Make sure that you are familiar with and have access to non-witness materials that may nonetheless come up during trial. For example, make sure you have pleadings, witness disclosures, agreements between counsel, etc. indexed and neatly organized. The rest of the traditional "file" that has no persuasive value may have procedural value in the case and should appear like all of your other trial materials, neat and accessible.

Before proceeding to the substantive preparation of your trial, a final word about the trial notebook, if you choose this procedure for organizing your trial, do not be afraid to use the copy machine. No organization is so well-tailored that any given piece of information has one, and only one, reasonable place. If you rely upon your memory, or upon a reference note, to get you from where you are in your trial notebook to where the one copy of the information can be found, you will defeat the purpose of the organizing tool. Your trial notebook should make your trial easier, not harder. If a particular piece of information pertains to more than one place in your trial, and has only one place in your trial notebook, you will spend half your time flipping through the notebook to the continual annoyance of the jury, the judge, and yourself. The second advantage of multiple copies is the organizational failsafe. If the multiplicity of copies causes your trial notebook to become unwieldy, it is time to reexamine the efficiency of your organizational scheme.

Begin at the End: Closing Argument Preparation

Preparation of the substance of the case for trial ought to begin with the general considerations and work down to the specifics. After choosing your organizing procedure and shuffling your information from the file categories to the trial notebook sections, you will have reviewed enough of the facts and law to begin the general considerations. In developing the trial notebook, we identified four areas of general consideration in jury trials: (1) opening statement for factual overview, (2) jury instructions for overall legal concepts, (3) closing argument for persuasion analysis, and (4) the "Ooops" lists for guaranteeing the legal minimums. The closing argument is the best general consideration for most lawyers in their initial preparation. Most beginning lawyers are least proficient in developing the persuasion analysis of a case and should, therefore, give it the important concentration of the first substantive item. Many experienced trial lawyers begin preparation with the closing argument because the spine of the closing argument is also the spine of the case.

The persuasive idea that tells the jury why your client should win is not only the spine of your closing argument; it is the relevance standard by which you will measure all potential evidence. Without sinking into esoteric chicken/egg analysis, it must be apparent that you will find the idea by which you measure facts for inclusion in your play by examining all of the facts available. Starting substantive preparation with the hunt for the "one idea" does not tell you which of the mountain of facts to look at—as it will later—but, rather, it tells you the perspective from which you should make your first examination of the mountain.

Once you have reviewed all the material, if your one idea is that your client should win because the defendant was negligent, or because the plaintiff was contributorily negligent, you might be right, but you have not found anything that will be of any use in persuading jurors that your client should prevail. The one idea must do more than repeat the applicable legal conclusion. The one idea you want the jurors to repeat in their deliberations (and that you will use for the spine of your closing arguments) must incorporate the most important facts in a way that compels the legal conclusion in common-sense terms. In a simple intersection collision, the theme for the plaintiff cannot be:

"Defendant was driving negligently when he struck my client's car."

The addition of facts alone will not complete the theme, although it adds something that the jurors need:

"Defendant was driving ten miles per hour over the speed limit when he hit my client's car on the right side."

To complete the idea, the jurors need a demonstration of the common sense of the legal principle:

"Defendant was driving ten miles per hour over the speed limit—almost half again the permitted speed—and as a result, my client did not have the time to negotiate the intersection or take the evasive action that the planners assumed would be possible when they decided the intersection did not need traffic controls."

Although the example is simple, the concept applies to all cases, regardless of the complication. In addition to a factual synopsis of the legal action or failure by the opponent, the theme must demonstrate to the jury why the law ought to be applied in the case. Try distilling your theme down to as few words as possible. For example, plug your theme into the phrase, "This is a case about ___." You might not argue it, but how would you complete that sentence? In the case above, what about, "This is a case about being careless, or reckless or distracted." Each of those words corresponds with different facts and maybe even legal theories. A careless, experienced driver is different from the reckless teenager and different from the driver distracted by a cell phone. All of those ideas tap into a common experience of the jurors and can become buzz words for your facts and legal theory. Beginning lawyers too often rely upon the force of the law or their own conviction that it is applicable. Persuasion requires that you demonstrate to the jurors that your proposition, in light of the facts, is the only reasonable and fair result. The jurors will decide for the plaintiff in the intersection case because the speeder took away your client's opportunity to avoid the collision. The legal concepts of negligence, duty, and proximate cause may form the basis for your thinking, but will not compel the jury to decide for your client. Even if you are in a negligence *per se* jurisdiction, the law and the fact of the speeding will not be enough to create a persuasive theme for the closing argument and the presentation of the case. If your one idea does not demonstrate why the law makes common sense in the case before the jurors, you cannot prevail. Closing arguments are constructed to answer the question: "Why should my client win?" Causation, be it a negligence, contract, anti-trust, criminal, or will contest is the key to persuading a fact-finder. The one idea you create for your case must factually demonstrate causation.

Once you have chosen your theme, you can begin to construct the rest of the closing argument. The construction does not begin with an examination of the law or the facts. It begins with the development of arguments that support your theme. The main purpose of closing argument is neither to rehearse the facts (that is the purpose of opening statement), nor to rehearse the law (that is the purpose of the judge's instructions). The purpose of closing argument is to rehearse the reasoning that makes your idea preferable to your opponent's, and it must be built upon a framework of sub-arguments that lead directly to the desired conclusion.

The sub-arguments that form the framework are deduced from the theme. This process causes you to examine the collection of law and fact. The examination, however, will be to augment the argument. This is mostly an exercise in perspective, but a most important exercise. You are not examining the facts and the law to discover what is there; you are examining the facts and the law to discover which sub-arguments are supportable, and which counter-arguments are necessary. Some lawyers can look at a group of facts and, like magic, understand all of the conclusions that might be drawn from them. Most of us cannot do that consistently, let alone in our first trial. Constructing the closing argument framework from the theme down to the supporting sub-arguments forces the lawyer to view the facts from the advocate's perspective—answer first, facts second.

Using the main theme as a relevance standard, divide the accumulated mountain of facts and law into three categories: "helps me," "hurts me," and "does not help either." The process requires that you examine each fact for all possible inferences in light of the theme. The sifting process should help you to pick up most of the sub-arguments for your closing argument framework, and alert you to areas of vulnerability requiring counter-argument. As you identify the arguments, write them down and list the facts that support them.

If you are lucky, the "does not help either" pile will be the largest. Although you cannot afford to sweep that material directly into the waste basket, you can put it in a big file or envelope in a place where it is inaccessible except in emergency. Beginning lawyers are loathe to discard any fact that they have found. No play falls so flat as one full of persuasion irrelevancies. If you are rigorous with the first persuasion analysis of the facts you have collected, you will benefit throughout your preparation and trial. You must, however, be sure that the throw-away pile of facts that "does not help either," does not contain facts that help each about the same amount. This is the first "theme relevance" exclusion of facts and law, and if it is slightly helpful to both you and your opponent, it cannot be discarded without further consideration. It may end up as a wash, helping as much as hurting, but it is hardly irrelevant.

The "help me—hurt me" judgments about evidence cannot be made without some assumptions about the theories your opponent might use. You ought to analyze your opponent's case like you have analyzed your own. Try to anticipate the main theme. Because you do not have the same control over your opponent's theme as you do over your own, you must identify the facts that hurt you with reference to the plausible themes your opponent might choose. (Consider how difficult the sifting process would be if you had, in addition to the three possible themes for your opponent, more than one theory of your own to add to the analysis.)

All relevant facts must ultimately be placed in the "help me" or "hurt me" pile. Those facts that cut both ways must be examined in light of the most likely theory for your opponent, and fall into one category or the other. In the last analysis, however, your theme will dictate whether you elicit, emphasize, or argue a particular piece of evidence. If you change themes or decide on a variation of a theme, make sure you go back and look at the facts again. Facts, like colors, look different depending on the background. This is also where it is critical that you read every deposition and statement in full for yourself. It is amazing what details, statements, and inferences jump off the page when you have a theme in mind and are preparing the case as a whole. Never rely on someone else's summary of a deposition or an encoding system when using litigation support software. Upon completing the initial fact division, you should have identified most of the important sub-arguments for the framework of the closing argument. Using the theme, the sub-arguments, and the categorized facts, you should be ready to tailor a first draft of your final argument, assigning priority and emphasis of argument as seems to you most appropriate, and filling in the supporting facts that flesh out the final product— the first draft of a closing argument.

Prepare the Jury Instructions Early

Draft instructions that reflect your legal theory of the case and that support your first draft closing argument. Since you know (with at least some certainty) what questions the jury will be asked at the end of the trial, it only makes sense to use your evidence to provide the answers to those questions. Imagine how easy law school would have been if professors handed out the exam on the first day of class. Students would spend the rest of the semester filling in the answers to the questions as they developed. If jurors know even the basics about what they will be asked to do at the end of the case, i.e. decide fault or damages or whether there was a contract, they will listen for the evidence that helps them answer those questions. If your evidence doesn't answer the questions asked by the jury instructions then you have a problem which is better fixed now rather than later.

Most jurisdictions have model jury instructions for civil and criminal cases. (In some jurisdictions, it is reversible error not to give an applicable model jury instruction.) The model instructions are a good and necessary place to start, so long as you do not rely upon them exclusively. If you have a matter that is not covered by the model instructions, go to the cases and try to find applicable language. (That is how most model instructions were drafted.) Some lawyers make an art of drafting jury instructions, and the day may come when your case demands that kind of time and talent. For your first trial, it is important that you draft your instructions early so that you can fill in any holes even in the discovery phase of the case. Make sure your pleadings and evidence support the instructions you request. Diagram the minimum evidence requirements for getting past a directed verdict, or establishing a defense and be prepared to get the court committed to the law of the case as early as possible.

For the first trial, you will be concerned with two kinds of instructions: "boilerplate" and substantive. The boilerplate instructions are those that are given in almost every trial, such as function of the court and jury, circumstantial evidence, burden of proof, credibility of witnesses, and jury procedure upon retiring for deliberation. After your first trial, they will be the standard instructions you automatically take from your instructions file. In many courts the boilerplate instructions will be those that the particular judge prefers and uses in every case. In your first case, you should review them with some care. Boilerplate instructions explain how the jurors are to consider the case and their role in it. You will get a clue about some of the things that you want to say to the jury during voir dire, opening statement, or closing argument by examining the boilerplate instructions. Be particularly alert for phrases from the boilerplate that provide a good vehicle for one of the sub-arguments in the closing argument.

The substantive instructions reflect the litigants' theory of the case. Be certain to ask for all that you need, but not for more than you can use. This is another opportunity to check your choice of theme. If you hesitate to throw out an instruction to which you are legally entitled, even though it does not fit your theme, your reticence may be a warning that you have some misgivings about your choice of theme.

Do not underestimate the importance of early attention to instructions. The legal framework of the case dictates the reason your client should prevail. Prepare your instructions separately, no more than one to a page. Be sure that they are numbered in the order that you want the court to give them. At the bottom of each instruction, put three blanks: Given _____, Modified _____, Refused _____. If the instruction is distilled from a case, cite the case; if it is from the model instructions, cite the number. Be sure that you have the original set for the court, a set for your opponent, and a set for your own trial notebook. If you are in a jurisdiction that allows written instructions to go with the jurors to the jury room, prepare an extra copy without notations or citations.

Instructions should be filed, and the court should note whether each instruction is given, modified, or refused. In most cases, you will know which instructions the court intends to give at least a half-day before they are given. Your instruction resolution sheet, noting your requested instructions, your opponents', and those that the court has agreed to give, will be completed during the instructions conference, and will be available so that you can note your exceptions at trial by quick reference. Review any applicable procedural rules that govern how you preserve error depending upon the court's action. In some jurisdictions this can be complicated, so, again, the earlier the preparation, the better.

Preparation of the legal theory is not complete until you have considered the possible forms of verdict, and decided which you prefer. In many jurisdictions, the court has considerable discretion about the form of verdict in civil cases. There is a body of lore as to which litigants prefer which verdict form—from general to special to general with interrogatories. Before digesting all of that material to make your own best judgment, remember: the party least favored by the strict application of the law is the one most likely to want as general a verdict as possible.

Finish at the Start: Opening Statement Preparation

Having completed a draft of the persuasive theme and the legal theory, many of you will want to move directly to the preparation of the testimony for your case-in-chief. The task is simpler if you sandwich the preparation of testimony between the first and last drafts of the opening statement. The advantage to considering the first draft of the opening statement before constructing the testimonial structure for your case-in-chief is that the opening statement forces you to consider the facts as a part of an entire story, rather than as previously collected and sorted units of evidence. By considering the opening statement first, you go through the fact-filtering process again and establish a factual array that reflects the persuasive theme developed in your first draft closing argument. With the exception of an occasional criminal defense, every opening statement presents the facts of the case through one of two possible vehicles: the story of the event, or the story of the coming trial. (Chapter 8). The story of the event presents the facts to the jurors by putting them back to the time and place of the events. The story of the trial presents the facts to the jurors by previewing the conduct of the trial. The purpose of both is to prepare the jurors to listen to the testimony with a perspective that will encourage them to eventually accept your arguments and conclusions from the facts presented.

The opening statement cannot include all of the "help me" facts, and there ought to be very few "hurt me" facts so damaging that they must be dealt with at the outset. The first draft closing argument will help you begin to rank the facts from most to least important. The prepared jury instructions will assist in identifying where the absolute minimum line should be drawn to ensure the legal theory. (In some jurisdictions, the failure to state facts in an opening statement sufficient to avoid a directed verdict results in a dismissal.) After the facts have been lined up in order of persuasive importance and identified for legal minimum, you must decide which of the facts above the minimum ought to be presented to the jury in the opening statement. This judgment is not a final selection tempered by the form of your opening statement or tactical judgments about emphasis of particular facts; it is an intermediate exclusion of facts that are too detailed, cumulative, or tangential to justify a place in the opening statement. For example, if one of the witnesses to an intersection collision will testify to estimating the defendant's speed at forty miles per hour, that testimony might not show up in the opening statement if a police officer is going to testify that the defendant was clocked at forty by radar. The opinion may be relevant and important, but unnecessary in the opening statement because it is only corroborative.

Before considering the presentation of the case-in-chief, there is a final overall view of the play that must be considered in preparing the first draft opening statement. In addition to the facts and law necessary for argument, identification of facts required to meet the legal theory, and ranking of facts by importance, the trial lawyer must have a sense of the human intangibles—the "sex appeal" of the case. Picking through the mountain of facts for those gems of humanity or emotional circumstance that will flesh out your client and your client's cause is the final step in constructing the first draft opening statement. Although these facts may not always be legally relevant in the most technical sense, they will always be critically relevant to your ability to prevail in the theater of trial. If the legal test of relevance is whether the offered evidence has some tendency to establish the party's contention or the opponent's contrary position, it is probably irrelevant whether the defendant in the intersection collision: is a teenager or an adult; is working in a library to pay for college or the child of a rock singer who has been given everything; or is an average student, of average ability, with average dedication, just like your child. Is there any doubt that these irrelevant facts will get into evidence, directly or indirectly, and have some affect upon the deliberations leading to a verdict? Although the importance of these facts may be apparent as they stand here, alone, it is difficult to recognize them and understand their importance as they lay hidden amongst the more substantive facts. You have not completed your overall preparation of the case until the "sex appeal" facts have been discovered and considered. As with the substantive facts, not all of the human facts are worthy of a place in your opening statement. The selection of those human facts will provide the personal picture that your opening will give the jurors of either your client or your client's cause.

Take the substantive and human facts that you have collected and put them into a first draft opening statement. If the facts you decide to include do not tell the jurors about what happened at the scene, or what will happen in the courtroom, or about an important person in the play, take them out of your opening statement.

The trial notebook procedure and the Closing Argument/Jury Instructions/Opening Statement method of case analysis are techniques for insuring that you have an overall view of what to present and how to present it. These techniques of perspective will not become less important after your first trial, but they will become second nature. You may find other procedures and analytic frameworks better suited to your method of work. There is less "right" and "wrong" to trial than to most other endeavors. In preparation, as well as in trial, *the* technique used is not as important as having *a* technique personally designed to do the task.

CHAPTER 4

PREPARE THE PLAYERS IN THE WOODSHED

Most of us, when we leave the theater, talk about the great acting performances, but do not even remember the name of the director who brought those performances out of the actors. Bringing the best performance out of the actors is the mark of a great director. It is no different with trial lawyers. Theater, of course, is pretend, while trial is our best attempt to reflect reality. Lawyers have real clients and present real witnesses. But, at trial, the real human dilemmas are resolved by how the jurors judge the performance of the players.

The trial lawyer can rely upon "truth" and luck alone or upon witness preparation to obtain a successful witness presentation. In choosing between the two, keep in mind that if your client's truth does not prevail, it cannot be explained away by the poor performance of a witness. The lawyer controls the case and is paid by the client to plead the cause. Witnesses do not "mess up," only lawyers do. The lawyer has but one way to avoid a poor performance by a witness: "woodshed" the witness. The term has survived from the days when our parents straightened us out in the woodshed behind the house—usually with the aid of small switch or a tough hand. Although the small switch and tough hand have gone by the way as tools of teaching, the trial lawyers who survive are those who know the value of putting witnesses in the woodshed.

In one sense, preparation of a witness begins from the first moment that you know of the witness' existence. Investigation, interview, preparation for deposition, and the taking of statements are a few of the preparatory events that might be applied to a witness. What follows after those preparatory steps have been completed, is the subject of this chapter.

It may be more precise to describe the preparatory steps as preparation of the case, rather than preparation of the witness. Discovery, investigation, and the first interview provide the substantive information upon which a case is built. The witness is preparing the lawyer to present the case more than the lawyer is preparing the witness to present testimony. The difference is important in dispelling a common misconception that inhibits beginning trial lawyers from fully preparing a witness after the witness has furnished information that helps to prepare the lawyer. It is unethical for a lawyer to tell a witness *what* truth to say; it is your job to tell the witness *how* to say the truth. Do not confuse helping witnesses to communicate the truth effectively with creating or altering the truth. Your job is to take the facts that you get and develop them into a cohesive story that explains the "what" and the "why" of your case. If you do not prepare your witnesses to convey their ideas effectively, your continued losses will one day drive you out of the profession. Preparation of the witness for trial, to be consistent with the ethics of the profession and the persuasive mission of the trial, requires the lawyer to teach the witness how to be a believable player on the trial stage. Preparation of the witness begins with preparation of the lawyer. Before the lawyer can operate effectively in the "woodshed" the lawyer must know how the witness needs to be "straightened out."

Order the Witnesses

The witness' position in your case and the relationship between the witness' testimony and that of your other witnesses are things the witness ought to know in most situations. If you have prepared an opening statement that tells the story of the trial, you may have already determined the order of witnesses. If you have prepared an opening statement that tells the story of the event, the order of witnesses is the next step in trial preparation. Unfortunately, many trial lawyers leave the order of witnesses to chance or availability. How would *Hamlet* play if the ghost showed up in the middle of the story rather than in the beginning? The order in which witnesses are presented directly affects the jurors' ability to recall and believe the case. Lawyers who present their witnesses in story order increase the likelihood of a verdict in their case, especially when the opposing lawyer fails to present witnesses in story order. So what does it mean to present witnesses in story order and how does real-world availability affect it?

If you begin considering the order of witnesses without first considering availability, you run the risk of creating a great plan that cannot be executed. While expert witnesses cause the greatest scheduling problem due to their tight schedules, other witnesses work, too, have children that need attending, and have other matters that will cause you more difficulty than you can imagine. Contact witnesses early, warn them of the likely trial dates, prepare them for the necessity of quick response to your beck and call during that short period in their lives when they are witnesses and take whatever action will give you the most flexibility. Discover any scheduling problems early and learn about the factors that control the witness' availability so that you can account for them in setting the order.

Assuming that you have a cooperative group of witnesses, you should begin order consideration with three standbys of persuasion: primacy, recency, and variety.

Primacy is the psychologist's shorthand for the proposition that first impressions matter. We remember best what we see first. The first idea stays the longest.

Recency is the psychologist's shorthand for the opposite idea. The final impression is lasting. Memories are short and latch onto the last thing. The last word is the best word.

"Variety is the spice of life." By breaking concentration patterns with variety, you can generate a new level of attention, creating more first and last impression opportunities.

A beginning lawyer may say that primacy and recency suggest filling the first and last positions with important witnesses, but that is not necessarily so. Primacy and recency tell you less about where to put important witnesses, and more about the natural importance of the first and last impressions. Although primacy, recency, and variety do not dictate the order of witnesses, they are powerful concepts of persuasion that ought not to be overlooked in choosing between various methods of organizing the case-in-chief.

Think about your audience; it is unfamiliar with your case. You have told them the story of your case in the opening statement. If you were directing this play, what would the opening scene be? How do you want your story to unfold? Stories must have a beginning, middle and end—primacy, variety and recency. Unlike a movie or play, the lawyer can only call each witness once (usually), so we have to choose witnesses carefully. Think about the personality types and strengths of your witnesses, how they will do on direct and cross. If you want your story to start with a big overview, don't start with a witness that arrived late in the game and whose natural tendency is to relate details. If your play is best presented in chronological order, the first witness will necessarily be the witness with first knowledge. If, on the other hand, you use a topical approach, the first witness may be the one with the most to say about the topic you consider the most important. The case may be sufficiently fragmented, with many witnesses having very small pieces of the whole, so that you must begin with the one witness that can give the jury a testimonial overview to match your opening statement. The reason for placing a witness first is not as important as having a reason that relates to the rest of the case, and that recognizes the advantage of primacy. Some cases even justify calling the opposing party as your first witness for cross-examination under the rules. (This is risky business. Unless you are quite sure that the party is not prepared to be called, will look bad immediately, or will present the most important part of your case, save this tactic for another trial.)

The major effect of primacy is the opportunity to set the perspective from which the jurors view the entire trial. You might choose the first witness merely to emphasize that your case is beyond challenge. One way to convey that message is to present a witness that is immune to meaningful cross-examination. After such an "uncontested" start, the jurors might lean back and wait for the rest of your case with the subliminal understanding that there is not really any contest. You may find it important for the jury to believe that some ambiguous physical facts—such as the skid marks that are open to different interpretation—are really helpful to you, and make that point by starting with the witness that can present the facts. The case may be of the kind that cannot be understood without reference to a diagram, or a model, or a contested document. You may find it useful to begin with the witness that can lay the foundation for the exhibit that will be referred to throughout the entire trial. The ability to call the first witness is a major advantage to the plaintiff in setting the tone for the case. The ability to present the plaintiff's case in its entirety before the defendant is able to present a single witness is a major advantage to the plaintiff in controlling the perspective for the entire case, so don't waste it.

The defendant cannot afford to ignore the plaintiff's primacy advantage. As the defendant you always know you are going second, so make it work for you. If at all possible, the defendant should make an effective cross-examination of the plaintiff's first witness, even if it is nothing more than a demonstration that the witness does not know anything of substantive importance. For example, a scene-setting witness who lays the foundation for a diagram, and knows little of the events at issue, can be interrogated about what the witness does not know. The examination will demonstrate to the jury that the plaintiff's first witness is not really a witness, merely a preliminary matter. Condition the jurors early on that you are always going to have to go second and that they should think about what you will have to say about the testimony they hear, using imbedded questions or ideas. Think about what the order of plaintiff's witnesses might be so that your cross-examination is telling your story effectively. In many smaller cases, the plaintiff may end up calling all of the witnesses in the case, so your story has to be told in reaction to the plaintiff's witness order.

Part of the primacy advantage is the effect on tentative decision making. Most people make a decision about a situation, even if unconsciously, as soon as they believe they have all the facts. At trial, that means the first tentative decision is made after the plaintiff's opening statement. Although the defendant may be able to neutralize that first tentative decision or persuade the jurors that they must not make it (at least consciously), the jurors are likely to have reached another tentative conclusion at the end of the plaintiff's case. Jurors start constructing a story of the case in their heads as the facts develop. They begin piecing together what they think happened and begin sifting through the evidence that confirms their versions or stories. As their stories get increasingly set in their minds, it becomes increasingly harder to change their minds. We all go through this process when making complex decisions. Think about decisions you made about where to attend college or law school, which job to accept, which political candidate to vote for. If you made up your mind to vote for candidate "A" would you change your mind even if candidate "B" called you the night before the election? Probably not. People tend to make tentative decisions and then evaluate future information in light of that decision. The more comfortable they become with their tentative decisions the more confident they feel about their correctness and the more they downplay contrary information. If the defendant's first witness does not provide an answer to the jurors' implicit question, "And what do you have to say about that?" there is a substantial chance that the jurors' tentative decisions in favor of the plaintiff will be further reinforced.

If the defendant puts on a case-in-chief, the defendant's attention to witness order becomes even more important than the plaintiff's. Recency (the sharp last impression) is usually most important for the defendant's decision about witness order. (It will matter as well for the plaintiff if rebuttal is planned.) In evaluating the effect of recency, remember that recency is not an attention-getting mechanism like primacy. Its power is in the lingering quality of having the "last word." The added attention you might expect from a jury that knows a witness is your last one requires that you do something to let the jurors know that there is nothing after this. The likelihood that the defendant will "save the best for last" means that the plaintiff needs an effective cross-examination for that last witness as much as the defendant needed one for the plaintiff's first witness.

You should give careful consideration to where you position your client, the protagonist. In the case of the prosecutor, the critical witness is the victim of the crime. (In the case of murder, it is the victim's surrogate—the chief investigator.) Your client is the most important witness even if the client has little factual information about the case. The play is the client's cause, and the jurors' reaction to the client will affect the outcome. The client's credibility will affect the credibility of all the other witnesses and evidence in the case. While you might put a particularly likeable or credible witness in a position to influence the jurors' view of the entire case, you may want to put the protagonist in a position that will do the most to enhance the protagonist's credibility. The client's testimony might be most effective if the jurors are first warmed up to accept it. It may be that the client is so good and knows so much that everything ought to follow the client. Whether you use the client to show off your case, or use your case to enhance the client, be aware of the unique quality of the client's testimony, no matter how little the client knows.

Order your witnesses by concentrating on a presentation that hangs together and understand that there are particular values to be considered in the lead-off, the clean-up, the client, and the chemistry between successive witnesses.

Prepare the Testimony, Then the Witness

After you have examined all the information in the individual witness' section of the trial notebook and know all that the witness *can* say, you must determine what the witness *will* say. The filtering process of the first draft closing argument and the first draft opening statement should have removed most of the irrelevant material. Of the remainder, the witness must testify to everything required for your legal minimum, opening statement and closing

argument to which no one else can testify. Just
because a fact is important and the witness can
testify about it does not mean it has to be part of
the witness' testimony. The witness should not testify to facts about which others can testify more
appropriately or more effectively, unless the testimony is important for corroboration or emphasis.
For example, if the passenger in the car that was
struck in the intersection collision knows that the
other car was speeding, you may not want the
passenger to offer that testimony if any other witness can establish the speed as effectively. In the
first place, the passenger's estimate of speed of an
approaching car is suspect. Secondly, if the jurors
think the passenger is stretching to make a point
they may discount everything else that the witness
has to say. Finally, the jurors may wonder why the
driver did not notice the same thing and stay out of
the intersection. Other examples may be less obvious, but the principle is of equal importance: The
witness should only testify to those things the witness ought to know.

The mechanics of preparing your witness examination notes will be dictated, to some extent, by
personal work habits. Most beginning lawyers, overly concerned about catching everything, write inter-
minable and detailed notes. A three-step process for
preparing trial examination notes will provide the
same confidence, but will give greater efficiency and
provide a smoother examination at trial.

The first step in the process is to scan the factual
material, making judgments about what the witness

can say and what you want the witness to say.
Make a one or two word note of each separate item.

The second step, after the factual scan is completed, is to prepare every question of your direct
examination by writing out the entire question. If
you prefer writing out the desired answer, too, go
ahead if you have the time. Use the scan to check
for all the facts to be elicited, but do not follow the
scan for order. The tactical considerations for direct
examination question order is more fully discussed
in Chapter 9. For now, it is sufficient to note that
the order of facts on the scan (probably following
the order from a major statement or deposition) will
not be the order of questions on direct, except by
coincidence. As important as it is to write out every
direct examination question, it is equally important
not to take it those questions to trial. Do not even
put them in your trial notebook. The simple reason
is that if you take them, you will read them. Reading the questions on direct is too inflexible, too
stilted, and too likely to encourage you to avoid the
important third preparation step of reducing the
questions to usable trial examination notes.

The third step in the process is the reduction of
the question-by-question direct examination to the
examination notes to be used at trial. When completed, the reduction may end up looking very much
like the factual scan, except that the order will be
different. Some lawyers prefer that the examination
notes contain one or two word keys to the general
area of inquiry. Some prefer that the key relate to a
specific question. Others prefer that the key relate

to a specific answer. Whichever you use, the document, when complete, will be the only aid that you have at trial and should be the only testimonial aid you use in preparing the witness. It is the front entry in the individual witness' section of the trial notebook. Make sure that your examination notes include any exhibits and proper foundations that need to be offered by that witness.

When you construct your trial examination notes, avoid the common preparation error of assuming that using only a few words means you should use only a little space. Using a few words for notes is a process to ensure that you will think at trial rather than read a script. It is not a process designed to fool the jury into believing you have a faultless memory. You will use the notes better if they are written large enough so that they can be read at a glance.

After your first trial, and certainly by your third one, your confidence and ability should be sufficient to consider skipping directly from the factual scan to the trial examination notes. For the first trial, however, do not skip writing out the entire question and do not take the questions to court.

The last step in preparing yourself to prepare the witness is a task that when completed for your first trial will be valuable for all of your subsequent trials and generally applies to the preparation of every witness. Make a short checklist of warnings and preparation exercises to ensure that your witness does not look ineffective during direct examination or foolish during cross-examination. The items on that list, discussed at some length later in this chapter, should remain a permanent part of your witness preparation repertoire. Put it at the front of the witness sections of your trial notebook, and use it to ensure that you cover everything with every witness before every trial.

Preparing the Witness for Direct Examination

Witnesses wear different labels, depending upon who produced the witness, who is doing the labeling, and why. Before the widespread adoption of the substance of Fed.R.Evid. 607, which allows any party to impeach any witness, there were two kinds of witnesses at trial: yours and theirs. When discussing the testimony of these witnesses with the jury, however, the advocate often uses other labels: "neutral witnesses with no interest in the outcome" (yours), and "biased witnesses with a stake in the result" (theirs). Witnesses fall into different categories that will influence how you ought to prepare the witness: your client; friendly witnesses; neutral witnesses you must call; hostile witnesses you must call; and friendly witnesses that your opponent must call. Most of your witness preparation will be with friendly witnesses, of whom your client is the friendliest. The remaining witnesses that you have an opportunity to prepare will usually be neutral witnesses.

This discussion of preparation assumes that the witness to be prepared is friendly. Although turning neutral witnesses into friendly witnesses is an important skill to be developed, it is beyond the scope of this primer. For our purpose, the neutral is useful as a benchmark against which to measure friendly witnesses. An investigating police officer is a classic example of a neutral witness. The testimony may favor one party, and if the lawyer is adept at personal relationships, the officer might be converted to a friendly witness, but the officer starts out as a neutral. The passenger in your client's automobile, on the other hand, is likely to be a friendly witness, even though there may be a technical conflict between the "non-negligent" driver and the passenger-friend who is suing everybody, including the driver. Occurrence witnesses that develop an opinion about the occurrence usually become friendly to the side their opinion favors, unless the lawyer does something to irritate them. The continuum from the friendliest to the neutral witness provides a measure of the cooperation you can expect, and the extent to which you can influence how—not what, but how—the witness will testify.

Three "truths" exist for all witnesses: (1) Witnesses are nervous about testifying at trial. (2) Witnesses, even the worst, have something good about them, and even the best have something bad. (3) Witnesses know a lot more about the substance of their testimony than they do about how to present it. Do not allow anything your witness does during preparation tempt you to modify your understanding of the three truths. Even the most self-confident witness is nervous about the prospect of testifying and being cross-examined. (The primary reason for asking all witnesses their name and address at the beginning of a direct examination is that the questions are ones that even the most nervous witness is likely to understand and answer properly.) A major goal of witness preparation is to put the witness in a proper frame of mind to be an effective witness. Witnesses can be insecure about everything from what the courtroom looks like to their personal appearance. Obviously, different tactics work with different witnesses. The tactic you choose should be calculated to produce a witness with a feeling of security about testifying. Help your witness address any areas of concern without trivializing them and give them specific advice. After all, you are reading a whole primer on your first trial. Confidence building is a continual part of preparation.

If lawyers could pick witnesses, all witnesses would be too good to be true. Happily, lawyers do not usually pick witnesses. (Experts are the exception.) One of the reasons that the system works is that the lawyer must work with the witnesses the case produces. There is something for a mother to love in every witness, and something for a sinner to hate in every saint. The advocate's job is to find the bright spot in that terrible witness and then to decide how to use it to put the witness in the best possible light. Similarly, the lawyer must recognize weak spots in the strong witnesses and, during preparation, either shore them up or find a way to minimize them at trial. Don't expect perfection from witnesses or for them to do more than they can. Witnesses, like all of us, get nervous and resort to all of their "bad habits" when pushed. Have realistic expectations about how a witness that is easily confused or angered when nervous will do on the stand. Remember how the witness appeared in deposition or when first interviewed. That is the person the jurors are likely to see. The more important the witness, the more time you need to spend helping that witness to relate the testimony effectively. Help the witness to anticipate cross-examination and provide specific strategies to deal with it. Have the witness practice sitting across the room from you in a setting that resembles the witness seat in a courtroom. Do everything you can to help the witness feel as comfortable and confident as possible.

Although witnesses know more about the substance than the theater of their testimony, they believe the opposite. Most potential witnesses are nervous because they expect to forget some of the substance or because they think the cross-examiner will be able to take the substance, tie it around their necks, and hang them with it. Most of them, at the same time, think they present themselves pretty well and that if they tell the truth, they will be believed. Although many of us are poor communicators, few of us realize it or want it called to our attention. Most of your final preparation will be about the theater. If you couch it in terms of substance, the witnesses will accept it hungrily. If you couch it in terms of changing personal communication habits, you can expect resistance.

When witnesses come to your office for their preparation sessions, they should have received and reviewed all previous statements, depositions, documents, and other pertinent exhibits. Be very careful, however, not to give any witness a synopsis sheet that you have prepared. Even if you have forgotten that Fed.R.Evid. 612 allows your opponent to inspect any writing that a witness has used to refresh recollection before testifying, your opponent probably has not. Do not allow witnesses to leave your office with a "copy of the answers" or any other document that indicates a proposed direct examination. Remember that you have an absolute attorney-client privilege only with your client. Depending on the law of your jurisdiction the attorney work-product exception should protect all of your preparations except that of expert witnesses. Typically testifying expert witnesses are required to disclose all information they have reviewed and all information that in any way forms a basis for their opinions. Be careful about any documents, pictures, letters or e-mails that you send or share with an expert. When preparing the expert be mindful of sharing any facts or opinions, strategies that, if pressed, you would not want repeated on cross-examination.

You need to know if your witnesses will be effective and should be mildly interested in whether they have reasonable memories, so do not allow them to have depositions and past statements at hand during preparation of direct testimony. You are not interested in whether they can read, just in whether they can testify. It is important to gain a feel for how the witnesses will testify in court—a very formal setting. For that reason, you should never prepare witnesses in their homes or places of work. In their own surroundings, witnesses cannot show you how they will react in court. There is a constant tension between needing formality to tell you how witnesses will do and encouraging informality so that witnesses will be relaxed enough to assimilate what you have to teach. Similarly, there will be a constant tension between giving witnesses enough advice and warning to cope with the trial situation, whatever it may be, and providing so much advice and warning that the witnesses are too frightened to perform. The first step to the resolution of those tensions is to understand the problem.

Tell witnesses their places in the trial. Witnesses should understand why they are being called to testify. The explanation should place them in the context of the lawsuit. Tell witnesses where they are placed in the lineup. When testifying in court, witnesses should have an idea of what the jurors already know and not feel compelled to repeat testimony. This is a good time to warn witnesses about sequestration. They need to know to bring a book or a newspaper to read while waiting. In addition, they need to know that they cannot listen to the testimony of others as a check on their own testimony. When telling witnesses about their places in the lawsuit and their spots in the lineup, be sure to find out about their schedules so that you cause a minimum of disturbance from their routines.

The first step in substantive preparation is to identify the major points of the witness' testimony, and make sure the witness understands that the remainder of the testimony is less important. Witnesses forget sometimes. If they know what really counts from the outset, what they forget is likely to come from the remainder. Furthermore, knowing what really counts is likely to reduce the witness' anxiety about remembering "everything"—a great aid to remembering "everything."

When you are talking about what is important, or after you have rehearsed the testimony, you must review matters that you want the witness to avoid. Not only is it important that you understand the ethical necessity of this review, it is important that witnesses understand it if they are to be comfortable with the instruction to avoid certain matters. Assuming that you have considered the wisdom of raising a piece of unfortunate evidence before your opponent does, and have decided against it, you must not leave the witness in the dark about it. It is unethical and illegal to tell a witness to lie. It is unethical and illegal to tell a witness to give a partial answer to a question that fairly calls for more. It is stupid and unethical to allow a witness to offer damaging information when no question has been asked that calls for the information. Tell the witness what you do not intend to ask about and what you do not think ought to be offered unless asked. The difference between not offering and hiding is the difference between legal and illegal, ethical and unethical. Tell your witness to avoid any matters that you will seek to exclude in a motion *in limine*, as well as the rules about subjects such as insurance. Above all, remind all witnesses to tell the truth as they know it.

There is no one method of witness preparation that works for all lawyers or for all witnesses. Three methods and one non-method account for most preparations. The non-method, unfortunately, is employed by far too many lawyers; it is faith in the witness' extemporaneous recitation of the truth. The apologists for the approach contend that if witnesses are a little nervous and disorganized their testimony will come gushing out with the unmistakable odor of the unrehearsed truth and a sympathetic jury will accept it. That the testimony will have an unmistakable odor is probably right. If you still believe in the tooth fairy, you should use the extemporaneous truth non-method of preparation.

Full rehearsal of direct examination and full simulated cross-examination are the two most common methods of preparation. A combination of the two, with varying emphasis, is not uncommon. Those who advocate the full dress rehearsal of the direct examination vary in the intensity and amount of practice. Some lawyers use videotape, playing it back so that the witness can see what is not working. Others do one complete run-through and call it a day. If you decide to use the full dress rehearsal (save the videotape for later), be sensitive to the memorization problem. Do not let the witness think that any question will necessarily follow any other particular question at trial. You do not want the witness to rely on an order or a script. The testimony cannot sound as if it was by rote. The endless rehearsal of a play is necessary because the actors are learning someone else's words. In your trial/play, the words are those of the witness. Do not, by over-rehearsal, transpose witnesses from people speaking their own words into people repeating memorized dialogue. If the testimony sounds memorized, the jurors will never know it was in the witnesses before the memorization process started. They will think that you, the lawyer, wrote a script.

The advocates of the full-scale simulated cross-examination contend that the preparation is as complete as with a full-scale direct, but is without the danger of developing a robot witness. In addition, the witness is "fire tested" for any cross-examination. The problems are that the lawyer does not have an opportunity to see how the witness will react to open questions that allow the witness room for a narrative response, and the attempt to elicit direct examination through cross-examination questions may petrify the witness. If you do opt for a full cross-examination preparation, have someone else do the cross. You want to preserve the witnesses' faith and confidence in you as their protector while they are on the witness stand. If you are more aggressive or "turn" on a witness while cross-examining, the witness may fear that you will do the same during trial.

Witness preparation ought to combine selected direct examination questions, simulated cross-examination questions, and some intelligent conversation. If you have prepared your examination notes for trial, using your notes as a checklist, review the substance of the witness' testimony through conversation about the events. Do not proceed in the order that you expect to use for examination at trial. By hopping around from topic to topic, you will avoid locking the witness into an order, while at the same time, fully satisfying yourself about the substance of the witness' testimony. The conversation is the time to plant phrases that you want the witness to use and root out expressions that you hope the witness will avoid. For example, if your witness keeps referring to "the accident," and you represent the plaintiff, you should suggest "crash" or "collision" or some other useful term that more adequately conveys what the witness means. Explain to the witness that "accident" has a different meaning in the law from what the witness is trying to say. At law, "accident" has a meaning inconsistent with the witness' belief that the defendant was at fault. The use of key words and phrases is important for emphasis, and for imprinting concepts upon the jurors' collective mind. The suggestion of another phrase is both useful and ethical, so long as you do not try to change the idea that the witness is attempting to communicate.

During conversation with witnesses, arrange a verbal signal, for use at trial, to tell witnesses that they have forgotten something. "Anything else" is a common signal. It is a poor direct examination question normally, so, "Did anything else happen," or "Is there anything else," will tell the witness: "You forgot something—think." It may be useful to explain some common objections to let witnesses know that the objections can provide a way for you to "talk" to them while they are being cross-examined. For example, your objection, "speculation, the witness wasn't working at the plant in 2008," is a great reminder for the witness to stop guessing about what the manual said, or what prior managers did. It can be a useful way of getting witnesses back on track if they are getting lost during cross-examination.

If, after the conversation, you are satisfied about the substance of the testimony, tell the witness the topical order of testimony and put the witness in a formal setting to test reaction "under fire." The client, and major friendly witnesses over whom you have control, ought to be taken to the courtroom for orientation. (Prudence dictates that you not tell the client or the witness that it is your first time, too.) If you are in a trial district where courts are often empty and you can control who comes and goes, you may wish to conduct a partial direct examination rehearsal in the courtroom. (Every time we tried it, our opponent's investigator or a future member of the jury panel wandered in.) Even if you do not do a testimonial run through, you should take witnesses to the witness stand. Let them sit in the chair. Show them where the court reporter sits, where the judge is, where the jury box is, and from where you will ask questions. Ask some innocuous questions to give witnesses a feel for the courtroom. Check voice level for witnesses, telling them how loudly you expect them to speak. It is helpful to put witnesses in the jury box and yourself on the witness stand to demonstrate the need for proper voice level and eye contact. Give some testimony while looking towards the lawyer's interrogation position, and then show them the difference by talking to them as they sit in the jury box. If you expect to use a diagram or exhibit with witnesses, show them where the exhibits will be, how they should refer to exhibits, and how they can get to an exhibit from the witness stand. Let them use the pointer. All of us feel more comfortable, and therefore, do better in familiar surroundings. Performance day is a bad day for a witness' first look at the stage.

After the witness has seen the courtroom (do not do more than one witness at a time), go back to the office to do the formal rehearsal of the direct and cross. Be sure the witness feels the pressure of the real thing, and then do a portion of the direct examination. Remember that you are looking for a clue to the witness' demeanor, not testing substance. Although there is little you can do to change your witness' manner, you can tell the witness what may not work as well in a trial setting as in conversation. These mannerisms may not work in conversation either, but do not tell that to the witness— you need cooperation!

Some witnesses will answer the question, "What happened after the blue car stopped?" with: "The driver pulled out without looking, ran right in front of the other car and caused an accident." If you have a volunteer/advocate, you must tone that witness down if you expect the jurors to believe that the witness is not so biased that the testimony ought to be disregarded.

The "actor" is more difficult to control. If your witness takes the trial as the first audition for a stage career, you will need some serious work and a delicate touch. One technique is a cross-examination that makes the witness look bad. The obvious dangers of this approach are: (1) it may not work and you will reinforce the testimony, and (2) it may work and the witness will be useless. Sometimes you can persuade this witness that the best actors succeed by understatement. Often there is nothing that will change the witness' behavior and you are forced to tighten up the direct so that the questions are just short of leading.

The most common witness characteristic you are likely to see, and one of the easiest to cure, is the incipient lawyer. The witness that qualifies everything must be persuaded that, "As I recall, yes," is less than you have a right to when you ask: "Does the sun come up in the east?" "I believe," or some other qualifier is not a good preface for a lay witness. It is your task to explain to witnesses that the qualification of every answer will make them more, not less, vulnerable to cross-examination. Even the professional witness, such as a police officer, needs to be reminded that the officer did not arrive someplace at "approximately 6:24." "Approximately 6:30," maybe, but not "approximately 6:24."

There are many other witness idiosyncrasies that the lawyer will encounter and must analyze and correct during witness preparation. You will only see them if you do enough formal examination of the witness to check the witness' examination demeanor.

Preparing the Witness for Cross-examination

Preparing the witness for cross-examination demands constant attention to telling the witness enough to be prepared, but not so much that fear sets in. A discussion of the following points, with examples as you go, and a short exemplary cross at the end, should warn the witness without causing a heart attack.

The number one problem for witnesses on cross-examination is explanation. Most witnesses explain when they should shut up, and shut up when they should explain. Tell the witness that the most important aid to answering cross-examination questions is to listen to the question, and answer exactly what has been asked—nothing more, even if it helps, and nothing less, even if it hurts. If you explain that this guarantees witnesses that they cannot then be made to look the fool, even if an answer is not helpful to the case, the witness will take heed.

Tell witnesses not to answer a cross-examination question until repeating the question to themselves and understanding exactly what has been asked. If they repeat the question to themselves, they are unlikely to answer more than has been asked. You can emphasize the problem of over-explaining by giving concrete examples. Explain the danger that the jurors will believe witnesses are partisan if they explain too much:

> Cross-examination question: "How fast do you think the defendant was going?"
>
> Answer: "That car was speeding at sixty miles per hour."

Show the witness why "That car was speeding" is an explanation that does not respond to the question of "how fast?" and will make it look as if the witness has an ax to grind.

The same witnesses that offer more than is asked offer less than they are entitled to give when the cross-examiner asks a "why" question. Encourage these witnesses to be expansive in answering a question that fairly requires or implies an explanation. "Why in the world would the defendant do that?"—even if asked with a smug sneer from the cross-examiner—calls for the witness to speculate about "why the defendant did," and anything the witness says is both fair and fully answers no more than the question asked. Tell the witness never to adopt an argumentative manner with the cross-examiner, but never to miss an opportunity to make an explanation (argument) if the cross-examiner invites it by asking a question that implies the witness' reasoning or conclusions are faulty. "Well then, if that is true, there is no way the defendant could have been where you said. Isn't that right?" is the kind of question that fairly asks the witness to justify the testimony, and the witness ought to do it, and do it, and do it, until the examiner understands why that kind of question should never be asked on cross-examination.

The witness should be warned not to get locked into an unreasonably precise or certain answer. If the driver of an automobile testifies during direct to going forty-five miles per hour, some cross-examiners are going to ask: "You weren't going exactly forty-five, were you?" If the driver insists on forty-five, no faster, no slower, the jurors are unlikely to believe it. If the driver says "about forty-five," the jurors, who never know exactly how fast the car was going, will believe the car was going "about forty-five" and that is good enough. Witnesses need not be more precise than common sense dictates. It is the lawyer's duty to tell them that.

There is a big difference between an approximation and a guess. "About forty-five" is appropriate when the witness knows that the car was going at that speed, but is unacceptable if the witness has no idea. Tell the witness again and again: *Never guess* when answering a cross-examination question. If the witness does not know the answer to a question, "I don't know" is better than any guess. If the witness knew and forgot, or should know and cannot recall, "I don't remember" is better than any guess. Cross-examiners dream about a witness who resorts to the guess. Be aware, when you tell the witness about "I don't remember," that the witness may fall into the trap of believing an "I don't remember" answer is a shield against all cross-examination questions. It is a good answer only when it is honest. Too many "I don't remember" responses will look like evasion.

The "never guess" rule should be applied to impeachment with a prior statement. Tell the witness that any question that asks, "Do you remember saying in a statement that . . ." is the beginning of an attempt to show the jurors that the witness said something at an earlier time that is different from what the witness said today. Tell the witness to answer "yes," only if the witness remembers the exact words, and if the examiner has repeated them properly. If the witness does not remember the exact words, the witness should not guess that the examiner must be right. Explain that a fair response is something like, "It has been a while, can you show me the statement?" or "Do you want me to guess?" If done politely, it stops the cross-examiner from making effective use of the provision of Fed.R.Evid. 613 allowing impeachment without showing the impeaching vehicle to the witness.

Warn the witness about the standard "trick" questions used by the lawyers in your territory, or by the particular lawyer in your case. For your first trial you will have to rely upon information from your colleagues. If you cannot find out what is common, consider this line of questioning, still used by some lawyers:

"Have you talked to anybody about this lawsuit?"

"Why are you testifying?"

"What did the lawyer tell you to say?"

Most witnesses believe it is "wrong" to talk to a lawyer about a case, no matter how much you tell them to the contrary, and they answer the question, "Have you talked to anybody?" with a hesitating and embarrassed "Yes" or a lying "No." Tell them to answer with a positive "Yes" or "Of course." Subpoena your witnesses so that they can respond to "Why are you here?" with, "Because I was subpoenaed." (This is not necessary with allied witnesses whose bias is obvious anyway.) Just as it is important for the witness to understand it is ethical for both lawyer and witness to talk to each other before trial, the witness should know, and be told specifically, that you expect the witness to "tell the truth." Aside from the ethical obligation, it is a nice phrase to hear the witness toss back to the witless lawyer who asks: "What did the lawyer tell you to say?" "The lawyer told me to tell the truth."

Three "procedural" matters should be covered with every witness that you prepare for cross-examination. Witnesses must understand that you, the direct examiner, have no function in cross-examination. You cannot respond to witnesses' pleas for help. A witness should not look to you for the answer to a tough cross-examination question, or by any gesture, give the jurors the idea that the witness looks to you for help. Nothing is so damaging to witness credibility as the notion that the lawyer has dictated what the witness has said. At the same time, tell witnesses about objections, and how the objection is the lawyer's weapon to help on cross-examination if witnesses pay attention. Insist that witnesses close their mouths tight the moment they see you on your feet or hear you objecting—even if the witness thinks that the answer will be helpful. Emphasize the importance of not beginning the answer, or the importance of stopping in mid-sentence, when you are objecting. The witness can use the time during which the objection is considered, to get composed, think of the next answer, or think of the last question. Remind witnesses to listen to your objection to see if it gives any clues as to how they might rephrase the testimony. The witnesses should know that they cannot begin or continue an answer after an objection until the judge—not the other lawyer, the judge—says "overruled" or "you may answer." Last, remember to warn the witness about sequestration.

Before leaving the subject of cross-examination, warn the witness, again, about the danger of explaining during cross-examination when the question does not ask for an explanation. Tell the witness about redirect examination. Assure the witness that if you think matters need explaining, you will have an opportunity to ask about it on redirect. If there are specific areas that you know are vulnerable, ask the witness about the inconsistency or other vulnerability. If the explanation is satisfactory, tell the witness that you will ask about it on redirect if, after cross-examination, it is necessary. Plan your redirect now with your witness if you anticipate needing one. Remind the witness that the key to surviving cross-examination is to think about what is asked, and answer only what is asked. Remember not to allow the witness to leave your office with a copy of the witness' deposition or statement. You need them for trial, the witness does not. If the witness does not yet feel secure about the testimony, continue the preparation; do not let the witness go home and worry about it.

Preparing the Client

Tell clients that they are on stage the entire time. Jurors will always look at clients throughout the trial, so their non-verbal behavior will speak as loud if not louder than their verbal testimony. Grimaces, faces, and physical speech of any kind while some-one else is testifying will cause the jurors to react negatively. If your client puts on a show at the counsel table, the audience will boo when it brings in the verdict.

You must also avoid having your clients whisper, "that's a lie," in your ear so that you cannot hear the lie the liar is telling. You need your clients' active interest, and every once in a while they will have good ideas or important facts. Give the clients a pad. Explain that you need their information and that they should write one idea, question, or com-ment on a page, tear it off and put it near you. Assure clients that you will look at the notes at the first opportunity. If you make that promise during preparation, and do not look at the notes at your first opportunity, the clients will start whispering in your ear again.

Two matters that you might find difficult to approach must, nevertheless, be handled with clients. The client's behavior is being constantly scrutinized. Jurors look for any way possible to match the reality they observe in the courtroom with who they think the client, the lawyer, and witnesses are when they think no one is looking. There must be an explanation somewhere why there is a prospective juror on the elevator every time your client makes an indiscreet remark about the case or uses offensive language. Every restroom, restaurant, phone call, parking space is a potential pitfall for everyone involved in the trial.

The second matter is appearance. An in-depth consideration of costuming is beyond the scope of this primer. Some lawyers believe that it is beyond the scope of what any trial lawyer ought to be concerned with. There are two rules, however, that can never hurt you.

Regardless of how informal the rest of society has become, the court is the temple of the law. Your clients should not necessarily go out to buy something to wear to court, but ought to wear whatever they would wear to a "dress up" place. Courtrooms are still traditional, so a tie, skirt or dress, what used to be "church clothes" are still best. Most juries will still include a significant number of seniors and baby boomers who still expect traditional courtroom attire. This is no time for anyone (lawyers included) to show off expensive jewelry, tattoos, or great legs.

No witness can carry off being someone else. If you try to manicure, haircut, and dress your college-aged drug defendant into the president of General Motors, you had better be sure that the image you are creating will ring true with the jurors. It will be difficult for the jurors to accept you client's testimony or your case if they believe that your client is putting on a show for the occasion. There is a fine line between dressing up for court and putting on a show for the occasion, but it is a line that must be discovered and honored. Your clients ought to be themselves at their best, but cannot be someone else—no matter how appealing that someone else might be.

The last warning for clients is about cross-examination under the rules. A party may call an adverse party for cross-examination in the former's case-in-chief. While the problem is more often one for the defendant, or in the case of the corporate defendant, its representative; the plaintiff should also be warned. As embarrassed as defendant's counsel might be when the corporate defendant's president is unexpectedly called as the first witness in the plaintiff's case, plaintiff's counsel does not feel great when the plaintiff, relieved from finally testifying, is called unexpectedly as a witness in the defendant's case.

Preparing the Expert

Expert witnesses are special at trial and present unique preparation problems. You may have an expert that came with the case, i.e. the treating physician or police accident re-constructionist; or you may have the expert that you chose, that you cast to play a specific part. The rules of procedure will govern when and how you must identify your expert. The rules of evidence will govern your expert's qualifications and the scope of the expert's testimony. Make sure you have a thorough understanding of both so that you do not suffer any unexpected restrictions on your expert's ability to testify.

Experts enjoy an undue amount of respect from juries. The "expert" that receives that respect from the jurors may not be the same person you have in mind when you think of an expert. For the jurors, an "expert" is a person whose opinion the jurors are more inclined to accept than their own about a matter at issue in the case. They are more likely to accept the "expert's" opinion because they believe the expert's training provides an insight that is unavailable to them. Notice that the jurors' definition does not require that the witness testify as an expert under Fed.R.Evid. 702, nor does it encompass everyone that does testify under Fed.R.Evid. 702. An investigating police officer, for example, will probably be considered an "expert" by the jurors after the officer is accredited, regardless of whether the officer is asked or offers any opinions other than those that would be admissible by a lay witness under Fed.R.Evid. 701. On the other hand, a psychiatrist, whose opinion about a party's mental state is admissible under Fed.R.Evid. 702, may not be viewed as an "expert" by jurors who believe that no one can be trained to really understand another human being's mind. An accident re-constructionist, in those jurisdictions that recognize such an expert, is at least initially more like the psychiatrist than the police officer, because the re-constructionist will be making the same judgment the jurors are asked to make with little, or hard to understand training that will cause the jurors to bow to the "expert's" opinion. If nothing else, this redefinition of "expert" ought to give you a clue about the importance of a meaningful qualification of your expert and the significance of who you choose to call an expert.

Remembering that we are still directing this play, the expert we hire is one of the few players we get to actually cast. Knowing the level of respect the jurors can have for an expert, make your selection count. Think of your play as it stands. What kind of witness will be of most help? Who will the other side bring? If your opponent's case has lots of theory, maybe you want someone practical. If your witnesses know bits and pieces of the case, you might want an expert that can help the jurors to see the big picture. Once you have chosen the best witness you can, your task is to get the jurors to believe the "expert." The hired expert's qualifications are critical to introducing the jurors to this witness, who lacks the natural credibility of having firsthand knowledge of events. Even with experts who come with the case, their qualifications can make them more believable than your opponent's expert, or other fact witnesses who contradict the expert's opinions. While you are required to provide enough of the expert's qualifications to build the foundation for the opinion, you should prepare the witness for the foundation testimony with an eye towards persuading the jurors that the expert's opinion is of the kind that should be accepted.

Preparation of the foundation testimony, as well as the substance, will depend upon what the expert has done with respect to the case and what the other side will be doing with expert witnesses. It will matter, as well, whether you are in a jurisdiction that follows *Frye v. United States*[1] or *Daubert v. Merrell Dow Pharmaceuticals*[2] in the approach to establishing and challenging expert witnesses. (The difference is an evidence issue beyond the purpose of this primer, but if you are presenting an expert you must know your jurisdiction's approach.)[3] Although you may be presenting a treating doctor in a personal injury case for an opinion about disability, you may be more interested in the doctor's testimony describing the treatment, the description of the

---

1. 293 F. 1013 (D.C. Cir. 1923).

2. 509 U.S. 579 (1993).

3. You will find a discussion of the difference at Chapter 10, Park, Leonard, and Goldberg, EVIDENCE LAW: A STUDENT'S GUIDE TO THE LAW OF EVIDENCE AS APPLIED IN AMERICAN TRIALS (Thomson West, 2d Ed.).

continuing disability, and the cost. On the other hand, you may be presenting an expert who has done nothing as a participant in the case, but is testifying to an opinion of what others have done, or about the present, past, or future condition of something or somebody. You might be so fortunate as to have the only expert in the case, but it is more likely that the other side will present an expert with a contrary opinion. In either case, the foundation for the jurors acceptance of your expert's expertise is critical. Do it right!

Experts usually have more difficulty with scheduling preparation sessions and trial appearances than do most witnesses (and, in any event, will be more vocal about the problems.) Be sure that you get a copy of the expert's résumé at your first contact, so that you have it well in mind when you corral the expert for a preparation session. Do not allow your expert to put you off with assurances that after having testified a thousand times, the expert does not need preparation. Every expert needs it, and even if the expert doesn't, you do. Since your expert's qualifications are the keys to credibility, the way you present them is critical. No one will pay attention to a dry recitation of where the expert went to school or a list of articles written. Weave in the credentials so that they are meaningful. There may be more than one audience for the qualifications. If you expect a challenge to your expert, you want the judge to notice. You may even preempt a voir dire objection if it is plain that your expert has the experience to back up the opinions offered. Go behind some of the items in the résumé and try to find a "human" element that can be used to emphasize the most important part of the qualifications. Look for specific experience, even if it does not sound particularly impressive, that relates to the subject of the opinion to be given in the case, especially if the other expert lacks that experience. An accident re-constructionist, for example, who was a police officer, even if it had nothing to do with accidents, should include that past as a police officer in the qualifying testimony. A psychiatrist who spent six months as an administrator in a state mental hospital for the criminally insane should be asked about that experience with some emphasis if the expert is testifying in a criminal trial, even if the reason the expert is in the case is thirty-five years of private practice and a reputation with colleagues as the best diagnostician in the state. Explain to your expert that you will resist stipulating to qualifications if the other side offers, and that you consider the manner in which the expert tells the jury about experience to be as important as any part of the testimony. Tell your expert that you will ask specific questions so the jurors do not view the recital as "bragging," but remind the expert to be forthright about experience. Ask the expert to think of the foundation not as a recitation of grandeur and accomplishment, but as a sharing of life experience. Your expert will say it better and the jurors will hear it more clearly.

When discussing the expert's testimony, you must arrive at a tactical judgment about whether the opinion will be presented before the facts supporting it, afterwards, or without factual support on direct examination. Fed.R.Evid. 705 allows the expert's naked opinion. The expert's ability to communicate the underlying facts, data, and opinion should shape your decision. Although there may be a circumstance in which the naked opinion is offered with all facts left for the cross-examiner to find, both facts and opinion will be more often in your direct and the question will be whether facts or opinion should come first. The facts and assumptions underlying the opinion, if well presented, may be as persuasive as the opinion itself. If you can present the expert's qualifications, then the information available, then the opinion, the progression will add to the credibility of the opinion. Some opinions are such that the detailed factual recitation does little to enhance them, and indeed, offering the opinion first makes the importance of the facts apparent.

The problem of presenting a "canned" recital is less with an expert than with other witnesses. The expert's testimony, unlike that of an occurrence witness, is better if it appears to be well thought out and calculated. If you have the time, go through the full direct examination, question-by-question, with the expert. As you proceed, be aware of some continuing problems with expert testimony.

Jargon is the major obstacle to the jurors' understanding of the expert's testimony. A little technical language shows the jurors that the expert is, indeed, an expert, but you should try to force the expert to speak in language familiar to the jurors. (There will inevitably be more than enough jargon for the small benefit of validating the expert.) In preparation, stop the expert on every single word with which you think the jurors will not be familiar and ask the expert for an ordinary term to convey the idea. A doctor might tell the jurors about "myostatic contracture of the Gastrocnemius," but the jurors need to know about the shortening of the large muscle on the back of the calf that resulted from the cast on the leg. This is, also, a good time to prepare yourself. Do not fall into the trap of using the expert's jargon in your questions. Resist the temptation to appear like a translator of a language that only you and the expert understand at trial. It can make both of you appear condescending to the jurors. When you are through with the direct examination preparation, be sure that you understand everything that the expert has said. If the expert can teach you, the expert will be able to teach the jurors.

Preparing the expert for cross-examination leads you to an irony. The problem with many experts is that they assume the cross-examiner does not know as much as they do about the subject, and that the jurors will accept their opinions because of who they are. At the same time, and no matter how confident they appear, most experts are scared to death of cross-examination. The fright is based upon the belief that the sneaky lawyer will blind-side them and make them look bad. Experts are more apprehensive about cross-examination than regular witnesses because it is the experts' *opinions*—not their eyesight or hearing—that is at issue. Their pride and reputations are at stake. Knowing this, you must work extra hard with the expert on the theater of cross-examination, or run the risk that the expert will make all the wrong responses.

The danger of the "hard position," the inappropriate explanation, and the imputation of bias are magnified with experts. In most scientific areas, the acknowledgement of uncertainty or the possibility of error is not calculated to increase acceptability. Most experts are accustomed to having opinions accepted without question by peers or those relying upon the expert. The common response to the smallest challenge is to circle up the wagons, stake out a small piece of ground, and defend it until the bitter end. Your experts must understand that if the issues were that clear you would not be in court. Help the expert to understand that an opinion will be more readily acceptable, and will better withstand the onslaught of cross-examination, if offered as one with which the expert is personally secure, while acknowledging that it is, after all, an opinion.

Because the opinions are their own, experts will be more protective of them, and more likely to see that a cross-examination question is about to undermine them. The result is that the expert is more likely to explain when the question does not fairly call for it. Redirect is much more common with expert witnesses and you must develop the expert's confidence in your ability to conduct the redirect in a manner that will let the witness have the last triumphant word. The expert will still do some explaining on cross-examination, no matter how successful you are in developing the faith in redirect examination. Although the expert is more likely to explain than the ordinary witness, to some extent explanation from an expert is less offensive, and if you can keep it to a minimum, your preparation will have been a success.

Tell the expert about the treatise rule, Fed. R.Evid. 803(18). Explain the use that the opponent can make of a treatise. Warn experts not to accept treatises they do not know about as authoritative, even if they suspect from the question, or the manner of the question, that they should. At the same time, discuss the manner in which the expert can acknowledge that there are other experts in the world, but in this case, the witness' opinion is the preferred one.

Some experts stumble badly over the fact that you have paid them. Remind them that you have purchased their time and their experience, not their testimony. Tell them to make a positive and unapologetic statement about fees if asked on cross-examination. Many lawyers like to handle the matter of fees during the foundation part of the direct examination so that the jurors make the "time and experience" connection to the payment of the fee. Whether this is wise in your case will depend upon the likelihood of the subject coming up on cross-examination.

The most important thing to remember in preparing your experts is that they are experts at what they do, not at what you do. Do not be over-awed by your expert. Prepare the expert's testimony so well that the jurors will be over-awed. Be sensitive to an expert's instinctive defensiveness and concentrate on preparation for cross-examination after both of you feel secure about the direct testimony.

CHAPTER 5

GATHER THE PROPS

Exhibits and diagrams present unique opportunities for emphasis, explanation, and simplicity in your trial/play. Physical evidence has an inherent force in excess of the substantive force of the information it conveys. The power of physical evidence derives from two sources of equal importance in preparing the use of such evidence at trial.

The most obvious source of power is that physical evidence is visual, not oral. Television's impact upon the way we learn has inflated the old adage about a picture's worth, from a thousand to a million words. The picture tells no more than it did in the past, but most of us now learn in paragraph size gulps by exposure to a visual symbol. As the members of the jury pool come from generations whose primary learning method has been visual, trial lawyers have to teach the story of their case in increasingly visual methods. Retention rates for information significantly increase when the message is accompanied with a visual. After a few hours most people will have forgotten 70% of a message they heard only orally. The old standard unit of learning, the sentence with a noun, verb, subject, object, and assorted adjectives and adverbs is no longer the primary, let alone the exclusive, mechanism for expressing ideas. All people are auditory, visual or kinesthetic learners. While visual and kinesthetic learners develop a proficiency at translating an auditory message it is not their easiest or best method of learning. If you knew that three people on your jury spoke Spanish and three more spoke French, you would try to communicate directly with them in their primary language if you could, instead of hoping that they were accurately translating the message you were delivering in English. Demonstrative and physical evidence give you the ability to deliver your message in a way that for many learners is their "first language." Visual learners will remember not only the visual language you use during trial, but the physical evidence as well. The better you translate your key theme and evidence into a physical form the more of your intended audience you will reach.

Making the effort to use and create physical evidence also helps in fighting juror boredom. We no longer live in a society that is used to long auditory messages. It only takes 15% of your brain power to process an auditory message; that leaves 85% of jurors' brain power focused on something else. While you don't want distractions, well placed and well done exhibits reinforce your trial message when jurors' eyes and minds are wandering the courtroom.

The second source of the power of physical evidence is its scarcity in most trial situations. The secret to *emphasis* is difference. Most trials are at least ninety percent oral testimony. Use the remaining ten percent (if you are lucky enough to have that much physical evidence) for emphasis. Physical evidence is *different*.

The relative power of physical evidence over oral evidence is independent of how effectively it is offered or of how significant it is substantively. The key to preparation of the props is to harness that power inherent in physical evidence to insure that it is working for you, not against you. All physical evidence is a visual aid to oral testimony, be it real (headlight glass picked up at the scene of an accident,) demonstrative (a photograph of the intersection,) or illustrative (a not-to-scale drawing of the intersection.) It is an aid independent of any substantive significance it might have.

The simplest and most often overlooked rule for the effective use of physical evidence is: If it doesn't aid, don't use it! The rule is based upon the inherent attention getting and attention holding qualities of physical evidence. If it does not aid the oral testimony just preceding or following its offer, you not only lose the advantage of physical evidence, you divert the jurors' attention from your important oral testimony to the naturally more compelling teaching of physical evidence that, by the way, is not teaching anything that you want the jurors to know. Do not allow the inherent power of physical evidence to work against you by competing for the jurors' attention with oral testimony that it does not aid. This diversion tendency is one of the major drawbacks to the current fad of technology in the courtroom. If you watch trials, you will see lawyers over-using Power Point or other presentation software. It is not because visuals are not effective; it is because the lawyers and their witnesses are competing with their own exhibits. When a lawyer flashes a slide, we are drawn to look at it. If it is filled with too much text or dazzling animation our focus is on it, not the witness or the lawyer. Effective use of technology is priceless; poor use of it is a distraction that most lawyers can ill afford. In your first trial, work on mastering actual physical evidence and maybe the use of a document camera, save technology for later.

The second reason not to use physical evidence that does not aid oral testimony is that it diminishes the impact of other pieces of physical evidence. Ten pictures are almost always better than one, but rarely ten times better. Before you diminish the rarity of a piece of physical evidence by the offer of more physical evidence, be sure the value of the second piece outweighs the emphasis value of the singularity of the first piece. Jurors view physical evidence as they do testimony, with a natural suspicion. They hold you accountable for every bit of evidence you produce, so when you attempt to bolster evidence you have already offered, jurors want to know why. If the first photo was the best, offering two more invites them to question whether the first one showed what you said it did.

The answer to whether, when, and how a piece of physical evidence ought to be offered during your case-in-chief, at least in the initial preparation stage, is found in your answer to the question:

What oral testimony does this emphasize, explain, or simplify? If the answer is "none," the answer to "whether" is "no." If, for example, the plaintiff in the intersection case believes the point of impact testimony may be helpful to the defendant, the plaintiff is unlikely to offer pieces of broken headlight glass found at the scene. Even though it is real evidence, and may be probative on the point of impact, the plaintiff's lawyer has no interest in emphasizing the investigating officer's testimony on that point. Similarly, a photograph of the intersection, taken from a direction from which neither car was traveling, and from which no witnesses were standing, shows something about the lawsuit, but will not be offered because there will be no oral testimony that the photograph emphasizes, explains, or simplifies. Physical evidence when integrated into oral testimony provides effective *emphasis*. Jurors don't like repetition any more than you would like to read the same sentence over again— any more than you would like to read the same sentence over again. Offering oral testimony and reinforcing it with an exhibit allows you to emphasize the testimony without repeating it.

In most cases, physical evidence should be offered in the middle of, or just before, the oral testimony that it aids. A major emphasis technique is to imprint oral testimony on a physical object. If oral testimony relates in some way to an item the jurors can see, and if the jurors are exposed to the testimony just after being exposed to the physical evidence, the witness' words may become imprinted on the physical object in the minds of the jurors. If the physical object, or its image, goes to the jury room at the end of the case, it carries the words of the testimony with it. Although there are situations that suggest that the oral testimony should precede the introduction of physical evidence, the latter being climactic; in most situations, the physical evidence should precede the oral testimony that it emphasizes, explains, or simplifies, in order to take advantage of the psychological imprinting.

The most obvious example of imprinting is a diagram. An investigating officer's testimony about positions of cars, location of glass, and length of skid marks will have a more lasting impact if offered with reference to a diagram of the intersection, than if offered by words alone. It would be acceptable to ask the officer what happened and what was found at the scene before introducing the diagram as an aid to the officer's testimony and that of future occurrence witnesses, but the officer's testimony will be better remembered if the diagram is offered first. A less obvious example of imprinting is the offer of the broken headlight glass found at the scene. Because the officer collected it, it might be offered as a part of the officer's general testimony about the accident scene. On the other hand, if the broken glass is offered just before the officer testifies to measuring the skid mark or just before the answer to the question (if permitted in the jurisdiction): "What is your opinion as to the point of impact?" the glass will carry back to the jury room the oral testimony about the point of impact.

How to offer exhibits and diagrams commanded a substantial part of the chapter on stage management because inefficient introduction of physical evidence diminishes the impact. How exhibits and diagrams are offered can, also, enhance the impact of physical evidence beyond its intrinsic value. For example, several pieces of physical evidence may have a greater composite meaning than the sum of the meanings of the individual pieces. The earlier example in which the officer picked up headlight glass and red taillight glass at the scene of the intersection collision, is one in which the plaintiff may wish to emphasize being almost through the intersection by offering all of the glass together, even though it did not come from the same car nor was it found in the same place on the street. If the clear plastic bag containing the headlight pieces is marked 1A, the clear plastic bag containing the red taillight pieces is marked 1B, and both are in a clear plastic bag marked 1, the exhibit will be introduced and go back to the jury room in a manner that will tell the jurors that the headlight and taillight glass "go together," without anyone there to remind them. The plaintiff's important contention of being almost through the intersection when struck is physically attached to the headlight/taillight exhibit.

Some exhibits require more than one witness to lay a foundation. Often, these involve chain of custody problems, and you cannot allow the jurors to see the item before the chain of evidence is completed. If the exhibit is of sufficient importance, the chain foundation may determine your order of witnesses. If you cannot reasonably proceed with all of the custody foundation witnesses before you need to use the exhibit, the court, pursuant to Fed.R. Evid. 104, might allow you to use it before the chain is complete, if you can make a persuasive offer of proof as to your ability to provide all the links. On the other hand, you may use the chain as a method to build anticipation. If you ask the foundation questions for the item at the same substantive spot for each of the witnesses, and very pointedly guard against disclosure of the most important aspect of the exhibit, you should expect to accumulate all the emphasis of anticipation when the exhibit is finally offered and accepted. In that event, it is imperative that the evidence finally be introduced as an "aid" to important oral testimony, to take full advantage of juror anticipation.

Diagrams and summaries represent a kind of physical evidence that require special preparation. Unlike real evidence and some demonstrative evidence such as photographs; diagrams and summaries are created as a part of trial preparation specifically for the theater of the trial. Some photographs are created for the same purpose, but more are the result of investigation without a specific trial purpose in mind at the time of the taking. Technology has increased the ease and availability of diagrams, charts and graphics. Just because you don't want the added pressure of running your computer during trial doesn't mean that you shouldn't take advantage of great exhibits. There are good companies that can assist you in designing charts and exhibits to emphasize your trial story. They might be able to work from already existing exhibits or they might design something based on the testimony. Good trial exhibit companies can help you translate difficult concepts into clear visuals or create subtle images that create lasting impressions. Judges and jurors can benefit from visuals that help everyone see the same thing and emphasize key themes or testimony. No matter how clear your description of the intersection, only a diagram or photograph ensures that all jurors see it the way you want them to. Words only have the meaning people bring to them. What is old or beautiful, large or small? What are four lines drawn together? A square, a rectangle, connected or not, vertical or horizontal? Even the simplest of words present different visual images to different people, so if it is important, control the idea by showing a "picture."

There are two kinds of diagrams: scale and not-to-scale. The former is created by a witness and offered as evidence to be considered by the jurors and reviewed in the jury room. The latter is created by a witness—though it need not be—and is usually offered "for illustrative purposes, only." The major effect of the "illustrative purposes" limitation is that the diagram does not become part of the pile of evidence that the jurors may consider and does not go back to the jury room during deliberations. The handling of diagrams or other matters offered "for illustrative purposes" varies from jurisdiction to jurisdiction, and in some cases, from courtroom to courtroom. Some illustrative, not-to-scale diagrams are considered evidence and are allowed in the jury room during deliberations in some jurisdictions. The foundation for such a diagram is provided by a witness that can testify that the diagram is a "fair and accurate representation" of whatever it purports to depict. If the information in the diagram is important for the jurors to understand, don't worry about whether it will ultimately make it back to the jury room. Beginning lawyers confuse admissibility with the simple foundation for a piece of demonstrative evidence. In most cases what is most important is that the jurors see the exhibit and hear the testimony, not whether it makes it back to the jury room. Do not miss the opportunity to visually display critical information because you believe it is only demonstrative and not admissible as substantive evidence. The use to which the diagram may be put is often determined by how fair and accurate the diagram is in the judgment of the court. More specifically, the test is often, "how misleading it isn't." An illustrative diagram that is not particularly accurate, but is not "misleading" on a matter at issue may often be allowed in the jury room with the rest of the evidence. The more common practice is to allow witnesses to refer to not-to-scale diagrams, mark on them, but not to allow them in the jury room if anything concerning distance or position is even remotely at issue.

If you plan to use a diagram for illustration in a jurisdiction where it is not allowed in the jury room, have a witness create it. The foundation for the diagram is provided by testimony that (1) the witness is familiar with whatever the diagram depicts; (2) the diagram fairly and accurately represents it; and (3) the diagram would be helpful in presenting the witness' testimony. Because no witness need testify to the method of conversion from scene to poster board of demonstrative evidence, the lawyer can draw the diagram without risking the ethical problem of choosing between being a witness and being a lawyer. But, don't you draw it. The ethical problem exists because the system cannot risk the appearance of an advocate who is also a witness. The persuasive problem is the same. The jurors are suspicious of evidence the lawyer "makes." Instruct the witness to make the diagram as close to scale as possible. No matter how much comment and instruction there may be about not-to-scale, if the diagram is close, the jurors will listen to the oral testimony the diagram aids as if the diagram were drawn to scale. If the diagram is not going back to the jury room, make it as large as possible, and make it the center of reference for every witness possible. The result of the diagram's dominance will be that the jurors will remember it and imprint oral testimony upon it. The image of the diagram and the imprinted oral testimony will go back to the jury room with them, even though the diagram remains in the courtroom. Remember that your goal is to control the visual playing field of the trial. If the jurors are picturing the scene the way you showed them, don't worry about whether the diagram is only demonstrative. Think about books that you read that were then made into a movie. Most of us can't remember what our imagined "book" Harry Potter looked like once we see the first Harry Potter movie. The credible visual image you present will be the one the jurors remember. Better, when they get back to the jury room and find it is not there, the jurors may ask for it, and your opponent will have to assess the risk that the jurors will figure out who said, "no," against the risk of letting them see the diagram.

Two factors control the desirability of a scale diagram. The first is availability. How much trouble is it to measure the scene or object, and create the diagram? The second, and more important consideration, is the effect of the exact measurements on your case. In some cases, the exact physical facts are obviously helpful to one party and harmful to the other. It is not always so, and it is not necessarily advantageous for the party who, on close balance profits most from the physical facts, to produce a scale diagram. If, for example, the plaintiff concludes that the physical facts are ambiguous and the case will be won by emphasis on the injuries and the plaintiff's personal description of the events, a scale diagram that invites the jurors to concentrate on the ambiguous physical facts at the expense of the plaintiff's narrative description is not useful. On the other hand, you might determine that although the physical facts are ambiguous, the ambiguity may not be easily communicated. You might determine that if the jury is unsure of the exact inferences to be drawn, it will draw inferences in favor of the party presenting the exact measurements—on the theory that if they did not help, the party would not have offered them. In determining the effect of the scale diagram on your case, remember that the trial/play is competitive. In the intersection case, if one side does not believe a scale drawing will help, the other side is likely to believe it will help.

Marking on a scale diagram can present a problem. Once the diagram is admitted as a scale replica, any not-to-scale mark on the diagram may destroy the foundation. If, for example, you want the investigating officer to mark where the skid marks appeared, you must do something other than invite the officer to draw a free hand line on the scale diagram. There are three easy ways to avoid agreeing to forego the scale foundation, and still have the officer mark on the diagram.

The first is to provide the officer with a scale instrument (a rule) for which you have received a stipulation, a court agreement to judicial notice, or testimony of the diagram maker that the scale instrument was the one used in constructing the diagram. (You will never have to resort to the latter.)

The second method involves the use of transparent overlays. Have the overlay marked with the number of the diagram and a sub-letter, for example, Plaintiff's 1A. Attach the overlay to the diagram. If the overlay is not the exact dimension of the diagram, make a description for the record that insures that the overlay can be replaced in the exact location if it has been once removed. Lining up corners is the easiest way. Have the witness mark on the overlay, and when the witness is finished, offer the overlay as a separate exhibit.

The third method is to demonstrate to the court that the not-to-scale mark will not be misleading, and should not, therefore, change the basis upon which the diagram has been admitted. This method works well when the proposed line demonstrates the approximate route a vehicle followed, a spot where a witness was standing, or the location of a physical object when that location does not directly affect the purpose for which the diagram is used. A skid mark, however, is exactly the kind of mark that no court is likely to allow by approximation on a scale drawing.

There are other, more elaborate, methods for adding to a scale diagram that may be justified in your case. Creation of other scale objects to be placed on the diagram is a common method. Remember, if you choose that method, that the foundation required for each object is the same as the foundation for the diagram. Each object must be separately marked and received into evidence.

Whether your diagram is scale or not-to-scale, do not try to put too much detail in the diagram. If it does not aid a point you wish to make, or is not needed for the foundation, do not put it on the diagram. Similarly, you should not attempt to show too much on any one diagram. Consider using two diagrams, or multiple, removable overlays for the basic diagram. Clutter transforms your visual aid into a visual hindrance. The oral testimony to be emphasized, explained, or simplified is lost while the jurors are trying to figure out the diagram. It is, therefore, critical to do your preparation with an eye to what all witnesses, yours and theirs, are likely to do to and with your diagram.

One way to insure that the unknowns of trial will not mess up your diagrammatic presentation is to anticipate and provide for multiple users. Transparent overlays and different colored pens are two common tools to accommodate multiple users. The overlays are a more cumbersome procedure, and unless you need the flexibility of removal, use the pens. When you expect more than one witness to mark on a diagram, ask the various witnesses to mark with various color pens and then write their names on the corner of the diagram with the same pen. If you use a different color pen for each witness, the jurors will have no trouble recalling who said what when they review the diagram in the jury room. When your opponent wants to have a witness mark on the diagram, insist that the integrity of the identification system is maintained.

Remember, however, that the pen marks stay. If witnesses are sequestered and if there is a chance that something to be marked on the diagram is at issue, it may be to your advantage to use overlays and insist that your opponent do the same when using the diagram. If the position of an object is in question, and you expect your opponent's witnesses to have inconsistent opinions of the location if they are forced to mark it without some suggestion as to the proper location, insist on the overlay procedure before the first witness marks on the diagram. If your opponent objects to the procedure, explain to the court that if witness number two is asked to make a mark after seeing where witness number one has marked, the attorney will be effectively leading the witness and violating the effect of the sequestration order. Once witnesses have been sequestered, most courts will not allow the attorneys to undermine the purpose of the sequestration.

It is as important to prepare the witnesses who will use the diagram as it is to prepare the diagramming method. Warn each witness not to refer to the diagram unless you invite the reference. If the witness looks at the diagram, the jurors look at the diagram. If you did not plan it, two bad things happen. First, the eye contact between the witness and the jurors is broken. Second, the imprinting effect of the oral testimony in conjunction with a diagram diminishes with use, and you do not want to waste it on something other than what you have selected—certainly not on a nervous gesture by the witness to relieve the pressure of looking at the jury.

It is particularly important that the foundation witness refrain from referring to the diagram before every mark on it has been explained to the jury. The lawyer controls this more than the witness. Even if the diagram has a legend, the jurors are not going to read it; and if they are, it will be during your witness' testimony. The most common mistake

beginning lawyers make with diagrams is to use
them before the jurors are ready. If, for example,
your investigating officer in the intersection case is
laying the foundation for the diagram at the beginning of the testimony about what the officer found
when arriving on the scene, lay the foundation that
the jury wants, not just the one the law requires.
Have the officer identify every mark and symbol on
the diagram, even if the full explanation is not
required for the legal foundation. The jurors will
have a complete understanding of the diagram, the
officer will be perceived as a precise and knowledgeable person, and the testimony will not be lost while
juror number three is trying to figure out what that
funny little cross hatch symbol means.

Prepare witnesses to specifically identify things to
which they point on the diagram. Every time that a
witness points to something without making a permanent mark, the record is incomplete unless somebody says something to describe the physical movement. When the plaintiff places the pointer on the
traffic light at issue without saying, "the one on the
southwest corner," the jurors will know what the
witness means, but the appellate court that reviews
the transcript will not. Another common method of
keeping the record, is for the attorney to say, as the
witness points to the traffic light, "May the record
reflect that the witness is pointing to the light on
the southwest corner." This fairly popular method
has the twin disadvantages of requiring the lawyer
to interrupt the jurors' attention to the witness,
and it takes more words. If the witness forgets, and

the record is critical on the matter, the lawyer has no choice but to complete the record. Prepare witnesses to describe in words what they do with a pointer so you do not need to interrupt. Better yet, prepare witnesses to mark on the diagram whenever the point is important. Aside from the obvious persuasive importance, the mark makes the record complete without need of oral description.

Be sure that your foundation witnesses understand exactly what you expect from them. This is one area of witness preparation that justifies question by answer review. It will not hurt if it sounds rehearsed, and will cause all sorts of stumbling if it is not. It will be easier if the witnesses understand that they must be able to tell you what the diagram is and how they know it is what they say. If the diagram is not-to-scale, the witness must be able to say that it "fairly and accurately" represents the intersection on the day of the accident and that the witness knows because the witness was at the scene, looked around, and has been at the intersection many times. If, on the other hand, the diagram is to scale, a witness must testify to measuring the intersection—maybe describing the method of measuring. A witness must testify also (it need not be the same witness) to the scale method used to consistently reduce the measurements to create the diagram.

If any exhibit is to be used for illustrative purposes, the witness must testify that the diagram, summary chart, or whatever, will aid the witness in presenting the testimony to the jury. (The actual legal foundation requires the court to find the exhibit will aid the jurors in understanding the testimony, but it is less condescending to the jurors if the witness claims the exhibit will help in giving the testimony rather than the jurors need the exhibit to understand.) Summaries are the classic example of the illustrative exhibit, although in many jurisdictions they are allowed to go to the jury room. Except for summaries of voluminous material that cannot be conveniently examined in court (Fed. R.Evid. 1006), summary charts are a restatement of evidence that has been presented to the jurors. Such a chart is a true aid, having no independent substantive value. Unlike a diagram, there is no transfer of an idea from words to lines; the transfer is oral words to written words. The summary is admitted, however, for the same reason the diagram is ultimately admissible: It will help the jurors understand. Using illustrative exhibits with experts is an excellent way to demonstrate and imprint their testimony. Typically, if a case involves a long series of financial transactions between many parties and the relationship of the transactions and the people proves a crime or civil liability, a summary of the various witnesses' testimony will be used to simplify. The creator of the summary chart is most often someone who has heard all of the testimony and can identify everything on the chart with the specific testimony that the jurors heard. The major investigating officer in a complicated financial conspiracy prosecution is the classic witness to perform this function. Of course, the summary is made during the prosecutor's preparation of the case, and reflects what the prosecutor expects to prove. If the case goes in as the prosecutor expects, the agent's testimony will include the summary chart. The effect is that the prosecutor makes two closing arguments. The first is through the mouth of the agent testifying about the summary chart. Computerized animations or recreations created by expert witnesses are frequently illustrative summaries of testimony, measurements, photographs etc. The animated re-creation of an auto collision prepared by a re-constructionist can be offered as illustrative, assuming all of the underlying data is complete. Tactically it may not make sense for your first case, but review current evidence cases addressing digital and computerized evidence if you anticipate laying a foundation or objecting to your opponent's offer.

Experts can use all sorts of demonstrative evidence to help the jurors understand their testimony. Models, charts, plastic body parts, anything that can get the expert out of the witness chair and into teaching the jurors is invaluable. Low tech versions that jurors can pass through the jury box can be just as effective as what people see on television shows. Jurors are used to seeing high tech trials in movies or on television. That doe not mean that you must use the high tech demonstrative evidence, but it does mean that expectations about physical evidence are more the norm than the exception.

Many jurisdictions encourage pretrial consideration of all exhibits. If you are in a jurisdiction holding extensive pretrial conferences, you can expect to review all exhibits and receive either tentative or final admissibility rulings. Most jurisdictions that have such pretrial conferences will, at a minimum, require an exchange and pre-marking of exhibits. This is the perfect time to get permission to use exhibits in your opening statement or voir dire. Courts are becoming more accepting of allowing non-controversial information to be displayed earlier in the case, so don't be afraid to ask if it will be helpful to your case. It is not time to whip out your 30 slide PowerPoint presentation, but a key photograph or diagram might help tell part of your opening better than a verbal description.

If you get a tentative or final stipulation or admissibility ruling, do not ignore the foundation for the exhibit at trial. The jurors want to know what the diagram or exhibit shows and how come the witness is in a position to know. Be prepared to face some resistance from the judge, who believes that all that nonsense was dispensed with at pretrial. Politely suggest to the court that the jurors need to know about the exhibit and that it might be better for the witness, rather than the lawyer, to "testify" about it.

Even if exhibits are not pre-marked at pretrial, you may decide to avoid the time consuming marking process during the trial. If you decide to have exhibits pre-marked just before trial, or if they have been pre-marked at a hearing, ask the clerk to mark them in whatever order you expect to first present them to a witness. This will allow you and others, to keep a current exhibit list with relative ease. It will also insure that you will not confuse the jurors or cause them to wonder what they forgot when you present exhibit number four for identification right after exhibit number two for identification.

Preparation of the props for your trial/play is neither complicated nor time consuming. It is not even important for the eventual admission of the exhibits. It is, like the preparation of the play and the players, important if you want the audience to like your play. The subtle relationship between the props and players goes to the credibility of each and affects how well the jurors remember the important parts of the oral testimony. In an increasingly visual society controlling the visual playing field is a critical part of the trial that should not be ignored.

CHAPTER 6

CHECK OUT THE AUDIENCE

The theater of the law gives the trial lawyer an opportunity for which most stage directors would commit serious felonies—the trial lawyer is allowed to kick some of the audience out of the theater. Old time lawyers, engaged in "pickin' a jury," developed an extensive mythology to explain the subtle interpretation of their own digestive rumblings. Some modern lawyers, steeped in the science of jury selection, employ social science technology to verify the subtle interpretations of their own digestive rumblings. Not one of them ever "picked" or "selected" a jury, and neither will you. Jury selection is done by the jury commissioners and the clerk.

You get to "unpick!" Exclusion of prospective jurors through the process of voir dire is done by lawyers. It is critical for you to remember that voir dire is not about picking jurors you like; it is an opportunity to exclude those you fear will boo the performance. The difference is more than semantic. The conduct of the voir dire and the preparation that facilitates it are quite different when trying to pick a jury you like, rather than trying to avoid a jury you will hate—and the former will interfere with the latter.

Too many lawyers, unfortunately, fall into the trap of trying for the unattainable. Operating under the illusion that they can pick a jury they will like, they concentrate on questions that will isolate favorable characteristics or they develop questions calculated to "educate" the jurors into attitudes that the lawyer likes. At the end of the day, unfortunately every voir dire ends the same way. The judge will give you a few minutes (literally five to ten) to look through the jury list and strike through the small number of names allowed as your peremptory challenges; and you will turn your strike list into the clerk; the clerk will compare your list with your opponent's and the first six or twelve remaining names constitute the jury—whether you like it or not! Do yourself a favor and prepare to exclude the worst jurors, so that you have a jury you can live with rather than one you will love. Prepare questions that will help you discover prospective jurors with the worst characteristics for your case—something that most prospective jurors are not likely to offer up from the get-go.

All juries are formed initially by a three-step administrative process in which lawyers have no part. The details of the process vary from jurisdiction to jurisdiction, but the major components are common. More importantly, the process generates most of the data with which you can begin checking out the audience.

The initial selection of prospective panel members is made by jury commissioners from a list of members of the community, usually lists like voter registration, driver's license, and sometimes utility or unemployment lists. There may be hundreds to thousands of names selected, depending upon the size of the community. The type of lists used contributes to the number, race and socio-economic characteristics of those called. These names are numbered, entered on a master jury list, and placed in a jury selection wheel or random computer database. The master jury list may be available to lawyers. If so, it is the first way to learn about the audience.

The selection of the jury panel (often called the venire) must be made at random from the master jury list. (If the process is anything less than random it is subject to challenge). The clerk generates the names from the wheel or database. A panel may be as small as twenty-four or as large as one hundred, depending upon the applicable statutes or the judge's estimate of the number of prospective jurors needed to complete a jury after strikes. Members of the panel are usually required to complete a personal data sheet and file it with the clerk when they are summoned. In most jurisdictions, the personal data sheets are available to lawyers scheduled before the panel. Some states require little more than name and address. Others, to the chagrin of the prospective jurors and to the joy of trial lawyers, require what would pass for a biography outline. Personal data sheets that require only name, address, age, marital status, educational level, occupation, and prior jury service are not uncommon. The personal data sheet is the best source of information for checking out the audience.

Juror questionnaires are also becoming increasingly common. The idea behind the questionnaire is to shorten the actual voir dire by having jurors answer common questions in writing ahead of time. Courts vary as to their willingness and procedure for using questionnaires so this is another subject that must be covered well ahead of trial. Questionnaires can either be generic by subject matter, i.e. standard auto accident questionnaire, or they can be specific to your case. Getting a judge to allow a specific questionnaire usually requires cooperation and agreement with opposing counsel so that there is agreement on the length of the questionnaire and the questions to be asked. There are numerous books and websites with sample motions for permission to use a questionnaire and suggested questions by case type that can work as a starting point. The questionnaire allows for sensitive matters to be covered privately and many lawyers believe that jurors will be more truthful in writing than under the pressure of a more public verbal answer. Whether you need a questionnaire is beyond the scope of this primer, but you should research the issue if you have some reason to believe voir dire will cover sensitive issues.

Batson v. Kentucky and its progeny have limited the once unfettered lawyer discretion in exercising peremptory challenges and have provided some constitutional limits to the jury selection process. You must understand the selection procedure in your jurisdiction and the sweep of the constitutional issues, especially if your case involves issues of a protected class and you anticipate the need to make a *Batson*-like challenge to the panel. Objections that the panel is not representative, was constructed with improper lists, lacks randomness, and the like usually must be made prior to the actual jury selection. Issues with respect to time limitations on voir dire, jury shuffles, and allocation of peremptories in multiparty litigation must also usually occur early. Know the process used to identify the specific panel names that will be assigned to your courtroom. (Methods of voir dire are discussed in Chapter 7.)

A copy of the master jury list should be obtained as soon as possible. You might not have access to the personal data sheets until immediately before trial. The master jury list, with jurors numbered as designated by the clerk, may often include the address of the prospective juror. Technology, web search engines, and databases have made juror research on such a list no longer a question of what information is obtainable, but rather, a question of how to sort out the information that will be useful. Today, a trial lawyer can learn more about a person than anyone should have a right to know. You can find out (or hire a company) to discover in seconds where prospective jurors live, the value of property they own, what primaries they have voted in, their education and almost anything else you think might matter. If you have the ability to generate concrete information in the days or weeks ahead of trial you can mine all that is available and then spend time separating out the useful for the potential jurors listed on the master list. At your first trial, you will probably have neither the time nor the need for the most exhaustive research of a master list. There will, however, be pared-down lists available. You will have less time to work with them, so be very specific about the information that can really help you to evaluate which jurors you want to strike.

After the panel has been selected, two important sources of information are available. You should be able to obtain the personal data sheets or question-naire answers for each potential juror on the panel. If the panel is not new, you can develop a panel "history" by examining the jury verdicts rendered by juries selected from the panel. Depending upon how many panels your jurisdiction draws at one time, how long the panels serve, and how much lead time between assignment of the case and trial, these two sources can provide an invaluable insight into your panel. Assuming that the personal data sheets of the jurors are available, and that the panel has served long enough for you to find jury verdict results, begin your preparation by collating the in-formation. The trick at trial will be to gather quick-ly all available information about a potential juror whose name is called. In addition, you will need a mechanism for comparing that information to all that you know about the other jurors who could be pulled next from the jury wheel. The best way to accommodate both needs is to develop a database or spreadsheet that collects all the information about any particular juror, develop a ranking system of exclusion based on the information that you have, and organize it either alphabetically or numerically according to the juror number assigned.

The first information added to the prospective juror's personal data should come from the jury verdict forms. Most jurisdictions maintain a verdict form file containing the actual verdict forms with the names of the jurors supporting the verdict along with the name of the jury foreperson. If you can obtain copies of the forms, enter on each panel member's data sheet the types of cases upon which the juror served, whether the juror was the foreperson, the verdict, and whether the juror joined it.

Other lawyers that have tried cases before the panel can be another valuable source of pretrial information about prospective jurors. If you know a lawyer who has tried a case before the panel, ask about the jurors. Most lawyers are happy to share the information. The lawyer may be able to tell you additional facts about jurors that were excluded during voir dire as well as those who served. In some jurisdictions the lawyers are allowed to speak to the jurors after the case, even though the panel is still serving. Those conversations are often illuminating about the juror even though the discussion is about another case. Many lawyers take notes during voir dire and about conversations after trial with jurors. Those notes may help jog the memory.

"Strength" and "friends" are two subtle pieces of information about jurors that are helpful and that the lawyer who has appeared before the panel might have identified. There are varying opinions about when one ought to exclude or hold onto a strong juror, but all lawyers want to be able to identify a juror that might control the jury. Similarly, juror friendships developed during jury service are important in determining what jurors to strike, and how to strike them.

There are many more sources of information about jurors. Keep in mind that as the amount of information grows the information interpretation problems grow exponentially. If you cannot interpret the information, it is meaningless. Many lawyers with wealthy clients who can afford the cost, and who believe in the "science," gather much more data than the basic suggestions set out for your first trial. Investigation of all panel members for clubs, church affiliations, and the like is not uncommon. Demographers of every description can be hired to take expensive polls of the general populace to determine, by scientific inference, the attitudinal make up of the jury panel. Jury consultants are available to do focus groups or mock trials. Much of this burgeoning social science technology is used by good trial lawyers to collect and evaluate data. Your client is unfortunate if your first trial is big enough to even consider the cost of such investigations, but the fact that others spend a great amount to do it should persuade you about the importance of collecting and handling the data easily available to you. Should you go on to try many and more complicated cases, you will learn how to work with personality profiling or demographic data. You will practice with it in every day encounters and continue to fine tune your instincts and your understanding of what behavioral and social science can and cannot tell you about a person. But in your first trial, stick with the basics.

Develop a juror ranking system using the pretrial information collected about the panel and a list of characteristics that you consider undesirable for your client's cause. Although the list will be different from case to case, you should make up a profile of the worst possible juror for your particular trial, and use it in your ranking system. Some lawyers choose to rank according to a preferred juror profile and concentrate on locating jurors with the desired characteristics; but that approach will result in a ranking that will not serve you well. If prospective jurors do not possess many of the preferred characteristics, they will be ranked low even though you have not identified anything worrisome about them. You never have enough strikes, unfortunately, to excuse every prospective juror about whom you know nothing worrisome, but who is just not what you want. Because you have limited strikes, your chore is to excuse people that will boo your performance, not choosing people that will cheer. The question you must answer when you have limited strikes is: "Can I afford to keep this juror?" To answer that question well, you need to have a ranking based on undesirable traits.

There is a mountain of lore and social science mythology written about prospective jurors and the best method for guessing which ones you do not want. There is no right or guaranteed way to engage in making personal judgments about the people you wish to exclude from your client's case. It does not follow, however, that you cannot develop a way with which you are more comfortable than you would be with random chance. Your client can use random chance or just "eyeball" people without you. You can bring a thoughtful analysis to the courtroom even if you are doing this for the first time. Jurors, like all people, make decisions based on their overall belief systems. In general if you can find out about their attitudes about the specific issues in your case, that is the most reliable information. Next will be their life experiences relevant to the case. Personality traits follow next and only after these three will general values and demographic information be useful. Think about the core of your case. A breach of contract case, for example, might be about trust or whether a handshake constitutes an agreement. If you have really digested your case into its core human components, it makes discovering similar life experiences among prospective jurors much easier and allows you to compare which experiences might benefit your case and which might not.

The comparison between the worse possible juror profile and the prospective jurors is a two-step process. The first ranking is based only on the pretrial information. Each juror should be ranked on a scale that is sufficiently discreet so that during voir dire, when you are making the final exclusions, the rankings will remind you of the mental process you went through when analyzing the pretrial information. A common system is to rank jurors from zero to four, with four the least acceptable. Many lawyers add an asterisk to designate those jurors for whom they would exercise their last peremptory challenge in order to keep them off the jury. As each personal data sheet is analyzed, record the ranking near the name so that you will find it quickly during voir dire. If you are using a panel list for quick comparison, record the pretrial ranking on that list too. (In some jurisdictions you will use the master jury list instead of a pre-made panel list. Which one you use will depend on whether the master list is small enough to be handled at trial.) This pretrial ranking of undesirability will be the quick reference against which you weigh the additional information that comes from the voir dire.

The second step in the comparison process is the ranking you make during the voir dire. "Voir dire," a phrase borrowed from the French, means "to speak the truth." The underlying assumption for the various methods of voir dire is that the prospective juror, upon interrogation, will "speak the truth" concerning the juror's qualifications to sit on the case. Many lawyers will tell you that jurors often do not tell the truth during questioning. Others will tell you that they are less interested in what the juror says than they are in how the juror says it, so it does not matter if the juror tells less than the truth. Whether you choose to make the personal judgments of voir dire based upon what the juror says, or how the juror says it, the information you receive will depend in large measure upon the questions asked. Developing a list of questions that will elicit juror response is the last step in preparing for voir dire. The questions that you prepare will depend upon the method of voir dire to be used, the information already available, the amount of time allotted by the judge, and the role you think voir dire plays in your lawsuit. Choosing who to strike and who to keep is an inexact science at best, but trial lawyers develop a sense based upon research and juror reaction during voir dire. No matter how they come by it, trial lawyers will tell you they excluded a juror because "there was just something I didn't like," or they did not exercise a peremptory because "the vibes weren't bad."

There are a host of voir dire variables and terms you need to know, starting with who does the questioning. The most common form of voir dire still involves questioning by lawyers. In many jurisdictions, however, and in almost all federal courts, judges control all of the questioning.

How long does voir dire last? There is a trend among judges to restrict the amount of time given to each lawyer to conduct the voir dire. In many places it can be as short as thirty minutes per side. How big is a panel? When the court asks the questions (and in some cases where the lawyers do the questioning) the clerk draws a number of names equal to the number of jurors needed, plus the total number of peremptory strikes for both sides. If the court anticipates a high number of strikes for cause it may increase the size of the panel. Similarly, if there are more than two parties, more prospective jurors are needed because each party may exercise peremptory challenges separately.

What is the difference between a strike for cause and a peremptory? A strike for cause is granted by the judge when potential jurors express a bias or prejudice under the statutory or common law such that they are disqualified from serving on the panel. There are numerous grounds for disqualification, so make sure you know them and know the "magic language" required in your jurisdiction to justify a strike for cause as well as your judge's process for handling the questions and objections. The peremptory challenges are yours to use for any reason except those prohibited by *Batson* and its progeny.

How does the process of questioning occur? The court, or counsel, questions the entire group. After the questioning is completed, each attorney makes strikes until the number of jurors left meets the statutory requirement. A significant variation on this method involves individual questioning of the prospective jurors with each side being required to make a peremptory strike, if at all, at the conclusion of the lawyer's questions to the prospective juror. In a few jurisdictions, and usually in criminal cases, the prospective jurors' names are pulled from the wheel one at a time, with the lawyers questioning the first prospective juror and making a strike decision, before the name of the next prospective juror is pulled from the wheel. If the case is one of high publicity, or if there is some danger of a question or answer "poisoning" the rest of the panel, the individual questioning of each juror is often done out of the presence of the rest of the panel. There can be more variation and it can be different with each judge even in the same jurisdiction. Because the questioning process can be fluid, make sure you are always aware of your "strike" zone. Be sure you know how many jurors are "in play" at any given time. Suppose your jury panel consists of forty and each lawyer gets six peremptory challenges to be used at the end of voir dire. Only the first twenty-four are "in play" as you start the voir dire—twelve prospective jurors who will be struck and twelve who will remain and constitute the jury. Since the clerk will read the names of the first twelve not struck, it is important not to waste a peremptory challenge on juror number thirty-two who never had a chance of making it on in the first place. If you are under time pressure, it is also important not to get engaged in a long discussion with jurors outside the strike zone. Obviously as the court grants strikes for cause or as peremptories are used the strike zone expands, so keep track and confirm with the judge or clerk if you get confused.

In any of the described methods, questions aimed solely at exclusions for cause, such as relationship with one of the parties or service on the indicting grand jury, are often asked of the entire panel before any names are pulled from the wheel for individual interrogation.

There are hundreds of textbooks and websites with thousands of lists of standard questions that can be asked on voir dire. Go back to the list above and try to find out the most useful information to your case as you can. It is better, for example, to know what the jurors think about the amount of damages you are asking for in your case than it is to know what they think about the McDonald's "hot coffee" case or tort reform in general. What does knowing that a juror's car has a bumper sticker that says "Visualize World Peace" tell you about a contract case or criminal case? Remember your primary tasks in voir dire. The first is to get as many "bad" jurors struck for cause as possible. The second is to identify as many "bad jurors" for your case as possible so that you can exercise intelligent peremptory strikes. "Bad juror" means jurors whose life experiences are such that they are likely to boo your case. In the world of voir dire, "bad" is good (to find).

Prepare your voir dire questions so that you speak less, and the prospective juror speaks more. This suggestion is not universally accepted. Some lawyers believe that the real advocacy purpose of voir dire is to educate the jurors, rather than to gather information to assist in their exclusion. If you have enough time in your voir dire you may be able to attempt both, but you have to gather enough information to exercise your peremptory challenges and that can only happen if the prospective jurors talk. Lawyers draft questions that are either statements of law followed by a question mark, or requests for promises from jurors about verdicts. The tendency to draft voir dire questions that educate more than they ask is increased when the lawyer is forced to ask questions of the entire panel, rather than of individual jurors. Similarly, criminal cases cause defense lawyers to begin educating the jurors about reasonable doubt as early in voir dire as the court will permit. If you adopt the educating approach you run the risk of keeping dangerous jurors. This sacrifice is not necessary because the trial itself should sufficiently educate the jurors. If, however, you decide that education is an important goal for your voir dire, frame your questions so that they give you some information about the juror in addition to giving the juror some information about your case. If, for example, your client in the intersection collision had a couple of drinks two hours before the collision, and you are concerned that the jurors might hold this against your client even though there is no causal relation to the accident, you may be tempted to educate the jury about the law's view of drinking and driving. "Do you understand that there is no law against having a drink or two and then driving a car, because a drink or two is not enough to influence driving?" may tell the juror your position on the law, but it will not tell you anything about the juror's position about drinking and driving. Before you tell the juror what the law is, find out how the juror feels about drinking and driving: "How much alcohol do you think someone can drink before driving is affected?" If you get an answer that you can accept, frame the "lecture" question as a follow up to the juror's answer. The more open ended your question the more likely you are to get the juror's to talk.

Two other techniques—looping and scaled questions—are helpful particularly if you don't have much time. Looping is a natural way of including other jurors in the conversation and allowing them to "educate" each other. In the example above if the juror, Mrs. Smith, answered, "I think two drinks is the limit," find out how other jurors feel about the answer, good or bad. You might ask what the juror seated next to Mrs. Smith thinks about the answer. (Always try to use juror names instead of numbers; no one likes being referred to as a number). You can "loop" through the panel discovering juror attitudes without ever making a judgment yourself. Since there are no bad answers in voir dire you can encourage openness and candor. Thank and praise jurors when you get what seems like a "bad" answer. If juror number twelve, Mr. Jones finally says, "I don't agree with Mrs. Smith, I don't think anyone should ever drive a car if they have had anything to drink," you might guess that Mr. Jones is not going to forgive your client for having a drink and then driving regardless of what the law says. Aren't you glad you heard that during voir dire instead of learning that he said it in the jury room and convinced a few more jurors! What seems like the worst possible answer is actually the best possible. You have discovered an unacceptable juror that if not dismissed for cause, will be the subject of one of your peremptories. You will respond with courtesy and with an eye to others who might share the view: "Thank you for sharing that view, Mr. Jones. That is exactly what this process is about. How many other people feel like Mr. Jones?"

A scaled question asks jurors to respond with a ranked answer such as agree, strongly agree, disagree, or strongly disagree. It works best if you can display the question or at least the choices so that you don't have to repeat them. It allows you to ask a general question about your case but get individual responses very quickly.

After completing the juror ranking based on pretrial information, and after you have completed drafting your questions for the jurors, prepare a name, address, age, and occupation list of the panel, a list of the areas of voir dire inquiry, and a diagram of the number of seats to be filled for voir dire. These items, along with the personal data sheets for each panel member, are the tools you will use at voir dire. Make sure your chart matches the way the jurors are seated, so that you can quickly fill in their names and juror numbers. Decide on your "shorthand" system for tracking their answers so that you can devote your attention to them and not your chart. It is even better if you can bring another lawyer, secretary or paralegal with you to take notes during voir dire. Encourage your client to observe as well so that you have as much information about how the jurors were responding when you go to exercise your peremptory challenges.

PART III
THE FIRST TRIAL

The anticipation during the week before trial—some would say the anxiety—is what makes old men and women out of young trial lawyers. The exhilaration when the judge takes the bench and the bailiff cries, "All rise," is the splash from the Fountain of Youth that makes those old trial lawyers young again. You and your client are on your feet, facing the bench. At the end of the bailiff's liturgy, the judge is seated, either nods or tells everyone to be seated, and the play is on. You are about to begin one of the most difficult and exciting of human endeavors.

As the clerk calls the case, the members of the jury panel, sitting in the courtroom behind the bar, waiting for their names to be called, have their first view of the set with some of the players in place. The judge will probably give the panel a brief introductory explanation of the nature of the case, the voir dire process, and the "mechanics" of being a juror. The length of that speech varies from court to court, with the experience of the particular jury panel, and with the completeness of the jury orientation pamphlet that has been furnished to every panel member. The court usually introduces the parties and the lawyers to the panel. Be sure that you stand and look at the panel when you are introduced. Your client should do the same. Now you are ready to begin to exclude those panel members that you do not want to decide your client's cause.

CHAPTER 7

THINNING THE AUDIENCE: VOIR DIRE

You are ready. You have thought about your questions and what kind of juror you need to strike. You have learned the judge's process and time limits. If you and your client are lucky, your first trial will not involve high publicity or the need for a larger-than-normal panel. You should have your jury box diagram, a diagram for identifying the seating of the proposed jurors, the jury panel list, and the personal data sheets in front of you. As each name is called, write it down on the proposed juror seating diagram and locate that person's personal data sheet from your compilation. If there is no room for all of the proposed jurors in the area of the jury box, the court will usually designate a separate section of the seating behind the bar to which the proposed jurors will move and from where they will be questioned by the lawyers. Review the data sheets, including the rankings you assigned during preparation. Compare the average rank for the eighteen to the average rank for the whole panel to get a quick judgment about the overall acceptability of the eighteen called compared to the rest of the panel. Order the data sheets from "worst" to "best," and put the "worst" to one side for first consideration in the exercise of strikes.

The art of voir dire as a persuasive tool, or as a fine-tuned mechanism for sending subtle vibrations to lawyers with sensitive antennae in order that they might make brilliant exclusions from the panel, is beyond the scope of this primer. There are some simple techniques, however, that can help during that first voir dire.

During questioning by court or counsel, watch the faces of the proposed jurors. Their expressions may tell you more than the information you have accumulated thus far.

The court will usually give each attorney an opportunity to make a short statement to the proposed jurors before the questioning begins. Better to say, "Hello, nice to see ya," without notes or hesitation than to do anything that looks or sounds planned or important. This is an introduction, and you ought to handle it like the first meeting with somebody at a social gathering. You cannot accomplish anything more than the briefest of introductions, and if you try for more, everything that you do thereafter will suffer from the failure of a reasonable introduction in the beginning.

The brief statement before questioning often includes a concise dispassionate sounding explanation of the lawsuit, not more than a couple of sentences, an entreaty for the jurors to speak out in response to questions, an explanation that the process of "prying" is not "personal" in motivation, and an explanation that the law requires the lawyers to make a certain number of strikes, which no juror should take personally. Be very careful about laying any of that on too thick. Every juror smart enough to decide the case knows that the questioning is intended to be "personal," and that a lawyer strikes a juror the lawyer believes will not favor the lawyer's client. Remember the personality that comes through to the jurors during trial, comes through for the first time in this short introductory monologue. Their first judgment of your courtesy, earnestness, and involvement is likely to last.

The particular questions that are asked on voir dire depend upon the nature of the case and upon the individual lawyer's judgment of the information that will be "telling" beyond the specific response. Be sensitive in how you ask questions. Questioning can be very invasive and embarrassing if done poorly. Think about how the jurors feel. For many this is their first time in a courtroom. They see the judge sitting up high in the black robes, a deputy with a gun, lots of official looking court personnel, the lawyer and clients. They are seated with strangers and are being asked to share their opinions in front of a crowd of people, most of whom seem better educated or at least more comfortable than they are. Getting jurors to open up and talk is hard work. A smile and open, friendly demeanor will go a long way in making people feel comfortable. If you are asking about potentially sensitive issues or paving the way for potential jurors to share biases, disclose something proportionate about yourself. In a civil case, for example, you might share that you were the victim of a crime once and so would not be able to be fair if this were a similar criminal trial.

Jurors are reluctant to raise their hands or otherwise answer questions directed to the entire panel. Because the more an individual juror talks, the more you learn; address questions individually if the court will allow. Using your completed diagram to identify individual jurors, address them by name. Remember not to use, "juror number four." If you skip around, asking different jurors in no particular pattern, the process will seem less contrived and more spontaneous. Just remember to spend the most time talking with those jurors most likely to end up on the panel. If you are under time limits, you can politely tell jurors far outside the "strike" zone that you would love to visit with them if you had more time, but it does not look like they are likely to be needed for this panel.

Cause strikes are made as answers are given that justify the strike. Know your judge's process. Some judges allow you to call the potential juror to the bench to ask the final questions to establish the strike. Others have it all occur out in the open. Know the "magic words" to satisfy the strike and under what circumstances you might be able to "rehabilitate" the potential juror. What happens after the strike for cause has been granted also varies by jurisdiction, so make sure you are tracking both the sustained and overruled challenges. If the challenge is not sustained, you will most likely exercise a peremptory challenge when the time rolls around. You cannot afford to leave on the jury a potential juror you have unsuccessfully challenged for cause.

After the interrogation is complete, the lawyers are required to make peremptory strikes. If the court will allow, ask to use the jury room or some-place where you can talk with your client and anyone else you had help with the voir dire. At any rate, do the striking at the bench, or in some other fashion in which the jurors do not know who struck whom. In some jurisdictions the list of potential jurors is passed back and forth between the lawyers for alternate striking until twelve jurors remain. In jurisdictions where the selections are made private-ly, try not to "double strike." A double strike is where both lawyers strike the same potential juror. Always err on the side of caution if you cannot predict whether your opponent will strike a juror that is truly "bad" for you. You do not need a wild card on the jury if you can help it.

If you are forced to make any kind of a strike publicly, do it with empathy and kindness. Not even jurors who did not want to do jury service in the first place want to be rejected. Most jurors develop friendships with other jurors. Except in the case where prospective jurors are seated together in the audience and are obviously talking to each other, you will not know the friendships that have devel-oped. It is important that your public strike of a prospective juror not be in a fashion that offends the "friend" who may still be on the jury. "Your honor, I think Mr. Jones would be more comfortable if he did not have to decide this case; the defense believes the court should excuse him," may work better than, "Defense strikes juror Jones"—but don't bet on it. Nothing works very well. Do not even attempt the "Mr. Jones would be more comfortable" version if Mr. Jones has not given you some responses that might reasonably be interpreted by others to mean that Jones has some bias. Do everything within your power to persuade the court that there is nothing to lose and much to gain if the court allows peremptories to be privately exercised. This is one of the few matters with which your opponent is likely to fully agree.

When voir dire is conducted by interrogation and strike of individual jurors, other considerations arise. There is an important difference between the strategy employed when the jurors are individually considered and the strategy employed when all eighteen names (if the jury will be twelve and each side must strike three) are pulled first. Under the one-at-a-time system, the first twelve jurors accepted constitute the jury. A lawyer need not use all available strikes. Having no idea of what name will be drawn next, the lawyer is necessarily more cautious in exercising peremptory strikes. Many lawyers believe that you ought to exercise all of your peremptories when individual challenges are made, with the goal of obtaining the best possible jury. Others believe that you ought to "save one for the monster," particularly in the case where the names are pulled one at a time and interrogation and strike precede the pulling of the next name. If, for example, you have eleven jurors accepted, and the juror being interrogated is a two on your pretrial rank and remains a two after questioning, you should not exercise the last peremptory challenge. The minute you exercise the last peremptory challenge in hopes of having one of the many ones or zeros come forward as the next juror, the clerk pulls the name of your opponent's lodge brother. The judge denies your challenge for cause, and you have eleven jurors, and one "monster," ready to boo your play from curtain to curtain.

If the full eighteen are pulled and then individually interrogated and struck, the need to hold onto the last peremptory is minimized. If the judge interrogates first for cause, there is almost no risk that someone other than the names you know will serve on the jury. You can use the last peremptory without concern that an asterisk you do not know will be a possible juror.

If your first trial is long, or if it is a criminal case that will take more than a day, the court is likely to have alternate jurors selected. The handling of alternates, the matter of additional strikes, and the method of selection are statutory in most jurisdictions. Be sure you know whether you must save a peremptory for the alternates.

Once the peremptory challenges have been exercised and before the clerk announces or swears in the panel, this is the time to make any *Batson*-like challenges to the panel and the way your opponent exercised the strikes. If you foresee race, or other protected classes being an issue in your case, be sure you know how to object and preserve error.

At the completion of voir dire, the clerk will administer the oath to the jury. This is often the time for a break, and it gives you the opportunity to take care of three important matters in chambers. If you anticipate a quick voir dire and no break, you must handle these before voir dire or approach the bench immediately after the jury is sworn.

In some jurisdictions the court will give the jury preliminary instructions as a matter of course. In others, counsel must request preliminary instructions. If there is something in your case that requires preliminary instruction, request that the court give those instructions before opening statements. Defendants in criminal cases usually ask for instruction on the presumption of innocence and the burden of proof beyond a reasonable doubt because most jurors are not familiar with them.

If you intend to invoke "the rule" (sequestration of potential witnesses), do it before opening statement. Witnesses can become as "educated" from listening to opening statements as from listening to testimony of others.

If you intend to use physical evidence or illustrative diagrams during opening statement, you should clear it with the court at the bench or in chambers. Although there is no real reason for distinguishing between the previewing of audio and visual evidence, the mistrial remedy being equally available, most courts will stop you from using physical evidence during your opening unless the court and counsel have had an opportunity to discuss it. Avoid having your opening statement interrupted by clearing the use of physical evidence with the court beforehand. In some jurisdictions, this is also the time to raise any *in limine* motions for the exclusion of evidence if it has not already occurred in the pretrial conference. If you expect that you will succeed in the exclusion of inflammatory material from your opponent's case, you may wish to ensure that it does not get into your opponent's opening statement and before the jury before you have complained. (Ideally the motion *in limine* should occur before the voir dire so that you know whether to deal with the possibility of the evidence in your questions or can preclude the other side from raising it in theirs.) After you have completed your bench or chambers matters, the stage is set, and the play begins.

CHAPTER 8

CURTAIN UP: THE OPENING STATEMENT

Opening statement is the first opportunity for the jurors to get into the play. Voir dire was a matter of personal survival. The judge's preliminary instructions were a preview of the type and style of the case. Once they have been sworn and instructed, the jurors are ready for the curtain to go up. They are ready to begin to listen, and to begin to decide about what they hear. Your opening statement will determine how well they listen to your entire case, their attitude about you and your client, and their willingness to decide in your favor. In that regard, the opening statement is just like the first scene of a play. If the first scene works, the audience will look forward to the rest of the play, begin to identify with the characters, and begin to draw tentative conclusions about how they would like the play to end.

Beginning lawyers often make one of two opposite, but equally disastrous, mistakes in presenting the opening statement. Many lawyers think that the opening statement is an opening argument and spend most of their time telling the jurors why their client should win. The others, knowing it is procedurally improper to argue during opening, and not believing that anything else will be particularly effective, give a matter-of-fact description of what they expect the evidence to be, in the order they expect to present it. Neither approach succeeds. "Arguers" ask the jurors to accept conclusions before they know the facts from which the conclusions are drawn and forces the jurors to a premature conscious consideration of who should win, which is contrary to the judge's instructions. "Matter-of-facters" give the jurors nothing more than an abbreviated version of the trial and then heightening the jurors' disinterest and the lawyers' own discomforts by explaining that what they are saying "is not evidence." The lawyer might as well say, "Do not listen to this because, (a) you will see it in more detail in just a minute, and (b) it does not count anyway".

An effective opening statement combines the aim of the "arguer" (to persuade) with the tools of the "matter-of-facter" (the facts) to produce an image of events that encourages fair-minded jurors to do what the lawyer wants, without the lawyer forcing the issue. None of us like to be pushed into making a decision and usually respond by pushing back. If you try to force the jurors to accept that this is "the only verdict justice will allow," or the "only evidence they can believe," the more resistant they become. For plaintiffs, the jurors should have reached a tentative decision for the plaintiff without being asked, and probably without being conscious of it. For the defendant, the same goal may exist in a particular case, but more often, the defendant's lawyer is trying to present enough to stop the jurors from reaching any judgments, tentative or not, until after the defendant's evidence.

The defendants have to work harder in opening statements to tell stories that diffuse plaintiffs' stories and lay positive foundations for their own. The defendant's open has to be more than a rebuttal of the plaintiff's or an articulation of why the plaintiff should not win. Telling jurors why green is a terrible color does not help them agree that blue is a better color. People don't make decisions from negative constructs; they need a positive solution even when they accept the negative. Deciding not to purchase a gas guzzling SUV doesn't mean that you will automatically buy a hybrid coupe. Accepting that the best jury research concluded that 80% of jurors decide the case in favor of the same party for whom they tentatively decided after the opening statements requires the defendant to do more than just hope that jurors will wait. The statistic does not mean that for eight out of ten jurors the trial is over after the opening statements and that everything that follows is irrelevant. After the openings, the evidence has to follow the way jurors have been led to expect. Jurors change their minds most often where there is a disconnect between the evidence produced and what was represented in the opening statements. Over-selling the case in opening is a sure way to destroy the natural benefit of tentative decision making. Remember, the tentative conclusion may not be a conscious one, and it is being drawn despite the judge's admonition to the jurors not to decide until after they have heard all the evidence. It is important for an understanding of the function of the opening statement to realize that a tentative conclusion will be reached. It is equally important not to appear to be forcing that tentative conclusion.

The rule of primacy has the greatest impact on the trial in the opening statements. Not only is it the first look for the jury and the one that is most likely to be remembered; it will set the tone for everything that follows. The plaintiff must do everything possible to take advantage of the first position. The defendant must understand the plaintiff's advantage and try to diminish and counter it.

The opening statement should be a positive, factual persuasion, calculated to achieve tentative juror agreement with the lawyer's position. Anything less is missed opportunity; anything more is too much, too soon.

"Positive" means that the opening statement should be a presentation of the party's position, not a quarrel with the opponent's position. This admonition is as applicable to the defendant as to the plaintiff. Although it may be easier for the party with the burden to make a positive presentation, it may be more important for the party without that burden. While there is little temptation for plaintiffs to quarrel in opening statements, the following defendants are often sorely tempted to begin punching holes in the plaintiffs' positions rather than positively asserting their own. If, however, the plaintiff has made a powerful factual presentation in opening statement, the defendant must make a positive statement to avoid being blown out of the case before having a chance to present any evidence. The defendant's opening statement is the only thing that stands between the plaintiff's opening statement and the plaintiff's evidence. If the defendant's opening statement merely snipes at the plaintiff's presentation, the jurors will have nothing contrary to the plaintiff's proof to consider or to wait for. Even in the defense case least conducive to a positive opening statement—the criminal defense in which you are hoping the government forgets something in its proof—there is something positive to be said. The defendant positively asserts the genius of America's system of criminal jury trials; explains why the defendant will not take the stand or produce any evidence as a symbol of the importance of the presumption of innocence; and enlists the support of the jury as the watchdog that casts a demanding gaze at the prosecutor's proof.

Maintaining a positive posture in the opening statement does not mean that you should not acknowledge the problems in your case, but it does mean that you should not acknowledge that they are problems. For example, if your client with the soft tissue injury to the back had a pre-existing back problem at the time of the collision, and you decide that you must tell the jury about that as soon as possible, you cannot raise it apologetically or defensively. "You will hear that Betty Sue had a bad back before her car was smashed from the rear by the defendant, but that does not mean she should not recover for her injuries," is not helpful. You might just as well have left it for the defendant to mention in opening statement; it could not be said much worse for you. The positive approach, on the other hand, will take the "surprise fact" away from the defense and at the same time cast it as something about which the plaintiff is outraged rather than defensive: "Betty Sue was just beginning to recover from a very painful back injury when the defendant smashed his car into the back of Betty Sue's. Her head was snapped back violently. The collision renewed that long cycle of pain and treatment that Betty Sue and Dr. Ficksit will tell you about."

The opening statement and the closing argument are exact opposites in technique, but the opposite sides of the same coin. Although the closing is almost exclusively argument, and the opening is almost exclusively fact recital, both must be built around the theme of your play—those few sentences that tell why your client should prevail. The effective opening, therefore, is built with the same structure as the closing argument. The first outline of the opening statement does not include facts you want to present; it contains points you want to make. After you have decided how many of those points should be presented in an opening, you find the facts that will make the point, and position them so that the conclusion will be obvious to the listeners.

Consider the defendant's opening statement in Betty Sue's whiplash case. The theme is that John Denter rear-ended Betty Sue's car because she made a sudden and unreasonable stop midblock in order to turn left into a driveway. The suddenness of the stop was caused by Betty Sue being distracted. The theme should be presented factually in the opening.

"John Denter was driving west on Baker at about twenty-five miles per hour. He was a couple of car lengths behind plaintiff's red Chevrolet. There were no other cars traveling in the same direction within a block either way. As the plaintiff crossed the Fillmore intersection, a hot air balloon was descending and about to land on a roped-off part of Fillmore just north of Baker. The KRZY radio station, about an eighth of a block west of the intersection of Baker and Fillmore, was having a big promotion. A lot of people were milling around in front of the station. There were clowns and gymnasts and other exciting things to draw the attention of those standing outside the radio station along Baker and, unfortunately, also the attention of the plaintiff. Across the street from the radio station was the hamburger drive-in where the plaintiff apparently wanted to go. John saw the plaintiff's brake lights come on suddenly as the plaintiff's red Chevrolet skidded before coming to an abrupt stop in the middle of the block. John slammed on his brakes the minute he saw the brake lights come on in front of him, but because of plaintiff's sudden, skidding stop there was not enough distance for John's car to stop without hitting the rear of plaintiff's Chevrolet."

There may be many other points to make and other facts that belong in the opening, but the jurors should now know, at least, that Betty Sue came to a screeching halt in order to make a left turn, and that the reason she stopped so suddenly was that her mind was on balloons and clowns, rather than on where she was going, and how she had to get there. If the theme is presented factually in the opening, it provides a consistent thread that can be rolled up and used in the closing argument. "Factual persuasion" is more subtle and difficult than persuasion through argument. Persuasion through argument assumes an audience that already knows and has had a chance to give some consideration to the facts that are the basis for the argument. Persuasion by factual presentation requires that you make the "argument" by the order and emphasis of the facts presented. You cannot draw conclusions and you cannot ask the jury to draw conclusions. The process by which you encourage the jurors to draw those conclusions is, therefore, very delicate. The reward for the opening statement that relies upon subtle factual persuasion is that the jurors view the conclusions they draw as their own, rather than as your suggestion, and they are less likely to let go of them easily.

A good opening statement is harder to do than a good closing argument. Jurors don't know you well enough to take you at your word if you tell them, Betty Sue was negligent or at fault. They have taken oaths to be fair and impartial. They have just finished voir dire, where they experience both lawyers asking different questions and expressing differing views of the case. They have been studiously watching both clients throughout, but haven't heard from either yet. Your opening has to keep emotional and intellectual pace with the audience. The audience has not been living this case the way you have been for the last year, or week. They have been plucked out of their ordinary lives and asked to decide this dispute. Imagine if someone stopped you in a grocery store and asked you to resolve a dispute, what would you want to know?

Most opening statements fit into one of two construction schemes: the story of the event or the story of the trial. The story of the event is a present-tense or past-tense recitation of the occurrences leading to the lawsuit. The story of the trial is a future-tense description of the trial as a vehicle for a recitation of the occurrences leading to the lawsuit. The construction which best fits your case will depend on the circumstances with which you are confronted. The story of the trial approach, for example, is probably less effective with a well-seasoned jury. The more exciting or dramatic the actual facts of the case, the less likely the story of the trial approach can fulfill the potential of the opening. On the other hand, if your lawsuit is fairly technical and the best thing that you have going for you is a very impressive expert witness, the story of the event approach does not provide the best vehicle for selling the expert in the opening statement. If the lawsuit is very complex, the story of the event approach may be unmanageable within the time for a reasonable opening statement.

Whichever approach you choose, the ingredients of an effective opening statement are constant. Although there are no rules that apply to every case, most good opening statements have common characteristics.

Facts are organized and words are chosen to create "images" in the minds of the jurors. Remember you will have auditory, visual, and kinesthetic learners on every panel, so you want to include language that will "speak" to each of them in their primary language. Visual learners, for example, upon hearing an idea will attempt to "see it" in their minds. Concrete learning is easier than abstract learning for that reason. Tell twelve people that "the man held the candle," and all will have a picture in their minds of both the man and the candle. If the concept is one that the mind can visualize, if it creates an image, the idea sticks. The adjective is the linguistic tool most useful for creating images. Twelve people may remember when you tell them "she walked up the stairs to the office," but not so certainly as if you tell them that "she climbed the twelve grey concrete steps leading to the office." Of course, imagery should be used sparingly to be effective. If your case is about an injury resulting from defective concrete, the image may be useful. If the case is about the breach of an employment contract by the man in the office, you hardly care if the jurors remember the steps, even though you may care that they remember that she went to the office to sign the contract. Remember that if a visual is important, you can use demonstrative evidence in your opening if it has been pre-approved by the judge.

Clients are portrayed in their best light. Commentators and advocacy lecturers have been heard to say, "Humanize the client." Defense lawyers representing corporate defendants do not say, "And then the defendant corporation shipped the oil." They do not even say, "And then Exxon sent the oil." Trying to neutralize the target-defendant problem, the defense lawyer is likely to say, "And then, Mr. Peterson, here, decided to fill the tanker." Do not confuse portraying the client in the best light, or "humanizing" with creating a client with whom the jurors can identify. All the Mr. Petersons in the world will not make juror number four think Peterson is Exxon. But avoiding the corporate name, and talking about people, portrays the defendant in its best light, by avoiding a constant reminder that the defendant is a wealthy target. Why else would you expect the plaintiff to keep referring to "the oil company?"

The most effective way to portray a client for whom you want to win the jurors' empathy is to describe personal facts. In a death case, for example, it is important to tell the jurors that the deceased husband had two children. It is better to say, "He left ten-year-old Billy and eight-year-old Pamela." If the children are important for damages, however, it is better to say that on the morning of the day he was killed, "he had breakfast with Billy and Pamela, and before he left for the office, he promised to get home early enough so they could take a bike ride before dinner." Every human being is involved in small personal events during the day that exemplify something of greater significance. Those small personal events are effective in creating juror empathy. Every juror knows that fathers are important for children and a small personal fact may convey that need and that element of damages more effectively than the statement that "they loved him very much."

The beginning ideas are important to the case. Although many lawyers begin the opening statement by telling the jury about the procedure to be followed in the trial, or by introducing everybody in the courtroom except the bailiff, most effective advocates begin the opening statement by telling the jurors something that they want the jurors to remember. The jurors will pay their most attention to you in those first few moments. The something you want the jurors to remember is rarely an explanation of what comes after opening statement or your associate counsel's name. You may well have reason to convey that information someplace in your opening statement, but not at the beginning. Many beginning lawyers do something meaningless for the first minute so that they can get rid of the jitters. It is not worth the price. The jurors will never listen to you more closely than they will listen to the first twenty-five words out of your mouth. Do not waste them. If the national news were covering your trial, think of those twenty-five words as the only sound bite to be played. That doesn't mean to add unnecessary drama, but it does mean that those twenty-five words should encapsulate your theme and answer the juror's question of what this case is about. Remember, your voir dire probably stressed more of your case's negatives if you were trying to weed out jurors who were going to "boo" your case, so these first few words are a critical time to tell the jurors the story of your case.

Effective opening statements, at their core, are stories. Culturally we learn through stories. Little Red Riding Hood went to grandmother's house, she didn't "proceed in a north, northeasterly direction to her maternal grandmother's house on June 17th." Facts are hard to remember, stories give us a way to hold the facts together. The opening starts with the theme, the case sound-bite, and weaves the facts into the trial story. Gathering the facts is the easy part; making those facts come to life before a jury is the hard part. The law acknowledges that stories make the facts more believable. That's why witnesses get to introduce themselves, why we don't just stipulate to bad evidence, and why appellate courts don't second guess trial court credibility decisions. Who the witnesses are and the visual images the jurors picture all make the distinct facts more or less believable. What do we do on first dates, or the start of new school years, but exchange the stories that make us who we are?

Your trial story starts with the identification of the theme, so that the jurors know into what "category" of human experience this story fits. The more universal the theme, the better all the jurors will relate to it. But be careful about introducing that theme or category of human experience with a reference that might be familiar to you but might not be familiar to all of the jurors. Sacred texts, such as the Bible, and cultural icons, such as Shakespeare's plays, have long been attractive to trial lawyers as references to introduce ideas. As juries become increasingly diverse it is important to distill themes to their essence and avoid the references that might not be familiar to some of the jurors. If, for example, you represent a younger brother suing his older sibling for "stealing" the value of a patent for intricate software technology, your theme inspiration of jealousy and rivalry might have come from Cain and Abel. But don't use the sparkling reference, even though it is apt, and risk alienating jurors unfamiliar with the Bible story. You don't need a reference for the universally understood core human emotions of jealousy and rivalry to make your otherwise technical patent dispute come alive for the jurors.

Think about what function you want your opening to serve. Does the jury need to be educated or can they make the critical judgment themselves? Do you want the opening to tease or empower? The task for the opening statement is to help the jurors develop the framework in which to evaluate the evidence in your client's favor. Consider a case in which you represent the state, suing a nursing home for continuing licensing violations. At the end of the trial, you want a jury that is empowered to level statutory penalties and sanctions. You might use the opening to talk about the numerous visits by state inspectors to the nursing home and the number of warnings and tickets the home received without ever changing its behavior. The factual recitation will set up your closing argument that only the jurors have the power, by imposing financial penalties, to protect the older citizens of the states and cause the nursing home to provide adequate care. Your facts and theme, of course, must fit the evidence you will present. Once you have done the hard work of sifting the facts and putting them together in a way that gives jurors the big picture in a way that makes them want to hear the evidence to follow, your framework is complete. It is time to focus on how you—lawyer at center stage—will present it.

Opening statements should be made without notes. The opening statement is the one part of the trial over which you have exclusive control. Nobody can do anything to the evidence or the procedure to mess you up. The opening can be fully prepared without fear of change by circumstance. If you have extensive notes with you during opening statement you will read them. People who take crutches with them, use them. Notes are a crutch. Aside from the fact that very few of us can read very effectively, the lawyer that reads sacrifices the implied belief in the client's cause that a "sincere" presentation conveys. The common advice, "be sincere," is not very helpful. It tells you how you ought to appear, but nothing about how it can be accomplished. One technique for appearing "sincere," is to make a presentation that is meaningful enough to the lawyer so that it is dragged out of the lawyer's head and heart, rather than being read from a yellow pad.

Effective opening statements never promise more than the advocate's case can deliver. The only thing worse than a meaningless opening statement is a powerful opening that promises more than the evidence produces. We have all experienced the disappointment of a movie trailer that was fabulous when the movie wasn't worth the price of admission. Every lawyer walks into the courtroom armed with the jurors' presumption that human beings are believable. Despite all experience to the contrary, and even in the face of the stereotype of the clever, tricky lawyer, human beings listen to each other with the presumption that what they are hearing is the truth until somebody or something demonstrates the contrary. Although you need not build up your credibility to a level above that of the presumption, you cannot afford to do anything that will lose the presumption of straight shooting and remind the jurors of the lawyer stereotype to which they have undoubtedly been exposed. If the opening statement promises more than the evidence produces, the lawyer loses credibility to a level below the "acceptable" line and the client's case suffers as a result.

Weak spots in the case are usually mentioned in opening statement. Not your opponent's weak spots, but your own. This is one of the techniques for avoiding the kind of oversell that leaves the jurors thinking that you promised more than the evidence delivered. This is a very touchy technique, susceptible to the kind of mistake that makes the cure worse than the disease. Mentioning the weak spots is often described as "taking the sting out", or "pulling the plug." The latter is accurate, the former is dangerous. There are two reasons for mentioning the weak spots: (1) you do not wish to look like you were hiding something when the other side mentions it; and (2) you do not want the fact to be unduly emphasized by being raised after the jurors think they know all there is to know about the witness or the occurrence. The first reason is based on the lawyer's desire to maintain credibility. The second reason grows out of a concern that if the hurtful fact is not mentioned by you, it will have greater impact upon the jurors than it is substantively worth. Any mention of the weak spot will take care of the first concern, but only the proper handling will ensure that the fact does not have an undue influence on the jurors. In politics, strategists help candidates "spin" bad facts. In a trial you cannot afford to be devious or untruthful about facts in a case, but you can place "bad" facts in context so that you preserve the credibility of the witness. You cannot satisfy the undue emphasis problem by "acknowledging" that the fact constitutes a weak spot. If you refer to it during your opening as a problem, or speak about it too early, you will highlight it for the jury more than your opponent could have. If your star prosecution witness in a drug conspiracy trial has three convictions for selling heroin, you need something better than: "You will hear that Robert Mafioso has been convicted three times for selling heroin, but he was there, and he saw what happened, and it will be your task to judge his credibility." If you plan to argue during a closing that the only way into a conspiracy is through a crook, use the same approach to pull the plug on the convictions in the opening statement:

Mark Corradi, the Drug Enforcement Administration agent who arrested Sanford, Mayer, and Brown while making undercover drug purchases as he progressed from one rung of this ladder to the next, will tell you that he never even met the defendant, Samuel Patten. The highest he got up the ladder of suppliers was Robert Mafioso, a man who sold him a full kilogram of heroin, and who had three times before been convicted for selling heroin. Samuel Patten was a very careful man, according to Mafioso. He will tell you that it was only because Patten was sure that Mafioso, with his record, was not an undercover officer that he was allowed to know who Patten was and what part he played in the sale of the heroin.

Every good opening statement celebrates substance over form. There are many stock phrases and ideas that are available for opening statements. Many of them were good when first used by a bright lawyer for a specific circumstance, but few of them were worth the universality that mindless copying conferred upon them. You will do yourself a favor if you avoid saying anything in an opening statement for which you cannot articulate a good persuasive or legal reason. The phrase, "what I say is not evidence," is a classic example of a statement that is often heard in openings, but rarely has any value. It is the law. The judge will say it. But it hardly adds anything to your presentation. On the other hand, if the plaintiff has just made an opening statement that you believe is bigger than the plaintiff's case will be, as the defendant's counsel, you may have a persuasive reason to use the hackneyed phrase:

"Ladies and gentlemen, what I say is not evidence. By the same token, what Mr. Fulvet has just told you is not evidence. Judge Canker told you just before Mr. Fulvet began that you were to decide the case on the evidence, and that what the lawyers said during opening statements is not evidence. Now if the evidence Mr. Fulvet produces through the witnesses is the same as he told you in his opening statement, you should find for the plaintiff. On the other hand, we believe the evidence will show that Mr. Oliver was traveling ..."

Since the lawyer's statements are not evidence, many lawyers preface statements of fact in the opening with the phrase, "the evidence will show." The phrase becomes rapidly tiring and annoying. If you are using the story of the trial approach to the opening, the phrase may have occasional value. Mix it up, however, with, "Agent Corradi will tell you," or "you will hear," or something similar. If you are using the story of the event approach, the whole concept of "you will hear," "the evidence will show," and the like is inappropriate. The story of the event is a first or third person story that will be badly mangled if foreign phrases like, "the evidence will show," are included. You should consider satisfying the technicality, the judge, and whatever persuasive value there is in letting the jury know that you are giving them a preview of what is to follow in the exciting evidence, by beginning your opening statement to the judge: "May it please the Court, it is my privilege to state the case for the government as we believe the evidence will show." Turn from the judge to the jury, and begin: "Mark Corradi bought two kilograms of heroin from ..." If you feel compelled to address the jury before beginning the story: "Ladies and gentlemen, Mark Corradi bought ..."

Three phrases that creep into many opening statements, although nobody suggests their use, tell the jurors that the reality they are about to see is really a put up job. "The story you will hear," "our witnesses will tell you" and "we submit" are phrases of fiction. A "story" is what a liar tells, not what an honest observer relates. "Our witnesses" tells the jurors that the witnesses have an ax to grind— yours. You may wish to say "their witnesses" at some time, but never "our witnesses." "We submit," implies that there is a contest about the reality. More importantly, it implies that there is another reasonable submittal. Although that may be true, it is not a phrase of persuasion. "We submit that he crossed the street while the light was red," adds nothing to, "He crossed the street while the light was red," except your admission that it might not have happened that way.

Whether you use the story of the trial or the story of the event for your opening statement, remember that every good story is better with pictures. If diagrams, pictures, or real evidence will be useful in your opening statement, or will make the jurors better prepared to like your play, use them. But be careful to avoid two problems. You may not use physical items that cannot be admitted into evidence. If you have any doubts about admissibility, ask the judge for a ruling before you begin. The second problem is more subtle, and is one for which there is no easy solution. The problem is that if you show too much, or tell too many details in an opening statement, you run the risk of having everything in the first scene and a jury that sleeps through the rest of the play. The opening is an effective preview, not the whole play. Remain mindful that while you know who all the players are and what all the pictures show, the jurors are still just trying to absorb the main story for the first time. Since they don't really know if or when they might see these exhibits again, they might focus on remembering them rather than absorbing the big picture of your opening statement. Only present what will help the jurors better understand the big picture and any key concepts they need to have in mind before the trial starts. The opening statement is a powerful factor in the success of your trial, and it deserves your most careful consideration.

CHAPTER 9

DIALOGUE: EXAMINATION
OF WITNESSES

Most of the information upon which the jurors will decide your case will come from examination of witnesses. Who wins the lawsuit will depend upon which pieces of information the jurors accept.

It is natural to say that witnesses determine the lawsuit, and at least with respect to credibility, that is true. Part of what makes trying cases so challenging is that you are hired as the lawyer-director-storyteller and yet you have to tell the story through other people. You have to persuade through a very structured question/answer, direct/cross examination format while following the rules of evidence and procedure. Your job is to break through that mold and allow jurors the opportunity to be persuaded by your witnesses. In order for jurors even to begin to be persuaded they must, first, be aware of the information and, second, believe it. Whether the jurors believe information from a witness depends upon the witness' credibility. In most cases, the testimony of important witnesses must be weighed against the contrary testimony of the other side's witnesses. Insofar as most of the witnesses enter the courtroom with the same presumed credibility, the witness that gains credibility during testimony—or in some cases, loses the least—will be the witness whose testimony is accepted by the jurors. No matter how much the jurors might like, respect, or believe the lawyer, the lawyer's credibility can do nothing to induce the jurors to accept the witness' testimony.

The advocate's skill, however, can have a major influence on whether the jurors are aware of the testimony so that they might then make a judgment about the witness' credibility. Even though a witness speaks, there is no guarantee that the jurors hear or understand what is said. Recent psychological studies indicate that people retain about 20% of what they hear. The advocate's skill in examination determines the information of which the jurors will be aware.

Examination of witnesses is conducted by lawyers to accomplish two opposite goals: (1) Build up the pile of evidence supporting your client's position which the jurors will accept. (2) Tear down the pile of evidence supporting your opponent's position that the jurors are willing to accept. The examination that builds up the pile is usually conducted with witnesses that you call to the witness stand and interrogate on direct examination. The examination that tears down the opponent's pile of evidence is usually conducted with witnesses that the opponent has called to the witness stand, and is called cross examination. The techniques for conducting the two kinds of interrogation are exactly opposite, because the goals are exactly opposite.

For any examination, there are only four kinds of questions that a lawyer can ask: (1) questions that call for a narrative response; (2) questions that define the subject of response; (3) questions that call for a specific response; and (4) questions that suggest the response. The questions are listed in an ascending order of interrogation control, and simultaneously, in a descending order of witness credibility. The narrative response question, "After seeing the collision, what did you do?" turns the courtroom over to the witness, allowing the witness to relate to the jury without distracting interruption from any quarter. While the witness talks, the jurors have an opportunity to size up the speaker. The subject defined response question, "What can you tell us about how the car looked after the collision?" puts the lawyer in a little more control of the response by limiting the subject about which the witness may testify. This still affords the witness ample opportunity to relate to the jurors and build credibility. Specific response questions like, "What color was the car that was hit?" allow the lawyer to gain much more control over the both the subject and the length of the witness' answer and affords the witness little chance to relate to the jurors. The response suggested question, "The car that was hit was green, wasn't it?" provides the lawyer with maximum control over the witness, limiting the witness' reasonable response to a "yes" or "no," and reducing the witness' chance to relate to the jurors to zero. Remember the example of the spotlight in the courtroom? Think about where the spotlight would shine given each of the four kinds of questions. Your question should control where the spotlight shines.

A question that suggests the response is called a leading question, and it is the subject of the rule that best explains the opposite techniques of building up and tearing down the pile of evidence.

Don't Lead on Direct, Lead on Cross

The rule is so simple that you would expect all lawyers to follow it with ease. Unfortunately, most beginning lawyers, and too many experienced lawyers who should know better, do exactly the opposite. They lead on direct and ask general response questions (narrative or subject defined) on cross, in spite of the Fed.R.Evid. 611 admonition that "leading questions should not be used on the direct examination," and "ordinarily should be ... on cross examination." Chances are that you will break the rule during your first examinations unless you give some consideration to the real reason for the rule.

The real reason for the rule that you should not lead on direct, but should lead on cross is not an evidence rule, it is a rule of persuasion. The rule of persuasion is based upon the understanding that "how" a witness says things is at least as important as "what" is said when you are trying to build up your pile of evidence acceptable to the jurors; and conversely, "what" the witness acknowledges, not "how" it is acknowledged is more important when you are tearing down your opponent's evidence pile. Most beginning lawyers believe just the opposite. They are overly concerned with having the witness say just the right words on direct and confident that if the witness will just appear whipped on cross examination the lawyer will have succeeded.

The strong urge to ask leading questions during direct examination comes from thorough preparation for trial, knowing which items are crucial, and having just the right words to make the story sing. If you add a strong suspicion that your witness will not say it nearly as persuasively as you would, you have a full understanding of why you might lead on direct.

You cannot persuade jurors by leading on direct because jurors cannot "accept" the information from the lawyer. The jurors may hear what the lawyer says, but they cannot "credit" it with any enthusiasm. The lawyer was not there, the witness was. If the jurors are to accept the information, they must be persuaded that the mouth they are getting it from belongs to the horse. Would you put a witness on the stand, make a fifteen minute monologue, and at the end, ask the witness: "Isn't that right?" If you chop the monologue into fifty small pieces, and ask, "Isn't that right?" after each small piece the effect on the jurors will be the same.

Even if you are one of those lawyers that juries find irresistible, you cannot substitute your acceptability for that of the witness. No matter which of the two of you, the examiner or the witness, is doing the talking, the jurors will base their opinion of the credibility of the testimony upon their assessment of the witness. If the witness does not have the opportunity to relate to the jurors, to be heard, to communicate, the jurors have no basis upon which to rate the witness' testimony above conflicting testimony from another witness. Everyone "buys" ideas from people they like. Advertising companies search for the right celebrity or pitch person to lend credibility to the products they are selling. You are not selling the jury a false bill of goods, but you are in charge of enhancing the witness's credibility so that the doors of persuasion will open. They can't open if you are standing in the way.

There is one more reason that lawyers want to lead on direct—it is easier. Why then, when it comes to cross examination, does the lawyer abandon the more easily asked leading question in favor of the more difficult general response question? It's the fault of the scriveners of movie and television lawyer dramas. We have been indoctrinated with the view that no cross examination succeeds so well as that in which the witness, without any apparent trickery by the lawyer, commits hari-kari in full view of the jury. Why does a witness commit this improbable act of suicide? Because the lawyer has so carefully boxed in the witness that the only answer to the question is the one that the lawyer has in mind and that no amount of explanation from the witness can avoid. Fine for the movies, but few witnesses ever destroy themselves with their own mouths and by virtue of their inherent badness.

The desire to see witnesses mount the platform, adjust the rope, slip their heads in the noose, and hang themselves all by their own mouths has been the death of too many lawyers, not to mention their clients' cases. A typical example is the testimony of an occurrence witness to the intersection collision. The witness, a lady of thirty-six, testifies that she was at the corner helping a small boy who had fallen off his bike, when your client's Ford went through the red light and hit the plaintiff's Chevrolet. She is the only witness other than the drivers, and if you can neutralize the effect of her testimony, you might win the case. Time for cross examination.

Q: Where were you at 4:00 p.m., Friday, June 5th of last year?

A: At the corner of Broadway and Second.

Q: Did anything happen that caught your attention?

A: First a little boy fell off his bicycle right next to me. Then there was a collision right in the middle of the intersection.

Q: Did you do anything about the little boy?

A: Yes, I bent down to help him, to see if he was hurt, and help him get back up on his bike.

Q: Did the car accident happen while you were helping the little boy?

A: Yes.

Q: Were you looking at a traffic light when the cars collided?

A: Just before and just afterwards. It was red for the Ford.

Without examining the method of the entire cross examination, consider how much better off the lawyer would have been if at least the last question had been "aggressively" leading, or the end of a series of leading questions.

Q: You did not know if the boy had been hurt, did you?

A: No.

Q: You were concerned about the child, so you bent down to help, isn't that right?

A: Yes.

Q: The boy was crying, wasn't he?

A: Yes.

Q: At the time of the accident, you were bending over to console the little boy and see if he was hurt, weren't you?

A: Yes.

If you cannot resist the temptation to ask about looking at the light, the leading question will do you less harm then the non-leading approach:

Q: At the time of the accident, then, you were not looking at the traffic light, were you?

A: No.

Another reason that lawyers do not like to lead on cross is that they are afraid that if they ask an adverse witness a question that suggests the response, the witness will "see it coming" and answer the other way. The more adverse the witness and the more loaded the question, the more likely that it is true. The answer to the problem, discussed more fully later, is not to ask the question. But if you decide to ask the question (no matter how much we tell you not to) it is better to lead. After eliciting that the witness was not looking at the traffic light at the time of the accident, this leading question and answer will not be as bad for you as they could be.

Q: So, for all you could see, the light could have been green for the Ford, couldn't it?

A: No.

Aren't you glad you asked? Bad as it is when leading you will not be hurt nearly as much as if you ask a non-leading question, usually with the sarcasm born of knowledge that the witness is trapped.

Q: Well, then, madam, if you were not looking at the light at the time of the accident, will you tell the ladies and gentlemen of the jury how it is that you could possibly testify that the light was red for my client's Ford?

A: Surely. Just as I told the policeman who came to investigate, the light was yellow as I approached to cross Broadway. Just as it turned to red, a little boy fell down, and I

> bent down to help him. Then the collision
> happened and I looked up. The light was still
> red in my direction, and that is where the
> Ford came from.

The worst thing about the answer is not that it does
not agree with the examiner's position. The answer
to the leading question did not agree either. The
non-leading question, however, gave the witness an
opportunity to tell her story to the jurors again and
in a persuasive fashion. You lead on cross because
you cannot afford to have the opponent's witness
relate to the jurors and gain their acceptance of the
testimony. You do not lose because the jurors hear
the other side's witnesses; you lose if the jurors
accept what they hear. Do not help your opponent
by letting the opponent's witnesses talk during your
cross examination.

The control that you wanted to exercise over the
information flow to the jurors on direct examination
is the reason that you should use leading questions
for cross examination. You have a much better
chance at controlling the information the jurors
accept if the spotlight is shining on you during cross
examination. Although control is of less importance
in building the pile of acceptable evidence for the
jury, it is the major weapon in tearing down the pile
of acceptable evidence that your opponent is building.

During all examinations, if you will remember
that the person who is doing most of the talking is
in control, and that the person that is in control

determines whether the acceptability level of the witness is increased, you will know when to lead. Do not lead on direct. Let the witness build acceptability. Lead on cross and, thereby; prohibit the witness from building acceptability.

There are exceptions to the "don't lead on direct, lead on cross" rule of persuasion.

Preliminary matters may be brought out through leading questions. In the direct examination of the lady who helped the little boy, the following question is permissible: "Were you on the corner of Broadway and Second at about four o'clock on the afternoon of Friday, June 5th?" Is it leading? Yes; it suggests the answer. The question is a proper direct examination question because it is preliminary to the testimony that really matters. Fed.R.Evid. 611 allows leading questions on direct "as may be necessary to develop" the witness' testimony. If the driver of the Ford was contending that the lady was never on the corner, the question would, indeed, be impermissibly leading. As asked, it is merely to facilitate getting on to the important part of the witness' testimony. To be sure, if there was an issue about whether the lady was really there, the direct examiner would want her to tell the jury she was there in a way that the jurors would believe and would not use a leading question. A "yes" answer without more is not particularly persuasive.

The rule allowing leading questions on preliminary matters is important to the direct examiner because of the short attention span of the jury.

Most examinations go too slow; leading questions make the examination go faster. By leading on questions for which juror acceptance is not important, the direct examiner increases the chances that the important testimony will be heard, will register, and will be accepted. Before you decide to lead on every preliminary question, remember that the jurors only get to know your witnesses by listening to them tell about themselves and what they know. Lead on direct for preliminary matters only when shortening the time of the examination is worth more than the testimony for which you ask the leading question.

Transitional questions are a form of preliminary question, but they often occur right in the middle of the most important testimony. You may, nevertheless, lead. The leading transitional question is an important tool for the direct examiner. The most difficult question to frame is the one that directs the witness to an area of interest for examination. "What did you do after the police had things under control?" is a better question than "What did you do next," but it does not tell the witness which of the five or six things she did you want to know about. If she talked to the policeman, looked closely at the cars, told the driver of the Ford to stay calm, picked up a piece of chrome from the boulevard, asked the little boy if he could get home by himself, and told somebody who came up to the scene what had happened, the question, "What did you do ..." may not be very helpful. "Did you go over to look at the cars?", is leading, helpful, and permissible.

Whether she went over to the cars is not at issue, and it does not suggest a critical fact to the witness. The question merely directs the witness to the area of inquiry. It tells the witness which of the many facts you want her to talk about next. "Was the front end of the Ford smashed in?", would be leading, because, in addition to directing the witness to a particular area of knowledge, it directs her to the specific answer within the area. "Did you see something?", is not likely to be impermissibly leading, while, "Did you see the front end of the Ford smashed in?", is leading. Transitional questions lead from one subject to another and help to "develop the testimony." After the witness has told the jurors all she knows about the collision at the intersection, and you want to ask about the statement she heard the defendant make the next week, ask a leading question: "Did you ever hear the driver of the Ford talking about the collision?" Leading? Yes. Objectionable? No. It is transitional.

The last major exception to the leading question rule has some surface irony, because it allows a leading question when the response is absolutely crucial to the case, and the witness cannot come up with the answer. The leading question is permissible under the evidence rule because it is the only way to "develop the testimony." It is persuasively permissible because juror awareness of a crucial fact, even if it is not delivered in a manner calculated to gain acceptance, is better than no awareness. Assume for a moment that the lady looked in the Ford and saw an opened bottle of whiskey on the floor. She told the police officer (who has not been called by either side) about the bottle. After asking her if she went over to look at the cars, you ask her if she saw anything. She says no, she does not remember seeing anything in particular. You now must try to jog her memory, and probably without leading her:

Q: Which car did you look at?

A: Both of them.

Q: Where did you look in the Ford?

A: All over, I guess.

Q: What did you see?

A: Nothing in particular, it was just a car.

If you do not ask a leading question, you are not going to develop the testimony. Leaving aside whether the evidentiary reason you can lead is because you are refreshing recollection, or impeaching your own witness, or just relying on the court's discretion to allow you to develop testimony, the next question will probably be: "Do you remember telling the officer that you saw an opened whiskey bottle in the Ford?" It is leading, but it is permissible because you have laid the necessary foundation by demonstrating that there is no other way to get the testimony from the witness.

If nothing else, the last exception to the rule against leading on direct ought to demonstrate the importance of the advice not to lead on most direct examinations. While the "yes" response to the leading question about the bottle is better than nothing, it is not much better.

The second half of the rule, "lead on cross," is also subject to an exception. You need not lead on cross if you do not need to control the witness' response. Although that is a very broadly stated exception, it will apply very seldom. Unfortunately, the exception calls for an exercise of judgment on the part of the cross examiner, and most beginning cross examiners have poor judgment about the need for control. Most of us are so sure about the argument that we are prepared to make and that we have the witness in a corner that we do not believe we need to control the answer with the form of the question. We believe that logic and good sense are exercising control of the response for us. Usually, we are wrong. During your first trial, you would do well to execute the rule and forget about the exception. Though we will, later, discuss the circumstances that may lead to the exception, the discussion will be aimed at demonstrating the importance of the rule, not the possibilities for the exception.

Conducting the Direct Examination

Direct examination is the easiest trial task to do in a minimally competent fashion and the hardest to do well. It is the most important part of the case in most instances. Remembering that people make decisions based on positive constructs, it makes sense that you win your case on direct not cross examination. The difference in effect between a minimally competent direct examination and a good direct examination is the difference between winning and losing the lawsuit. The difference in appearance between a minimally competent and a good direct examination is not so easily detected. Many trial lawyers never learn to distinguish one from the other, but most winners do.

Direct examination competency usually falls into three categories: (1) good enough to get the information out of the witness' mouth, (2) good enough to have the information from the witness understood by the jurors, and (3) good enough to have the testimony persuade the jurors. Every lawyer is capable of accomplishing the first level before entering law school. Many lawyers, unfortunately, remain at the level long after they have been out of school and into court. Great cross examinations and exhilarating addresses to the jury show off the lawyer as advocate, become the stuff of thrilling war stories and are the skills that beginning lawyers are just aching to conquer. Direct examination success is not so alluring. It is not uncommon to hear the adage that "all a good direct needs is a good witness." Every time you hear that, you know that you are listening to a lawyer whose direct examinations depend entirely upon the skill of the witness. Since few of us are lucky enough to have great actors and actresses with fine minds and powers of observation standing on the corner when the Ford runs the red light, we must learn how to have a fine direct examination when we have an ordinary human being for a witness.

With few exceptions, every good direct examination must contain the answers to the famous laundry list of questions for news gatherers: Who? What? Where? When? Why? and How? If the answer to one of those questions is not contained in your direct examination, you must have an articulable persuasive reason for the omission. The "What?" is the minimum that must be produced to traverse a motion for directed verdict, the rest of the list constitutes the full substantive expanse of the direct that moves it from the "got it out of the witness' mouth" category into the "jurors will understand" category.

Reaching the "persuades the jurors" level of competence requires attention to the theater of the examination and concentration on how the testimony is being presented. There are two factors, other than the skillfulness of your witness preparation, that affect the theater of your direct examination: (1) the presentation of the witness in the best light, and (2) the presentation of the facts in a memorable pattern. The jurors need all of those to find in your favor. The jurors must hear the testimony (speak their language), understand it, remember it, and trust the witness that delivers it. A good director makes sure all of that occurs.

The testimonial personality of your witness controls many judgments about the length of the examination and the form of the questions to be asked. Although you can smooth rough edges off a witness during preparation, the lawyer's woodshed is not equipped for major rebuilding projects. If your witness is one of those that comes across as a liar even when testifying that the sun rises in the East, your examination will be shorter and your questions will be mostly specific response questions:

"What corner were you on?"

"What color was the car?"

"How long were you there?"

On the other hand, if you have a witness that the jurors will believe immediately, the interrogation will be longer and filled with open-ended narrative and subject-defined response questions:

"After you heard the crash, what did you do?"

"After you heard the smash of the two cars coming together, did you hear anything else?"

Although few witnesses will be so bad or so good that you will be compelled to let the nature of the witness completely circumscribe your examination options, the nature of the witness will always have an effect on the shape of the examination. Every examination idea or questioning pattern that follows must be considered in light of the witness that fate has made available for examination.

Jurors have short attention spans. Fifteen to twenty minutes is about the best you can expect. A very good witness early in the trial might stretch that out to a half hour. Imagine that your jurors have a remote control in their hands and can change channels when they become bored. How long can you keep a witness on the stand before they would switch to something more interesting?

The jurors may have to sit in the box, but they don't have to pay attention. Unless you keep them engaged, their minds will wander to work, or to children, or to whether court will finish in time for them to run by the dry cleaners.

Jurors learn better by looking than by listening.

Although a change of witness or the introduction of a visual exhibit might rejuvenate the jurors' attention and begin another attention cycle, each successive cycle is likely to be shorter than the preceding one.

Jurors are more attentive, and their faculties are sharper, at varying times in the day. There has never been a juror, for example, that was sharp right after the lunch hour.

These observations should lead you to two important techniques of direct examination. The first technique is to design your direct examination of any witness, even your best, with consideration for the limitations of the jurors' powers of perception. The second is to conduct your direct examination with your eye on the jurors for telltale signs of interest, fatigue, boredom, excitement, and the full panoply of listener response that will be obvious if you watch the jurors watching your witness. Use techniques like blocking and headlining to help your audience. We retain information better if we learn it in small chunks rather than large quantities. Phone numbers have the dash because we can remember small three and four digit strings of numbers rather than one seven to ten digit string.

Blocking refers to creating smaller blocks of the direct so that the audience can retain it better. So you might have separate blocks for personalization, context, and action or observation. Headlining signposts and summarizes the blocks, so that the jurors know both when you are shifting subjects and what to retain out of each block. When jurors are tuning in and out of the testimony, this makes it easier for them to catch up.

Some general techniques apply to all direct examinations. Although not every examination should be as short as possible, every examination should exclude matters within the witness' knowledge that are persuasively irrelevant. If for example, four different pictures of the Ford showing the damage from different angles are in evidence, there is little reason to ask the lady who was on the corner: "Will you tell the jurors about the damage to the Ford that you could see when you went over to look at it?" It matters not that she saw the damage, that she saw it first, or that she was the person that called the newspaper that sent the photographer. If she is not the witness through whom the exhibits are offered, there is no persuasive advantage to taking up valuable juror listening time with something they already know about and have accepted. On the other hand, the legally irrelevant facts that the lady lives just two blocks from Broadway and Second, is a housewife, and has a boy seven and a girl four are facts that you want before the jury. Although they do not go to credibility in the specific manner that legal relevancy might require, the character of the witness will be judged in part by how she performs, and in part by who the jurors think she is. Choose facts to personalize your witness with regard to what you know about your jurors. If you know that one of your jurors went to the same college, or had the same hobby, use it as part of your personalization block. The more jurors relate to your witnesses as one of "them" the easier it is for the jurors to relate to the witnesses' testimony. Be selective in the human details you bring before the jury. Good direct examinations contain all the persuasive facts, but are not cluttered by persuasive irrelevancies. Rarely will you ask a witness to tell the jurors everything the witness knows about the facts relevant to the lawsuit.

Although the jurors have only a twenty minute attention span, some witnesses have forty minutes worth of testimony to give. Do not be afraid to provide a breathing spell in the middle of the testimony. The witness that will testify for forty minutes, let alone the witness that stays on the stand half a day, has some items of testimony that are more important than others. Construct the direct examination with an eye to the two to five minutes after twenty, when the jurors are likely to have tuned you out. This is a good time to ask the least important questions. If exhibits must be marked, or if you anticipate the other side asking for a bench conference, try to put them at the time you expect juror attention to be low. One of the advantages of trying cases to a jury of twelve is that not all of the jurors will be tuning you out at the same time. It is helpful, nevertheless, to shape your interrogation with an understanding that juror attention is cyclical.

Each witness' testimony is a play within a play. Usually the witness appears only once, delivering all the lines and developing all of the rapport with the audience at one sitting. Care must be taken to insure that the most important lines are delivered after the witness has developed some rapport with the jurors. There are times, however, when it is useful to have a witness deliver the most shocking or the most important lines right after the witness' name and address. Although there is no universal answer to organizing a direct examination, a persuasion-based organizational framework is a prerequisite to a successful direct.

Commentators have developed some general rules for organizing direct examinations. Chronological presentation is easier for the witness, and coincides with the way in which jurors will most easily recall information. On the other hand, it can be boring and lead to inclusion of persuasively irrelevant facts. Topical organization, by contrast, allows you to construct the examination based upon the interesting points to be made by the witness. But time switches can be confusing. Who the witnesses are, why they have been called, and where they fall in your lineup of witnesses is more likely to help you to organize your direct examinations than any general rule approved by fifty-one out of one hundred trial lawyers. Your witness order is the only real way you have of relating your trial story. Your story unfolds for the jury as first time listeners only through your witnesses.

The lady on the corner, for example might be able to testify most persuasively by telling just exactly what she saw in the order that she saw it:

> "I approached the corner as the light turned yellow. A little boy came alongside on his bike. As he tried to stop for the light, he fell over. I thought he might be hurt, because he was crying a little. I bent over to see if I could help, and just then I heard a terrible crash. I looked up and saw the two cars coming to a careening halt in the intersection. The Ford that had gone through the red light was still headed west, but the Chevrolet it broadsided was knocked almost through the intersection to the east."

On the other hand, if an occurrence witness observed four negotiating meetings about a disputed contract, a topical approach may make the testimony easier for the jurors to accept.

Q: Was anything decided?

A: Yes, they agreed that Bill would paint the house during July, and that Sharon would pay him $200 after each of the sides was, in turn, completed. I remember it well because we were all sitting in the bar after a long day of water skiing. After they shook hands, Bill said, "There goes my month of water skiing."

Q: Was this during the first discussion?

A: No, that was not the first time that they had talked about it. Sharon had been after Bill to paint the house since the first of April. I can remember at least four different times that they talked about it.

Q: When was money first discussed?

A: During the third conversation, I think we were in the same bar. Bill had excused himself, and Sharon told me that she could not understand why Bill would not do the whole house for $700.00 as long as she was going to buy the paint. When he came back, she offered $800.

In addition to occurrence witnesses, you may have character witnesses, damages witnesses, expert witnesses, special problem witnesses such as young children, witnesses to lay the foundation for exhibits, and witnesses of many other descriptions. The first considerations in organizing the direct ought to be the nature of the witness and the witness' testimony.

Regardless of the organizational framework for presenting the substance of the testimony, most direct examinations should begin with an introduction of the witness. Once you have chosen the facts to personalize your witness relay them in a way that helps the witness feel at ease and lets the jurors get to know the witness. What you choose to bring out will differ with each witness and may vary according to the witness's function. Expert witnesses, for example, may require a longer educational block than an occurrence witness. Every witness of any description should be introduced so that the jurors have some reason to accept the testimony.

The first part of every introduction is the name of the person being introduced. In many courts, the only way to get the name and address of the witness into the record is to ask the witness. Name and address fill the bill. In addition, it is a polite way to proceed with your introduction of the witness to the jurors. Although you may find occasion to ignore the advice to first fully accredit the witness—"Mr. Newton, why do apples fall from trees?"—the witness' name must be first. As you use that name throughout the examination, resist the temptation to appear friendly with the witness by using the witness' first name. Unless the witness is a small child, your client in some cases, a witness who is obviously your lifelong friend, or some other special case where first name informality is obviously appropriate, refer to the witness as, "Mr. Newton," "Ms. Newton," "Miss Newton," or "Mrs. Newton," but not "Isaac." ("Sir Isaac" would probably be appropriate for the definer of gravity, but that is a point too subtle for a primer.)

The introduction of the witness tells the jurors "why" they should accept "what" they hear from the witness. The "why" they should accept from the testimony of the witness will be found in the "who," "where," "when," and "how" of the witness. It is as important that the jurors have a reason to credit cocktail waitress Mary Ellen's testimony that the man acted like a drunk when he bought his last highball before going out and running over your client, as it is that they have a reason for believing physicist Einstein when, as an expert witness, he tells them that $E=mc^2$. Mary Ellen's five years as a cocktail waitress are as important to the dram shop case as Einstein's impressive resume is to the validity of his theory. Personal facts tell the jurors something about who the witness is and why the testimony should be accepted.

The "where" and "when" about an occurrence witness usually answer the question, "how do you know?" This important part of the introduction is often called, "setting the scene." Although you may have a witness whose sole function in the case is to "set the scene," the foundation for any occurrence witness' testimony includes the "where" and "when" of location to demonstrate that the witness was in a position, at the relevant time, to make the observation. You should "set the scene" for each individual occurrence witness, not because it is a necessary evidentiary foundation, but because it will usually enhance the acceptability of the "what" the witness presents to the jurors.

Although most direct examinations will start with introducing the witness to the jurors and explaining why the witness is worthy of their attention, it is a rule of order that can be violated in the proper circumstance, with persuasive result. Assume, for example, that you are defending the intersection collision case and that you have an occurrence witness that each party, for its own reason, did not tell the jurors about during their opening statements. After eliciting the witness' name, you may find it more persuasive to get right to the "what" of the witness' testimony, and fill in the reason the witness should be believed after the jury has been jolted by the unexpected testimony.

Q: Mr. Baker, did you see an accident on the corner of Broadway and Second, last June 5th at about 4:00 p.m.?

A: Yes, I did.

Q: Will you tell the jurors what you saw?

A: I saw a Chevrolet on Second go through a red light so fast that the Ford that was entering the intersection on the green did not have time to stop.

Once the jurors have assimilated the direct contradiction with the plaintiff's witness who was standing on the corner, the importance of the inconsistency will force them to ask themselves: "Where was he?" Now that you have their inquiring attention, fill in the testimony. Have the witness explain that he was in his office on the second story of his house on the corner, that his attention was called to the intersection by the little neighbor boy he saw approaching the intersection, that he had a clear view of the entire intersection, and that the reason he did not go out afterward to talk to the police officer was that he tripped hurrying down the steps and twisted his ankle. By going straight to the core of the witness' testimony, you satisfy primacy and variety. By ending the direct with a strong point in a way that makes it hard for the cross examination to begin, you have accomplished recency as well.

Some of your witnesses will be less than you would choose if you could invent them. Even with the most unattractive witness, you must give the jurors some reason to accept the witness' testimony. Whether you should include the less attractive facts about your witness in the introduction of the witness to the jurors depends upon the same analysis as the question of "pulling the plug" during opening statement. During examination, however, where the witness will be confronted with the fact by the cross examiner, there is more dramatic reason to "pull the plug" during direct if you can do it in a fashion that will soften the blow.

One way to soften the blow is to blend the bad fact about your witness in with the rest of the direct examination. Even if you blend it in so well that the jurors are not consciously aware of it, and certainly not of its importance, they are likely to remember it when your opponent raises it on cross examination, and you will not appear to have been hiding something. If you present the bad fact in a positive, rather than a defensive attitude, you may dissuade your opponent from going after the bad fact on cross examination. By taking the sting out in advance, it can make the cross examiner look either like a bully or repetitive. Juries will tend not to like either, especially if they liked your witness.

Consider, for example, the worst fact that you can have about an occurrence witness: a prior contrary statement by the witness. Although there is nothing you can do to erase the prior inconsistent statement, you can lessen the effect. If the first time that the jurors know that the lady on the corner told the little boy's mother that the Chevrolet ran the red light is on cross examination, your case that the Ford ran the red light is in some trouble. Consider the advantage of a direct examination that deals with the subject by blending it in with the lady's total testimony. The following questions might be asked after full introduction and testimony that the Ford went through the red light, and that the lady waited for the police to arrive:

Q: What did you do when the police officer arrived on the scene?

A: Well, I saw a number of people who had been on the corner talking to the officer about what happened. Then the ambulance arrived and the people from the two cars were able to walk into the ambulance. The officer was busy measuring the distances that the cars were from each other when it came my turn to describe what I saw. Just then, Teddy, the little boy that had fallen off his bike, came over to me and said that his leg hurt. I looked at his knee and there was a pretty ugly bruise, so I decided to take him home right then.

Q: Where does Teddy live?

A: Just across the street and down about half a block on Second.

Q: Did you take Teddy home as you had decided to do?

A: Yes. He began to cry, and I became concerned about him. His knee was pretty swollen, and he was favoring that leg quite a bit.

Q: Was there anybody home at Teddy's?

A: Yes, his mother. I carried Teddy in the house, and she became quite upset.

Q: Do you know why she was upset?

A: She saw Teddy being carried, and must have thought he was part of the accident, because she said, "My God, he's been hit."

Q: Did you leave Teddy with her?

A: Not right away. She was almost hysterical, and I wanted to calm her down so she could wash up Teddy's knee and put a disinfectant on it. I put Teddy down on the couch, sat her in a chair and told her that there had been a collision between two cars, and that Teddy was on the sidewalk next to me when he fell off his bike.

Q: Did that calm her down enough so that you could leave?

A: Not right away. So I kept talking about the fact that there had been a collision between two cars, and that Teddy had not been involved. I kept telling her about the collision, hoping that she would realize that Teddy had just fallen off his bike. I finally got her to understand that he hurt himself falling off the bike and not because he had been hit by a car.

Q: What did you do after Teddy's mother pulled herself together?

A: I went back to the corner to tell the police officer what I had seen.

Q: What was the officer doing when you arrived back at the corner?

A: He was not there. There was a wrecker moving the cars, but the police car and the ambulance were gone.

Q: Did you ever talk to the police about the accident?

A: No. There were three or four other people who had talked to the officer on the scene and I did not see any reason to call and bother the police department.

When the cross examiner asks your witness about telling Teddy's mother about the Chevrolet going through the red light, at least the jury will have been aware that there was a conversation, and the circumstances surrounding it. The witness will be able to explain the contradiction on cross examination without much difficulty because the foundation for a reasonable explanation had been presented on direct. If the cross examiner is good, and the witness does not have an opportunity to explain on cross, the opportunity will be more natural on redirect than it might have been if the jurors had not been "conditioned" on the subject during the direct examination. Remember, there are only limited possibilities: (1) Teddy's mother is mistaken, she was too shook up to get things right. (2) The lady was so concerned about getting Teddy's mother calmed down and was concentrating so hard on that task that she was not paying much attention to the details she was relating. (3) The lady is a liar. If you are stuck with (3), you are stuck. If (1) or (2) is the proper explanation, the witness will get the opportunity to say on cross or on redirect:

"I really don't remember the details of what I told her, I was just trying to get her to understand that Teddy fell off the bike on the sidewalk and had not been hit by any car. I might have said the Chevrolet went through the red light. I was concentrating on getting her to understand that Teddy was not involved. If she says that I said that, I surely would not want to say she was not telling the truth. She was pretty shook up at the time, though. More than I was, I think. I'm sorry, I just do not remember telling her that the Chevrolet went through the red light. It was wrong if I did."

If you are going to try to pull the plug on a damaging fact, you must be sure to do it with a careful ear for the timing of the discussion and the fullness of the disclosure. Before you decide to raise it, give careful thought to whether you really think it is a problem your opponent will raise. Juries tend to "side" with the witness. If they are thinking about what part they would play in your drama, it is not the part of lawyer, it is most likely the part of witness. Everyone has baggage they would not care to have displayed in open court, especially if they are just witnesses who came with the case, those who just happened to be there. If the matters are personal or have nothing to do with the facts the witness is relaying to the jurors, you might decide to leave it alone and let it backfire on the cross examiner. If it is a boil that needs to be lanced; how and when you do it can keep it from backfiring on you.

If you begin an examination with an explanation of the problem, or if you interrupt a line of examination and make an obvious transition to the problem, you will have highlighted the problem at least as well as your opponent could have on cross examination. In addition, you will have implicitly acknowledged that there is something to it. In the case of the good Samaritan lady, if she testifies on direct that she actually told Teddy's mother the light was green, she remembers too well. She will have pulled the plug, but will have no reasonable explanation for the inconsistency. If she says on direct that she told Teddy's mother the light was red, you are left with the argument that Teddy's mother was too distracted to remember, but must make it in closing argument in light of the fact that the first person to signal that there was a contradiction between the Samaritan's testimony and the mother's, is the Samaritan—an unlikely chronology unless the Samaritan was trying to cover up something.

The most common advice concerning the organization of direct examination is that it should end on a high note. Ending on a high note does two things. It takes advantage of the principle of recency, leaving the jurors with a last idea of substance; and it makes it difficult for the cross examiner to gain good juror attention to the first few cross examination questions after you announce, "Pass the witness, your honor." You want to make it hard for cross examiners to start their cross examinations in the way they had planned. It may be because the testimony was sympathetic and the jurors are feeling the emotion of the moment. Sometimes you have the opportunity to ask a question that ends the direct examination by leaving the jurors hungry for the answer to a question not asked. In an action to recover insurance for a burned building, for example, where the defense is that the plaintiff burned the building, the direct examination of the plaintiff might end with some mystery:

Q: Mr. Plaintiff, if not you, do you know who burned your building?

A: Yes

"Pass the witness, your honor."

The cross examiner starts with a dilemma: fall in the trap, ask the witness, and suffer the answer or avoid the trap and leave the jurors dying to know the answer while the cross examination does nothing to satisfy them. You might not have as dramatic an opportunity, but the lesson is: finish strong!

The testimony of the witness is what the jurors want to hear, and the manner of the witness' testimony will determine whether they accept the testimony. It does not follow, however, that the examiner can merely turn the witness on at the beginning and off at the end. Even if you have the world's best witness, you cannot ask the witness, "What happened?," and interrupt the narrative response twice with an "and then" before the witness comes to the end. In the first place, you are likely to hear an objection from your opponent that the question calls for a narrative response. Secondly, an examination that is entirely witness narration loses precision. Direct examinations can be hard for lawyers in part because we are not the focal point, but also because it requires us to help draw out each witness' part of the story in a way that showcases that witness' strengths. That means your approach has to differ depending on who you have on the stand and what testimony you need to elicit. Since your questions are your only tool to accomplish the goal, you have to develop a variety of approaches and learn when each is appropriate.

A question that calls for a narrative response, as an example, carries a couple of cautions. The court might not allow it if your opponent makes a Fed. R.Evid. 611 objection. While most judges will exercise their discretion to allow some narration, the objection is likely to be sustained if based upon the argument that counsel will not be able to make a timely objection to inadmissible evidence included in the narrative response. Judges know that an objection after the jurors hear the testimony may be good for the record, but useless for the trial. You might persuade the court to allow the narrative with an assurance that the witness will not offer whatever evidentiary evil concerns the objector, but there is another concern, and it is yours. There is a persuasive reason to be cautious about total witness narration: it shows off the witness, but it does not show off the facts. Further, to the extent that it highlights any facts, they are the facts that the witness emphasizes, not necessarily those facts that the lawyer believes are the most important.

The most effective presentation of a witness, capable of narration, combines the credibility advantage of narration, with the fact emphasis and control advantage of questions that call for specific responses. In addition to giving the examiner control over selection of facts to be emphasized, it allows the witness to tell the story twice without a successful objection that the second time is cumulative. Consider the advantages of the layered approach to asking for a narrative response, and following the narration with a series of specific answer questions to highlight testimony:

Q: (after eliciting name, address, and law enforcement experience of an undercover narcotics agent) Agent Holmes, will you tell us how you operate as an undercover drug purchaser for the state police?

A: I try to blend into the society so that I lose my identity as a police officer. Although not everybody that buys and sells drugs fits the same description, there is a segment of society, identifiable by dress, hours they keep, places that they frequent, in which it is easier to buy and sell drugs than is normally true. I try to become a member of that segment of society so that somebody selling drugs might contact me as a potential buyer. The toughest thing about making a drug arrest is catching the pusher in possession of the drugs or in the act of trying to make a sale. Drug dealing is not as open and obvious a crime as burglary, and the only way that we have found to make a dent, is to put people like me in the segment of society most likely to be dealing in drugs so that I can be on the scene when a sale is made. I rarely make an arrest on the first sale of narcotics because the seller is usually the lowest man on the totem pole of a group of people involved in the sale of drugs. I try, by asking to buy larger quantities than I think the low man will be trusted with, to work my way up that totem pole until I deal with the man at the top, the one who is supplying everybody else down the line. That is the time I try to make arrests, and catch everybody from the one on the top of the totem pole, all the way down to the one on the bottom. Sometimes, I cannot climb the totem pole by asking for larger quantities. In those cases, I try to make an arrest of one of the low men and gain cooperation for an introduction to that low man's supplier.

Q: Did you arrest the defendant, Sidney Teller?

A: Yes.

Q: Will you please describe the events leading up to the arrest of Mr. Teller.

A: Mr. Teller's arrest came at the end of a three week operation during which I made three different purchases of heroin from four different individuals. I made the first buy on Friday, August 2nd from Bill Mantou. He sold me thirty grams, and when I tried to get over him to his supplier by asking if he could sell me a half kilo in a couple of days, he said he would make the sale. I arrested him, and through the state's attorney's cooperation, made an arrangement to trade an introduction to his supplier for a reduced charge. Mantou set up a meeting with Jack Pushar. On the second meeting with Pushar, I was able to buy the half a kilogram of heroin. I told Pushar that I represented a syndicate of buyers, and suggested that I might be interested in regular purchases of a kilogram or more, but that I needed assurances of ability to deliver. Two days later, Pushar met me with a kilogram and was prepared to sell it to me. I told him that I was not interested unless we could make the continuing deal, and that my partner and I had to meet with the source to be sure that we would be supplied, and that this was not some kind of a sting operation by the police.

Q: Did Pushar put you in contact with his source?

A: About four days later, Pushar contacted me during dinner in a restaurant, told me to get my partner on the phone and have him meet us. I called Agent Bellows and told him to meet me at Luigi's in ten minutes. When he arrived, Pushar drove us, in his car, to a spot at Riverview Park. There we met Teller. After we talked, he left to go to his car. Pushar then sold us the kilogram of heroin. He and Teller were both arrested.

Once the agent has given the jurors an overview, the advocate can retell the story by emphasizing the specific important points. If the first narrative is very broad, as in the example, the more specific questions that follow may call for shorter narratives. Without making any judgment about the appropriateness or completeness of the inquiry, some examples will help to demonstrate the advantage of the layered approach to the examination.

Q: Agent Holmes, where were you when you made the purchase from Bill Mantou on August 2?

A: In an alley behind Luigi's.

Q: Why were you in the alley?

A: Mantou insisted. The alley is a half alley that is not visible from the street. Mantou asked me to come out the back door of Luigi's, and meet him at the end of the blind half alley in a spot behind a couple of large packing crates.

Q: Where did you arrest Mantou?

A: In the alley after I could not get him to buck me up to his supplier with a bigger purchase.

Q: You said earlier that Mantou set up a meeting with his supplier. Will you tell us how that happened?

A: After Mantou agreed to make an introduction in exchange for a reduction in his charge from sale to possession, we returned to Luigi's. Mantou made a phone call . . . .

Q: Excuse me, Agent Holmes, who did Mantou call?

A: I don't know. I asked, Mantou didn't tell me, he said that I didn't need to know, and I didn't press it.

Q: If you were trying to work your way up the totem pole from one supplier to the next, why didn't you insist on knowing who Mantou was calling?

A: He only promised to set up the meet, and he made it pretty clear that the name of the person he was calling was not part of what he had agreed to supply. I was afraid that if I pushed him I might be putting him in a position where he could not afford to trade the introduction for the reduced charge.

Q: Why not?

A: If the person on the other end of the phone was anyone other than his supplier, and we then got close to that person, it would be pretty clear that Mantou had supplied the name. If he didn't supply the name, the only way we could get it would be after we had involved Mantou's supplier, and then Mantou would not be the only possibility for giving the name. I was afraid that Mantou would take his time on the sale rather than risk having the person on the other end of the phone think that Mantou had supplied a name.

Q: Did you meet Mantou's supplier sometime after the call was made?

A: Yes.

Q: Will you tell us about that meeting?

A: (Answers concerning the activity with Pushar through narrative and more specific questions and answers.)

Q: What did Pushar do when you told him that you wanted to deal directly with his supplier?

A: He told me that he did not have a supplier in the country, and that he could guarantee shipment so long as there was any heroin in the United States.

Q: Is that the way you left it with him?

A: No, I kept pushing and he finally said that he would be in touch.

Q: How did he say that he would get in touch with you?

A: He didn't.

Q: Did he say how he would get in touch with you?

A: No.

Q: Did you purchase the heroin he had with him?

A: No sir, I did not.

Q: How did the meeting end?

A: He left first, and about a minute later, Bellows and I left.

Q: Why did you just let him go?

A: Because so long as he was willing to contact us again, there was a chance that he would lead us to his source, or demonstrate that there was no other United States source.

Q: You said earlier that Pushar contacted you at Luigi's four days later. Was that arranged?

A: No.

Q: Why were you at Luigi's?

A: Every contact that I had been able to make with Mantou and Pushar had been in or around Luigi's. If Pushar was looking for me, I wanted to be easy to find.

The layered approach to narrative overview and following specific detail questions can be varied to meet the persuasion requirements of the situation. Generally, the more complicated the fact situation, the more important it is to have a very general narrative first, followed by extended questions eliciting specific responses. If the fact situation is not complicated, the narrative can be much more detailed, with specific questions following only to highlight the most important facts.

Q: Officer, would you describe how the blue pickup was proceeding as you began to follow it?

A: We picked it up on Twelfth and Regent, heading east on Regent. The truck was in the curb lane going about fifteen to twenty miles an hour. As we followed it, between Twelfth and Twentieth, it switched lanes from the curb lane to the center lane about twelve times. Its speed varied from fifteen to twenty miles per hour on a fairly regular basis, going up and down about twelve to fifteen times. The brake lights were on about half the time. When we crossed the Twentieth street intersection, we put on the flashers and tried to pull the truck over. After another block, it was still proceeding in the same manner. We turned on the siren, and the truck came to a stop in about a quarter of a block.

Q: What did you do after the pickup was stopped?

A: I got out of the squad car, went up to the driver's side and tried to get the driver to come out of the truck cab. After a minute, he lowered the window, asked me what I wanted, and finally came out of the truck. He was slow and unsure getting out of the truck. When he got out I ran a short sobriety test on him and then arrested him for driving while under the influence of alcohol.

Q: Officer, what is the speed limit on Regent?

A: Forty miles per hour.

Q: Was there any other traffic heading east on Regent in the vicinity of the squad and the truck.

A: No sir, not at 3:30 in the morning.

Q: Please describe for us the twelve lane changes that you observed between Twelfth and Twentieth.

A: They weren't complete lane changes, and the truck never signaled a lane change. The pickup started in the curb lane, but was right on the line between the curb and center lanes. Each time it changed lanes it went from just one side of the line dividing the lanes to the other, most of the time not having the entire truck cross over the line. Every time that the truck started back towards the curb lane side of the lane dividing line, the brake lights would go on and the truck would slow to fifteen or sixteen miles per hour. Every time that the truck went towards the center, the brake lights would go off and the truck would speed up to eighteen or nineteen, sometimes twenty miles per hour.

Q: What kind of a sobriety test did you run when the driver got out of the truck?

A: I asked him to touch his nose with his forefinger, (demonstrating), to pick up a quarter that I put on the street, and to walk on the street alongside the curb.

Q: How did he perform the tests?

A: He poked himself in the eye, fell over and could not pick up the quarter, and kept walking up and tripping on the curb as he tried to walk along the street.

Another popular method of combining the flow of the narrative with the detail of specific questioning is to punctuate the narrative by interrupting it with specific questions. This does not provide the layered effect of the narrative followed by detailed questioning. On the other hand, it brings the detail to the juror immediately, and generally, takes less time than the layered approach. There is no rule to suggest which is better, or which is applicable to any particular kind of fact situation. The trade-off considerations, however, are the speed and punchiness of the interrupted narrative against the repetition and thoroughness of the layered approach. As a general proposition, the interrupted narrative requires the narrator to provide more specific details during the initial narrative. If there are too many interruptions for details, the interrupted narrative becomes all interrupted and not much narrative:

Q: Officer, would you describe how the blue pickup was proceeding as you began to follow it?

A: We picked it up on Twelfth and Regent, heading east on Regent. The truck was in the curb lane going about fifteen or twenty miles an hour. As we followed it, between Twelfth and Twentieth, it switched lanes from the curb lane to the center lane about twelve times. Its ...

Q: Excuse me officer, would you describe those lane changes for us?

A: Yes. The truck kept moving across the lane dividing line between the curb lane going east and the center lane going east. It rarely got completely over the line one way or the other, usually about three quarters of the truck.

Q: Did the truck signal the lane changes?

A: No.

Q: Did you observe anything else, officer?

A: Yes sir. Every time the truck changed lanes, it made a speed change, going down in speed with the brake lights on as it moved toward the curb lane, and increasing in speed with the brake lights off as it moved towards the center lane. When we crossed the Twentieth street intersection, we put on the flashers and tried to pull the truck over.

Q: What happened after you put on the flashers?

A: The truck went another block without stopping, so we turned on the siren. The truck stopped within about a quarter of a block from where we turned the siren on. I got out of the squad car, went up to the driver's side and tried to get the driver to come out of the truck cab. After a minute, he lowered the window, asked me what I wanted, and finally came out of the truck. He was slow and unsure getting out of the truck. When he ...

Q: Pardon me, Officer Kellum, how long were you outside the window before the driver lowered the window?

Although it is hard to argue for any universal rule of questioning technique, it is a rare direct examination that is not enhanced by using a narrative-specific mix that is layered or one that proceeds by interruption. Integrating exhibits into the direct is also another way to layer the witness testimony. By having the witness provide the initial narrative, you can use exhibits to punctuate the specific testimony. If the witness will be on more than twenty minutes, and more than one narration is advisable, you might consider mixing up the two methods. If a long continuous narrative is needed, it is possible to interrupt that narrative by asking for more specific responses, as needed, and then go back and layer the examination by picking up additional details that were left out. The technique chosen will depend upon the length of the narrative, the importance of the details, the skill of the narrator, and most of all, upon your own sense of pace and timing. Those judgments come with experience and depend upon the specific courtroom you are in and the particular jurors that are listening. Consideration of the problem in advance will heighten your perception and bring you closer to the day when your judgment will be confident, if not correct.

Questioning styles are unique to the interrogator, and every generalization about questioning technique must be prefaced with a caveat that you may be the interrogator for whom the generalization is inappropriate. There are, nevertheless, some generalizations worth thinking about and certainly worth following in your first trial or two, where competence, not brilliance, is the goal.

Direct examination questions ought to be short enough to be easily understood by a nervous witness. Another advantage to the short, simple question is that you have to think more about your entire direct examination in order to draft a short, yet useful, question. Another major advantage of the short, simple question is that it is hard to lead while asking it. Two good techniques for insuring that you ask short, simple questions that are not leading are: one idea per question, and start the question with what you want to know. The chances are that the next thing you want to know from a witness is who, what, why, where, when, or how something happened. The way to avoid asking a question like, "Did you go over to the car after you were sure everything was safe?" is to begin the question with what you want to know: "Where . . ."

A major weapon against the long unwieldy question is simple language. This is particularly difficult for law students and beginning lawyers. By the third year in law school, most of us are well schooled in word inflation. In addition, we are beginning to feel our importance. We would like others to understand we are important. Thus, "I'm important" language fills our questions.

"Could you tell us by whom you are employed?" instead of "Who do you work for?"

"At what point in time did you have occasion to observe the vehicle negotiate the corner?" instead of "When did you see the car turn?"

The words that you use tell the jurors something about who you are and who you think they are. There are arguments about whether you ought to talk up or down to a jury, and about whether you will appear condescending by doing either. The most important consideration is whether the witness and the jurors understand the question. Until you have the experience to make a discerning judgment about yourself and how you look to jurors, use simple, every day language. Leave the complex pseudo-educated phrases and lawyer talk at home or in the office. Do not bring it to court.

The simple question is most difficult and most important when the witness is an expert. Expert

witnesses, quite naturally, use their calling's jargon
when speaking, including in court. You are obligat-
ed to watch out for the jargon, and ask the expert to
explain every unusual term until you are sure the
jurors understand the meaning. Many lawyers, unfortunately, compound the problem by using the
jargon during examination. If the expert uses a
jargon term, it is natural to ask a question about
the answer in the terms of the answer. In addition,
we sound awfully smart when we can use the expert's language. Thus:

Q: Was the abrasion posterior to the pelvic area?

A: No, the scrape was in front of the hip.

If you slip and ask a jargon question, pray that you
have a doctor who will, despite your use of the
doctor's jargon, answer in English. Stop yourself
from using a commonly employed method of "translating" for the jury, "Doctor you and I know what a
placental abruption is, but will you turn to the
jurors and explain it to them?" This kind of translation can make both you and your expert look condescending and can have the effect of excluding the
jury from the testimony. Mastering the art of the
plain question can be difficult, but it is a critical
skill for an examiner on cross as well as direct
examination.

The first trial is not too early to be concerned
about asking questions that in addition to being
understandable are persuasive. The words you
choose, the concepts you present, and the emphasis
you create will determine whether you have pre-

sented merely an understandable examination, or a persuasive one.

Shakespeare thought that "a rose by any other name would smell as sweet," but any plaintiff's lawyer can tell you that two cars meet in a "collision" or a "crash," and every defense lawyer knows that you call that an "accident." The name matters. "Accident," in common parlance, and in the law, means no fault, unavoidable. "Crash" may not mean anything in the law, but most people visualize bad damage for which somebody is to blame. The concept of subliminal persuasion through code words has been verified by psychological testing, and has caused the Federal Communications Commission to prohibit subliminal advertising. The specific words you choose can evoke specific responses from your audience, both jurors and witnesses. It is no accident that the plaintiff's lawyer may talk about the "violent snap of the neck that jerked Betty Sue's head almost into the back seat when the defendant plowed into her car from behind," just before the defense lawyer talks about the "whiplash (sometimes, soft tissue injury claim) from the accident." The consistency with which seasoned successful trial advocates choose their language is not coincidence. Word choice is not limited to the violent personal injury arena. Two opposing lawyers asking about an alleged oral contract are likely to characterize the meeting between two parties as "conversation" on the one hand, and "negotiation" on the other. Those characterizations usually have a direct relationship to the themes of their cases. You want language and themes that jurors will repeat when they are back in the jury room persuading their colleagues.

Opinion testimony is a common area in which beginning lawyers fail to make a persuasive examination. The failure is more often in the examination of a lay witness than in the examination of an expert. Although Fed.R.Evid. 705 allows an expert to state an opinion without first setting out the facts upon which the opinion is based, few lawyers approach the examination of an expert that way. On the other hand, when the opinion is that of a lay witness that is admissible under Fed.R.Evid. 701, most beginning lawyers work so hard at getting the opinion before the jury, they either forget to lay out the complete factual basis or do not believe the facts are of any use once the opinion is in. The facts will be more persuasive to the jurors than the conclusion of the witness. Ironically, it is the lay opinion where the facts are likely to be omitted and the expert opinion where the facts are included. Even if the witness is a police officer, a kind of pseudo-expert, the officer's opinion that "the man was drunk," is not as persuasive to the jury as a description of the facts the officer observed:

> "The man stumbled getting out of the truck. Then he had to prop himself up with his left arm against the door to keep his balance. When he got out, I could smell beer on his breath and see his bloodshot eyes. He could not say his own name."

It may be that the stature of a police officer gives an opinion credence, but if you have to make a choice between the officer giving an opinion or presenting the facts, choose the facts. Your own experience will tell you that you hold more dearly to conclusions you reach on your own than you do to conclusions you adopt from others. If you think again to jurors back in the jury room, you want them to have command of the facts so that the opinion is shared by them and the witness. The more jurors can relate facts to their own experience, the better basis they have for evaluating (and agreeing with) the opinion. If you delete the facts, you are forcing them to accept the opinion solely on the credibility of the witness.

A direct examination cannot be persuasive if it sounds improbable or rehearsed. Questions that ask for improbabilities on direct examination make the examination sound rehearsed. The problem with an examination that sounds rehearsed is that the jurors are left with the impression that they are seeing a performance from the witness. Even if a police officer has written in a report that he received a call at 6:17 p.m., you are probably better off asking the officer, "What happened at about 6:15 that evening?" than you are asking, "What time did you receive the call?", and getting an exact answer: "6:17." Unless it is a logged call, or an event that is other-wise automatically timed involving a matter where minutes are at issue, your witness may lose credibility by being more exact in an answer than the situation requires. The extra exactitude will sound like something the witness prepared for, not like something remembered. You can guard against the rehearsed sound of improbability by taking care not to ask questions that call for a more perfect response than you need. If your witness just happened to look at the speedometer at the time that matters, ask: "About how fast were you going?" You are likely to hear: "About forty." If you ask, "How fast were you going?", the witness, trying hard to be completely truthful, may say: "I was going forty-two miles per hour." Most jurors are not willing to believe that people make that kind of precise reading, even if they might do it themselves. Do not inadvertently invite your witness to sound implausible. This is another reason not to bring your "script" of the direct to the courtroom. Work from your outline, or a list of the answers you need the witness to give so that the direct will be impromptu in front of the jury.

Lawyers are constantly searching for techniques to emphasize special portions of the direct examination. The possibilities range from the effective use of the whiteboard to the bush league device of repeating the witness' answer to make sure the jurors heard it.

Q: Where did you go that evening?

A: To the Kasbah.

Q: To the Kasbah? (or worse: Ah, the Kasbah.)

A: Yes, to the Kasbah.

If you believe that a witness' answer ought to be repeated so that the jurors do not miss the answer or its significance, you need not tread upon the questionably ethical ground of commenting on the evidence. A proper way to accomplish the same result has the advantage of not sounding "cheap." Use the answer as a part of the following question.

Q: Where did you go that evening?

A: To the Kasbah.

Q: What did you do at the Kasbah? *or* How long did it take you to get to the Kasbah? *Or* Describe the Kasbah for us.

If the portion of the answer you want repeated is in a narrative, interrupt just after the part you want to emphasize, and repeat the portion of importance as the first part of your question.

A: . . . and then I saw them get out of the bed.

Q: After you saw them get out of bed, what did you do? or When they got out of bed, what did they do? or Did you see them do anything after they got out of bed?

If you are using the blocking and headlining approach discussed earlier, you will have natural opportunities to recap and highlight testimony without being so obvious.

Q: Now that we talked about what you saw after they got out of bed, let's talk about what happened when they went downstairs.

Another variation on the bush league approach to repetition is the "I beg your pardon, I did not catch the answer. What did you say?" question. It is important that your witness speak up; but the attempt to get the witness to speak up and repeat an answer you know the jurors heard is too transparent to be effective. The feigned inability to hear trick does, however, point up the importance of the witness' voice level. If you do not hear an answer, you must have the witness repeat the answer so the jurors hear it. If you are faking it, or if you use some other obvious device, you will get the emphasis of the second hearing, but with it some loss of the presumption of credibility with which you started.

When you come to an important part of the testimony, or at any time when your witness is not looking at the jury, you will pick up the jurors' attention and gain some emphasis by beginning a question with: "Will you please tell the jurors ..." If you have a particularly recalcitrant witness who insists on looking at you, you might walk behind the jury to do your questioning, if the court and the courtroom design make it possible. The witness will then be forced to watch the jury in order to look at you. If the courtroom design will accommodate this questioning position, save it for when you come to that part of the testimony that you want to emphasize.

In addition to varying your position, and the position of the witness if you are using a diagram or some other prop, you can achieve emphasis for particular questions by changing voice tone, pitch, and cadence. A low whispered question is sometimes the loudest sound in a courtroom. Being able to control and vary your voice can be a tremendous asset and is typically one of the most noticeable differences between great lawyers and their lesser counterparts. Being able to sense the emotional changes in the courtroom is priceless. As you develop you can become more comfortable in displaying more emotional range because you are more comfortable knowing that you are still in control of the courtroom, even if you are the defense lawyer having a quiet moment with the plaintiff widow. Once you develop the skill, showing appropriate emotion in the courtroom can be a sign of your humanity and can increase your credibility with the jurors.

The sketch pad or whiteboard that allows the witness to draw a rough quick illustration can provide emphasis for critical questions. You may even be able to create an easy piece of demonstrative evidence by making a list of key terms or events on a piece of paper while the witness testifies. With a treating doctor, for example, you might make a list of the tests the doctor performed to help illustrate the testimony and to use in your closing argument.

Many examinations end on a last question of importance. It is common for lawyers to warn the jury that the last question is coming and that it is important: "Mr. Brewer, I have just one more question. (Dramatic pause!) What were you doing in the bed?" You may be able to find something a bit fresher and more effective, but do not overlook the importance of letting the jurors know that you are coming to the exciting conclusion of the direct examination. If you can find no substitute, and fall back on the "one more question," do not ask two— or more.

Q: Mr. Brewer, I have just one more question. What were you doing in the bed?

A: I was hiding under the covers because the lightning scared me.

Q: Are you really afraid of lightning?

A: You promised only one more question. Can I go home now?

The problem with asking two questions instead of the promised one is not that you lied or cannot count. You lost your big finish with the second question. Make sure that your last question will not draw an objection that is sustained. There is nothing more deflating than to have built up the question, only for it to end with a fight among the lawyers and the judge ruling against you. If the objection is overruled, you are fine to go back, set the stage again (implying without saying, "Before we were so rudely interrupted") and re-ask your question. If the objection is sustained, try to go back to testimony that will not be objectionable so that you can still manage a strong ending. This underscores why you treat each witness as a scene in your play and you have a good finish for each scene.

Some witness' testimony can be emphasized by the use of a document to refresh recollection or as part of the introduction of the document itself. A police officer, housing inspector, hospital nurse, or any witness that makes reports or writes concurrent notes can use those notes without losing any credibility. If an occurrence witness arrives with notes and reads testimony, that witness will quickly be dismissed by the jurors because the witness had no understandable reason for writing at the time and it appears to be a created script. The officer, and others who write to preserve information, do not face that credibility problem.

If you wish to emphasize a portion of an officer's testimony by reference to a document Fed.R.Evid. 612 might provide an opportunity. Find a small detail in the officer's report that has something to do with the matter you wish to emphasize, but is not important enough for the officer to remember. When the officer is testifying about the matter, but does not remember the small detail, you may ask if the report might refresh the officer's recollection. The report, handed to the officer, will focus the jurors' attention and remind the officer of the forgotten detail.

On the rare occasion that the officer does not actually remember the investigation (trial might be five years and five hundred other investigations later) Fed.R.Evid 803(5) allows the officer to testify from the report. The foundation to allow this use of the report emphasizes why the officer's testimony from the report is credible. The writing, after all, was done before anybody was thinking about lawsuits. It must be accurate.

Emphasis does not necessarily mean you have to be "theatrical." A whisper in an hour of shouting is the emphasized point, not the consistently, loud words. Emphasis can be achieved in many ways. But if it is gained by all of them at one sitting, there is no emphasis. Emphasis, by definition, means that 80% will be less well remembered than the 20% that is emphasized.

The most intriguing point of emphasis in most trials comes from the "special" witness: the widow, the rape victim, the criminal defendant, the small child, the victim making an in court identification. It is the witness that might cry, or be obviously brave, or be ashamed, or express some other emotion with which the jurors will empathize, that creates the most important emphasis problem for direct examination. The witness, by definition, is assured of the jurors' attention. That assurance of attention provides a rare opportunity to sell your case to the jurors. Timing is the key. Any witness that is likely to be emotional and drain the jurors of some emotion during testimony must be handled delicately so that the emphasis of difference and climax is not lost. A widow, for example, that begins crying the moment she takes the stand and does not stop until she is excused, emphasizes nothing, and runs the risk of being pitied and dismissed as "just a widow." The examiner has control of the witness' emotion in most instances. The special witness is likely to take the stand bravely, attempting to hold herself together at all costs. The examiner's manner can reinforce the effort. The examiner also has the key questions that will break down the witness' control. Use them sparingly, and time them to your best advantage; but use them.

The rape victim is a tragic, but classic, example of the special witness that must be handled properly if the prosecutor is to put the rapist behind bars. In most cases, the prosecutor needs to inquire about the details of the assault. Most victims will lose composure when discussing the details. That pain is an important truth for the jury. If you can present the witness initially as any other witness, eliciting background information and non-assault information of importance, you will build both the anticipation and the contrast that will never allow the jurors to forget the tragedy to be related or the accusation that will follow it. The emotional loss of normal examination routine conveys a kind of truth that is hard for human beings to ignore. The witness' loss of control is not as important for the sympathy that it might engender as it is for the jurors' perception that what they are hearing under stressful circumstances could not be incorrect. When you approach this delicate part of the examination, do not overplay it. It does not need the artificial help of, "I know this is hard for you." After the witness has explained the assault, ask a few questions that will allow her to regain her composure just enough so that when you ask the last question: "Is that man in this courtroom?" the witness will be resolute in pointing to the defendant, not vengeful, just resolute.

You will present the "special" witness most effectively if you identify the testimony that is special and plan the examination so that you build up to the most important point, then finishing the examination with a last question that brings the special point back to the mind of the jurors.

The flip side to the special witness that works in your favor is the witness that you know is not going to perform well. In those circumstances, you may consider managing the jurors' expectations about the witness before the witness takes the stand. Just as you consider taking the sting out or pulling the plug on specific weaknesses, you may have to spend a minute or two of voir dire or opening statement raising or lowering expectations. The more important the witness, the more likely you will want to manage the jurors' expectations about the performance beforehand.

> "Ladies and Gentlemen, you will hear from Jeremy today on the witness stand. This is the first time he has been in a courtroom and he is very nervous. When Jeremy gets nervous, he fidgets in his chair and looks down at the floor (or stammers, or repeats himself) so you might see that happen today. He wants to tell you what happened so that you hear it from him, he is going to do his best to look you straight in the eye, but it may not happen."

Or you might use the same idea to raise expectations about the other side's witnesses and lower those about your expert.

"You will hear from two experts in this case, Dr. Smith and Dr. Jones. I will be presenting Dr. Jones who practices here at Hospital General. Dr. Jones has never testified in front of a jury before, he spends his days treating trauma patients at our emergency room. Dr. Smith who is here on behalf of the plaintiff on the other hand has testified twenty times just this year and one hundred times over the last eight years. He has special rates that he charges for testifying in front of juries and is a professional expert witness."

If you give careful consideration to three touchstones of direct examination, you will conduct your part of the direct examination persuasively: (1) take out all of the irrelevancies; (2) give attention to the pattern of your questions and the shape of the entire examination; and (3) be precise and parsimonious in choosing points to emphasize.

Conducting the Cross Examination

Any examination of a witness presented by the other side (or of the opposing party presented during your case-in-chief) is a cross examination. It is, technically, a cross examination when you examine your client's spouse, or some other witness that has more good things to say for you than for your opponent, if your opponent called that witness for direct examination. But the examination of a friendly witness that the other side was forced to call is not why we want to be trial lawyers. We become trial lawyers to conquer. The dramatic scene in which the trial advocate slices deftly through the cover-up to expose the lying witness is the stuff of which lawyers' dreams are made. The dreams over-emphasize the importance of cross examination as the ultimate determiner of the dispute, but accurately portray the nature of most cross examinations. Cross examination is the ultimate confrontation theater. It is the gunfight in the street that leaves one person dying in the dust.

"Dying in the dust" is the key to understanding the force of cross examination and to developing a useful perspective for trial. There are no cross examination winners, only cross examination losers. The importance of cross examination in the outcome of the trial is not due to substantive gains. The gain, for either side, is in the theater of the confrontation, and the effect of the perceived "loss" on the force of the loser's presentation. Even when you turn a witness completely around, you make no substantive gains, you only nullify any substantive gains the opponent might have from the witness' testimony. It will be rare when you turn a witness' testimony. Most successful cross examinations that leave the witness "dying in the dust" do not achieve a recantation. The demonstration of bias, the admission of omissions, and the failure of detail are much more common reasons that jurors refuse to accept the testimony of a witness that you have successfully cross examined. When the jurors refuse to accept the witness' testimony, the witness and your opponent lose. If you are farther ahead after a successful cross examination, it is not because you have gone faster; it is because your opponent has gone slower. The difference is more than a word game.

If the lawyer understands that there is nothing to win on cross examination, the lawyer maintains a critical advantage over the witness. Witnesses believe that they must win something on cross examination. They view cross examination as an ordeal over their credibility and believe that they must prove something and make points on cross examination. In short, they assume the burden of proving truthfulness, believing that if the examination is a draw, they will lose. The result is that witnesses are more nervous on cross examination than they ought to be and are likely to take risks that only those who believed they had something to prove would chance.

The lawyer's equivalent of the witness' unreasonable assumption of the burden of credibility, is the unreasonable dream of cross examination victories. The lawyer's ego, if it is involved in the cross examination, will neutralize the advantage that witnesses have conferred by thinking that they must win. The lawyer whose worth depends upon winning the cross examination will, like the witness, approach the cross examination with too much at stake, be too nervous, and take unreasonable risks chasing a dream.

Volumes have been written about the difficulty of cross examination, and a kind of mystique has developed that scares beginning lawyers. Confidence, unfortunately, is a prerequisite for a successful cross examiner. The good news is that cross examination is relatively easy if a few simple rules are followed. The confidence that you need to cross examine should be enhanced by the knowledge that the task is not beyond even the lawyer who has yet to try the first case. The beginning lawyer does not need to know enough or be good enough to win anything on cross examination. The beginning lawyer must only avoid losing; and that can be done simply by putting safety first. Although there are cases that require the lawyer to plunge into a risky cross examination, they demand experience and judgment to continually reassess the risk as the examination proceeds, and the sharp skills to extricate the lawyer from danger. Those cases are so rare that the beginning lawyers do not need to worry about them until they have enough experience to have developed the judgment and the skills. Beginning lawyers should only cross examine within the safety rules.

The hallmark of every successful cross examination is lawyer control. So long as the lawyer, not the witness, controls the pace and the substance of the cross examination, the lawyer cannot lose. Control is the lawyer's safety device for cross examination. Great cross examiners have many techniques for controlling the examination. Some manage with their style or poise. Others maintain control with flawless judgment about when to tighten up the reins on the witness and when to allow the witness to ramble. Still others are so good at reading a witness, they can tell when pressure will work and when it will not. Whatever it is that the great cross examiners use to control the examination, you have not got it—not yet. The beginning lawyer exercises control of the witness and the examination by following the safety-control rules to the letter. The result may be that some opportunities are lost. The beginning lawyer may maintain a more restrictive posture than is necessary to control the examination, but the beginning lawyer that follows the safety-control rules does not lose the examination.

Assuming that lawyers have enough control over their own mouths so that they will not say anything substantively damaging towards their clients, they can insure ultimate safety and control in cross examination by not allowing witnesses to say anything either. Indeed, there are times when, "No questions, your honor", is the best cross examination. If the witness has finished the direct and it has not hurt you, nothing can be more effective than to convey to the jurors that whatever the other lawyer thought was just accomplished meant nothing. The key to creating that impression is your confidence. Stand tall and make your announcement, without looking nervous or insecure, or like you are secretly too afraid to take on the witness. It is your attitude that lets the jurors know that whatever the witness said adds nothing that matters to your opponent's case.

Most witnesses, however, will have helped your opponent enough, or be vulnerable enough, so that the risk of allowing the witnesses to open their mouths again is justified by the chance that you can put their feet in them. If the safest way to insure against losing a cross examination is to keep the witness from saying anything at all, the next safest technique is to ask questions that allow the witness to answer in one word. Not only is it the safest way to cross examine, it is also the most effective. The less the witness talks the more the lawyer controls. Remember your spotlight. If it stays focused on you, the witness will be left in the shadow and the jurors will look only at you. The more you let witnesses talk, the more likely it is that the spotlight will swing their way and you will lose control. Even the great cross examiners ask questions that call for a one word answer at the critical points in the examination.

The one word answer, in most cases, is either "yes" or "no." The only way to insure the safety and control of a one word, "yes" or "no" answer is to ask leading questions that fairly call for no other response. The lawyer will lose a cross examination if the witness has a reasonable opportunity to explain. If the lawyer's questions fairly call for a "yes" or "no" answer, there is no room for witness explanation. The key word here is fairly. It takes work to design questions that the jurors can recognize really do fairly call for the one word response.

The question that gets the "yes" or "no" response is a declaration, but in a form that requires the witness to agree or disagree: "The sun rises in the East, doesn't it?" Cross examination is not really an "examination" because the lawyer is not really "asking." Although the lawyers are not privileged to speak during witness examination unless they are asking questions, the cross examination question is question in form only. Cross examination questions are the lawyer's tools for making declarations. It is important that the declaration be one that does not fairly call for uncertainty on the part of the witness. Agreement or disagreement, either one, is better than uncertainty. Uncertainty calls for an explanation. "The sun rises in the East, doesn't it?" cannot fairly be answered with uncertainty if the matter at issue is the direction from which the sun was shining at the time of an early morning accident. On the other hand, if the question was put to Galileo at the inquisition on his view of the Copernican theory, the declaration might not be entitled to automatic agreement. An answer of, "Yes and no," or "Not exactly," or "It only appears that way," would be reasonable. Notice that each answer is more than one word, and that each leaves the jurors uncertain of the answer and anxious for an explanation. When the witness begins to explain, your safe harbor is lost.

Many beginning lawyers, armed with the knowledge that they should make declarations that call for agreement or disagreement, try to force the witness to answer "yes" or "no":

Q: She agreed to buy the magazines, didn't she?

A: Well, she signed . . .

Q: Ms. Brantley, just answer the question yes or
no.

Two bad things will happen every time the lawyer
tries to restrict the witness to a "yes" or "no" in
that fashion. First, the judge, jealous of the preroga-
tive to control the manner of interrogation, will
"approve" the witness' forthcoming explanation by
telling the lawyer and the jury that the lawyer has
no right to try to restrict the witness: "Counsel, the
witness has a right to explain the answer." Next,
the jurors, thinking that the lawyer must either be
afraid of the explanation or just plain rude, will
listen with more than usual attention as the witness answers:

"Well, she signed the paper that the man stuck
under her nose, but she said that she was not
going to agree to buy all those magazines for five
years. From what I could see and hear, she
thought she was signing up for a one month trial.
Does that answer your question?"

Although the lawyer does not have the power to
restrict the witness to a "yes" or "no," the court
does. Fed.R.Evid. 611. The court, however, is unlikely to exercise that power in favor of the cross
examiner except in the most aggravated circumstances. If you are asking well designed short and
tight cross examination questions, you should never
have to ask the judge to intercede; the judge will do
it for you. The beauty of good cross examination
questions is that witnesses lose credibility for trying
to explain their way out. You will succeed only if

you have framed your declaration carefully to avoid over-statement. If the above magazine question, for example does not try to incorporate the arguable result of "agreed to buy," and is restricted to what the lady did, Ms. Brantley will not be allowed to ramble on with her explanation:

Q: She signed the document, Plaintiff's Exhibit Number One, that I just showed you, didn't she?

A: Well, she signed the document, but . . .

Mrs. Brantley looks like she is trying to be evasive or argumentative. At this point the jurors probably already know the answer to the question and will start to tire of her refusal to answer. Once this goes on a few times, with questions that are equally fair but restrictive it might tire the judge too. Some judges will give you the relief you ask, some will not. Prudence may dictate that you make your plea at the bench, though you might imagine a witness whose conduct makes it useful to make the request to the judge in front of the jury. In any event, your chances are much better of persuading the judge when your questions clearly do not fairly call for an "explanation."

Even if the judge is unwilling to honor your request to keep the witness' answer responsive to the questions, the narrowly framed declaration provides its own self help. If the witness explains in response to a question that does not fairly call for an explanation, the jurors will quickly conclude that the witness has an ax to grind, a position to champion—a bias! Although it is unlikely that you would want to be explicit in demonstrating that bias to the jury, the unreasonable explanation is likely to strike the jurors that way even if you do not go through the questions and answers:

Q: She signed the document, didn't she?

A: Well she signed it, but she didn't think she was signing to buy all those magazines for all those years.

Q: Ms. Brantley, excuse me, but I didn't ask you what you think she thought, did I?

Answer irrelevant

Q: Ms. Brantley, I asked you if she signed the document, didn't I?

Answer irrelevant

Q: You know the answer to my question about the document, don't you, Ms. Brantley?

Answer irrelevant

Q: Would you do the jurors and me the common courtesy of answering the question that was put to you? Did she sign the document?

If the witness is refusing to answer with that safe one word "yes" or "no," the court is not willing to restrict the witness, and you cannot risk the seeming belligerence of being explicit about the witness' bias, take solace in the fact that the jurors are at least as perceptive as you are. If your questions do not call for an explanation, and she keeps explaining, the jurors will tag her as the "explainer" that she is, discounting her testimony with a silent: "the lady doth protest too much, methinks." You can try a few additional reins on the explaining witness such as: "So your answer is yes (or no, depending on the question)? Mrs. Brantley, perhaps you did not understand my question to you, my question was...." Repeat the question verbatim (another reason the short question with plain language and one fact is perfect). If she is really recalcitrant, you can try: "Mrs. Brantley, we can do this the long way or the short way. I think it will be easier if you will just answer the question I ask." The key to the approach you will take is to ask good cross examination questions that are clear to everyone in the courtroom and then to calibrate the degree of your response to the behavior of the witness. It is always better, if possible, that the judge or the jurors (silently), rather than you, call witnesses on their behavior.

The declaration with which you ask the witness to agree should be short. It should contain only one idea. It should not be subject to misinterpretation. The jurors will believe the witness should understand the question, and will expect a straight forward response. If the question is too long, you are likely to have the witness ask you to repeat it. If the request is a fair one, you have lost a little—not in substance, but in theater. The witness has demonstrated that you do not know what you are doing. As a matter of safety and control, "I couldn't follow that, could you ask it again?" is more than a one word response. The witness has you doing what the witness wants, rather than the witness doing what you want.

The same thing is likely to happen if the question, no matter how short, contains two ideas. The witness is likely to ask you which question you want answered, even if you have asked about two ideas that are guaranteed to get the same response: "yes" to both or "no" to both.

If the question is subject to more than one interpretation, the witness will not ask you to repeat the question, but the answer will be more than one word. The witness will answer the interpretation the witness prefers, not the interpretation that you want. You lose the safety and control of the one word answer. The original magazine question (She agreed to buy the magazines, didn't she?) was short, dealt with one idea, but was subject to two interpretations: (1) agreed as a matter of law, and (2) agreed as a matter of fact. The witness gives the answer the witness wants.

By breaking down every topic into its component parts, you can insure that your questions are short, have one idea, and are not subject to misinterpretation. Every question should force the witness to make one of two choices, either agree with you and answer the question or risk losing credibility. Remember you are happy with either one! Your ultimate goal is that at the end of your cross examination the jurors do not believe the witness and discounts the witness' direct testimony. Does it matter if the jurors discount the witness' direct testimony because of the substantive answers to your cross examination questions or because the witness was so difficult that the jurors wrote off the witness? The tendency for beginning lawyers is to be so caught up in getting the exact answer that they miss the big credibility game.

Assume, in the intersection collision example that you wish to make the point that the witness who claims to have seen the accident was one hundred feet away behind a tree that is five feet in diameter. Further, that she did not say anything to anybody at the scene. You insure the safety and control of one word responses by making declarations about small, certain parts:

Q: You were standing on the sidewalk at the time of the accident, weren't you?

A: Yes.

Q: You were waiting to cross the street, isn't that right?

A: Yes.

Q: You were facing west, I believe?

A: Yes.

Q: There was a tree directly to the north of you, wasn't there?

A: Well, I don't know if it was directly north.

Q: If you had turned a quarter turn to your right you would have been looking straight ahead at a tree, isn't that right?

A: Yes.

Q: The tree was two or three feet from you, wasn't it?

A: Yes.

Q: That tree was about five feet wide, wasn't it?

A: I didn't measure it.

Q: It was a big tree, wasn't it?

A: You could say that, I guess.

Q: You were standing about one hundred feet from the accident, weren't you?

A: I don't know; I didn't measure it.

Q: You were about a third of a block from the accident?

A: Yes.

Q: You did not talk to the police, did you?

A: No.

Q: You saw other people around the scene of the accident, isn't that right?

A: Yes.

Q: You did not tell any of them that you saw the accident, did you?

A: No.

Q: You went to Mr. Whiplash's office five months after the accident, didn't you?

A: Yes.

Q: And you told him that you saw the accident?

A: Yes.

Q: Until you told Mr. Whiplash, you had never told anybody that you saw the accident, had you?

A: No.

Breaking the idea down into each of its component facts takes away any opportunity the witness would have to explain or deflect the question. Each question places the witness at the credibility fork in the road. If the witness argues or tries to "protest too much" she loses credibility; if she denies your declaration ("Yes, I told three friends about the accident later that day,") you are ready to impeach. You get what you want. You have impugned the believability of the witness no matter which path she has chosen.

The pace of the interrogation has an impact on the lawyer's ability to maintain the safety and control of the one word answer. Silence invites a witness to explain just as much as a question that asks "why?" If you ask: "You did not tell any of them that you saw the accident, did you?" and then leave empty language space after the witness answers, "No," the witness will fill that empty language space with an explanation of why she did not say anything to anybody. You will be helpless to cut off the explanation because your silence implicitly invites it, and the witness' failure to inform anybody requires explanation. Unless you press forward with another question to which you fairly want the answer, the jurors have time to ask themselves: "Wonder why she did not say something to somebody?" If they have the time to ask themselves that natural question, the witness has time to answer it. If you have the next question in mind when you ask the first, you will maintain the safety and control of the one word answer. When the witness answers "yes" or "no," and then takes a breath to explain, you begin the next question. Just about every witness that is going to offer an explanation will take a breath after the initial "yes" or "no." If you start the next question when the witness takes that breath you will not seem rude or to be interrupting. Indeed, the witness' attempt to explain will seem to be interrupting your naturally flowing next question. Interrupting is rude, and is not viewed any more favorably by jurors than by anyone else. The trick to control is to be the person who is interrupted, not the person who is interrupting. If both speakers press on the person that started first will prevail in the minds of the jurors because they are fixed on the first voice. In cross examination, always be prepared with the next question. Control through pace of interrogation only works if you are asking proper cross examination questions.

Another technique for closing up the implied language space to explain is to develop a rhythm to the questions. If you maintain a rhythm, and keep it for any length of time, it will mesmerize both the witness and the jurors. Leaving for a more advanced discussion the chance of getting a witness to make a mistake under those circumstances, the rhythm becomes the norm, and the witness' explanation breaks the rhythm. By breaking the norm, it is the witness that is "out of place" with the explanation, not the lawyer that is "out of place" with the next question.

In addition to the implied language space, physical space invites explanation. At least, the lack of physical space discourages explanation. Your physical presence can help you close up the implied space to explain. In most courts, it is improper for a lawyer to cross examine a witness from a position close up to the witness. Unfortunately for real cross examiners, the television and movie stance at the witness box, peering down at the witness, is so intimidating that few judges will allow it. It does, however, point up the value of closing the physical space between the witness and the examiner. If the physical space is closed up, the psychological space to explain is similarly closed up—at least in the mind of the witness. Even though you are unlikely to have the luxury of coming right up to the witness, you can accomplish much of the same by taking a physically aggressive posture. If you are going to lean, lean forward, not backwards. If you have a choice, move closer to the witness, not further away. Do not let furniture get between you and the witness. Even if you cannot approach the witness, you can probably move to the side, or the front, of an examination lectern. The physical presence of cross examination is forward moving even if you are stuck in a chair. Use your body movement, pace, and tone to bring a forward energy to your cross examinations.

Each of the techniques is designed to limit the witness' response to a safe one word answer. The one word answer is safe because the lawyer stays in control. Maintenance of control must be a consistent matter between the lawyer and the witness. If the witness gains control in any small area, there is a chance that the witness will gain control of the interrogation. You might, for example, ask a question that is not as short as prudence would dictate:

Q: Was it your testimony during direct examination that at the time the red car was in the intersection, the yellow car was still west of the cross walk line and had not entered the intersection?

The witness may ask you to repeat the question or to rephrase it. That is what the witness wants. What you want is an answer to your question. Do not do what the witness wants. Do not ask the question again. Unless the question was beyond comprehension, do not rephrase it. If the question was understandable, and a second hearing of the question will show that it was understandable, ask the court reporter to please read the question back to the witness. If the question was, indeed, understandable, the procedure implicitly tells the jurors that the witness was not paying attention; and it tells the witness that the lawyer will ask the questions. The importance of having the court reporter do the reading is not a desire for accuracy. The importance is having the cross examination proceed as you want it, not as the witness wants it.

If you take the safe, controlled approach to cross examination, you should be aware that there is a danger of the appearance of domination. Although you want to be in control, and you want to limit the witness to one word answers, you cannot afford to appear as if you are unfairly dominating the witness. If you appear to be unfairly restricting the witness, you will suffer the same backlash problem as in the unreasonable unilateral attempt to limit the witness to the "yes" or "no." This is another area in which you must be sure to calibrate the cross examination to the type of witness. You can soften the effect of your questions by your tone, pitch, speed, and body gestures. You do not cross examine the grieving widow, a child, or any other witness that seems vulnerable the same way that you cross examine a corporate executive, criminal defendant, or any other witness that does not exhibit vulnerability.

The final safety-control rule is a warning about something you should not do. Never argue with the witness. Of all the rules and techniques for trying lawsuits, this is the most difficult for lawyers to follow. Truth is, few of us follow it all the time. You will see some very good cross examiners break the rule and profit. A beginning lawyer cannot have the judgment that is required to make a good enough risk analysis to justify a question that argues with the witness. Every-time that you try it you will run an unreasonable risk, and even if you succeed, there is little profit. The urge to argue with the witness comes from the idea that you should win a cross examination, the dream of completely annihilating a witness, and the lawyer's belief that there are "points" to be made on cross examination. The last of these is the least valid. Points are not made on cross examination; they are made in closing argument. Why argue by asking the witness a question and giving the witness an opportunity to argue back, when you can argue in closing argument when the witness is long gone? In the example of the witness, the tree, and the accident one hundred feet away, the last question you should ever put to the witness is:

Q: So the tree blocked your view of the accident, didn't it?

The best answer you can hope to get is "yes." The worst (and most likely) is "no" with a detailed explanation of why not. You cannot reasonably stop the explanation because the jurors will be curious. It should be obvious that the tree was in the way, if your questions supported the inference. Be happy with the inferences you can create on cross instead of going for the confession. Inferences can be more powerful. Once you have finished your cross examination the jurors will come to the conclusion that the tree was in the way on their own. Since they thought of it instead of you forcing it on them (over the distracting protestations of the witness) it is inherently more believable. Inferences can also be more memorable. Jurors tend to remember inferences as if they were actually part of the testimony and can be more likely to remember the inference than actual testimony. Let the power in the infer-

ence work for you instead of inviting an argument.
Even though your opponent will attempt to rehabilitate the witness on redirect by asking if she could
see around the tree; don't you ask the question
during cross. Among other reasons, the jurors may
have already decided the tree was in the way regardless of the witness's explanation.

There is no adequate way to demonstrate with
the written word the theatrical difference between
the explanation coming at you during cross examination and the explanation made later during redirect examination. The key to understanding the
problem is in the confrontational nature of cross
examination and the reminder that there are only
losers on cross examination. When you ask the
woman who has testified that she saw the accident,
the question: "So the tree blocked your view of the
accident, didn't it?" you are arguing with the witness. The dialogue is really: (Witness) "I saw it."
(Lawyer) "You could not have seen it." By arguing
with the witness, you set up the confrontation potential of cross examination. There is an explicit
argument before the jury and somebody must win
and somebody must lose. The witness, unfortunately, is in the best position to win. The witness not
only gets the opportunity to explain because you
have invited it; but you do not have an opportunity
to respond. When the witness says, "It was no
problem, I could see around to the left as the yellow
car smashed into the red one," you cannot say to
the witness, "Wait a minute, if you were two feet
from the tree and the tree was five feet wide and

the accident was one hundred feet away, a straight line drawing will demonstrate that at a hundred feet the tree blocked sixty feet of the scene in front of you." You can only ask questions. If the tree blocked the witness' view, the witness is not going to admit that to you on cross examination. Wait until closing argument to make the point. You will not be stuck with the witness' reasonable rejoinder that she could see around to the left, and you will not be saddled with the jurors' memory of your cross examination loss when the witness burst your logic bubble.

The temptation to argue with the witness is fueled by the lawyer's knowledge of the closing argument to be made to the jurors. Having thought it out, the lawyer knows that logic supports the argument. The lawyer develops faith in the logic of the position and believes the logic alone will offer the safety and control needed to face the witness with the question. Unless the witness agrees with the question—it happened last in 1376—the logic offers no control, the witness explains why the other side of the argument is correct, and the lawyer loses the theater of the cross examination.

A question need not be as obviously confrontational as, "So the tree blocked your view of the accident, didn't it?" in order to be a question that argues with the witness. Any question that expresses doubt about the witness' premise is argumentative. The question that every lawyer knows not to ask on cross examination, "Why ...?", is essentially argumentative. The question asks the witness to explain something. In cross examination, the direction to explain implies that there is no reasonable explanation other than the position of the interrogator. Of course, there is, and the lawyer usually hears it right after asking, "Why?", or, "Tell the jury how that is possible?" Not even the knowing sneer on your face, calculated to show the jury that you know the witness is cornered or about to lie will protect you once the witness starts explaining. Jurors picture themselves as potential witnesses, not potential lawyers. In any argument between the lawyer and the witness, the jurors' sympathies will be with the witness.

Control, through declarations that call for a one word response is important in cross examination because you cannot exercise control through preparation. Direct examination control is achieved through extensive preparation of the substance of the testimony and of the witness. Cross examination cannot be controlled through preparation; it must be controlled through execution. Preparation for cross examination, nevertheless, is as important as for direct examination. The execution of control on cross depends upon the preparation before trial. Preparation for cross examination, though individual in the sense that individual witnesses are examined, involves an overall attack on the opponent's case. Just as direct examination preparation requires a theory of the case first, cross examination requires a theory of both your case and your defense. Cross examination questions either support your theme and defense or they undermine your opponent's theme. If the questions don't have a direct relation to either, they aren't needed. You must prepare to cross examine the case before you prepare a cross examination of an individual witness.

The first step is to determine what you need to accomplish with all of the cross examinations in the case. To do that you must make some assumptions about what the opponent's case is going to look like. After you have enough knowledge of the opponent's case so that you know how you would try it were you the opponent and how you will attack it, go to your evidence rules.

Cross examination is a tool for diminishing the size of the opponent's pile of evidence. If you can keep that pile from growing by keeping evidence out on direct, you can conduct the safest of all cross examinations: "No questions." Review all of the opponent's case alongside your evidence rules and make notes of evidence you can exclude and the rule or argument that will exclude it. If it never gets in, you never have to cross. There are at least two other evidence considerations that you should deal with at the beginning of your preparation: the rules of impeachment and the problem of "opening the door" to otherwise inadmissible evidence. Fed. R.Evid. 613 provides for two different methods of impeachment with a prior inconsistent statement (discussed in detail later in the chapter) and you will want to employ one method or the other, depending upon the witness and the circumstances at trial. Evidence that is inadmissible under the rules of evidence becomes admissible on redirect examination if you inadvertently "open the door" by raising the matter during cross examination. If the opponent has something that will not be helpful to you, but is not admissible under the rules of evidence, be sure that you remember in preparing for cross examination to ask no questions that would "open the door" for your opponent.

The second step in overall cross examination preparation is total fact and witness analysis of the case. Part of this was completed when you worked out your drafts of opening statement and closing argument. Some of the arguments that you will offer about the opponent's case and witnesses depend upon your ability to make certain declarations or realize specific admissions on cross examination. You should catalog those items to be sure that none are missed. In addition, you must work through all the depositions, statements, and other information you have from or about the opponent's witnesses so that you can integrate your attack through all of the witnesses. Witnesses on one side will invariably know something about the same events. Often they know them differently. Compare what a manager might have said as opposed to a lower level employee or what a current versus a former employee might have said. Compare what witnesses say with what their manuals, documents or websites say. Compare their stories. Do they know them too similarly to be believed? In many cases, the conclusions that one witness draws depend specifically upon what other witnesses were doing. Can you alter their testimony by changing a critical fact? Look at what your opponent's witnesses can offer that might help your case. Not all cross examination must be destructive. Evidence is always more believable if you can get the other side's witnesses to offer it. Does the plaintiff complain that there was no training but one of her co-employees has pages of signed attendance sheets from training seminars in her file? Compare testimony to common sense. If it doesn't make common sense to you, it might not be believed by the jurors. Make sure you have looked through every available source of information. The best cross examination questions are the ones the witnesses and their lawyer don't expect. The devil or smoking gun is buried in the details. Thoroughness frequently gets rewarded in cross examination. After you are sure you know how all of the witnesses for the opponent integrate or conflict with each other and with your witnesses, you are ready to prepare specific cross examinations.

You can prepare to cross examine an individual, you cannot prepare the cross examination of an individual. You can predict the area of direct examination for a specific witness, but you cannot predict the words that the witness will use or the witness' manner. It is the witness' testimony before the jury that is cross examined, not what the witness has said in the past, or what you think the witness might say on direct examination. Therefore, your preparation must be complete enough so that you are prepared to attack an unexpected assertion, or take advantage of an unexpected blooper. To do so requires two things: superb preparation before trial and intense listening to the witness during trial. Fortunately the two go hand in hand and you can do both. If you are truly prepared, you can actually listen to the witness' answers both during the direct examination and your cross examination.

The foundation of the preparation before trial is a complete review and abstracting of everything the witness has said in deposition, statement, conversation, or any other manner related to the case. Because you may need to refer to any part of it quickly, you should abstract and index any deposition or extensive statement. You should make notes of shorter material such as letters or conversation. Any method of organization that allows you to find the former statements quickly will do. Many lawyers prepare the abstract by dividing a piece of paper vertically, putting the abstract of the former statement and the index on the left, leaving the right side for notations made during direct examination. If you have a particularly long deposition containing items that you know you will want to use for cross examination, you should tab the deposition in addition to doing the abstract. Make sure that for every topic on which you can imagine cross examining the witness you have the page and line number of the deposition or document ready to go in case you need it. Nothing keeps witnesses in line better than you knowing their testimony better than they do.

After abstracting everything the witness has said about the incident or case, review the background of the witness and the witness' relationship to the case. In a dram shop case, for example, the person serving an obviously intoxicated person and the bartender who made the drink both work for the defendant. The person serving the drink will present different problems from those posed by the bartender who merely filled the server's order. Both may have a bias because they work for the defendant, but the server will be more of an advocate for the opposition. It is the server's observation (or lack of it) about the patron's intoxication that is being challenged. Moreover, the cross examination of a server with fifteen years of experience may be very different than the one of a physics major working tables to pay for college.

Once you have full knowledge of who the witness is and what the witness has said in the past, you should try to make a specific prediction of the direct examination. This will help you to review your general prediction for the opponent's case, and forewarn you about the areas you need to cover with cross examination or other evidence. At the same time, you should identify all areas of witness vulnerability. After you have decided what you think the witness will say on direct examination, and where the witness is vulnerable, you must establish cross examination goals.

Preparation of cross examination goals is the most difficult and most important cross examination task. Unfortunately, specific advice about cross examination goals is of little use for more than the specific cross examination about which it is given.

The general advice for developing cross examination goals must be taken with the understanding that specific situations should control. Some general advice may be inapplicable and some just wrong for a specific cross examination.

The only fairly universal rule for cross examination goals is that everything the witness says on direct need not be confronted on cross examination, and every vulnerability apparent in the witness need not be explored. For the beginning lawyer, and maybe for all but the great cross examiners, prepare a good, not a great, cross examination. If you shoot for everything, or if you try to pull off a winner, the chances are great that you will fail. Not only will you lose the cross examination in front of the jury, you are likely to give up a small loss that you could have pinned on the witness. Remember the shorter the cross examination the less likely you are to lose control, so two or three points are plenty. Compare the points you know you can establish with your theme. Which points help establish something positive about your case, as opposed to those that suggest why the jurors shouldn't accept your opponent's? Which points can you make through impeachment with a prior inconsistent statement? Ask yourself a few questions. What information do the jurors need to understand this case (as opposed to what does my ego want to prove)? At the end of the cross examination do I want the jury to believe this witness on any issue? What do I want to say about this witness in my closing argument?

In preparing for cross examination you should write out your cross examination goals and rank them both as to desirability and difficulty of attainment. If you are lucky, the most desirable goals will be the easiest to obtain. If you are in the real world, you will be forced to give up a little of one for a little of the other. Take a long look at the two rankings and gauge the value of the goal against the difficulty in achievement in order to decide which goals to pursue. Then prepare the cross examination.

The ranking of cross examination goals identifies your areas of inquiry. The next step is to decide the order of inquiry. A cohesive order is not as important on cross examination as it is on direct. The same principles of primacy and recency apply to cross examination. If you are hoping to elicit some testimony from the witness that is helpful to your case it is better to do it at the beginning of the examination. Few witnesses are very agreeable after you have impeached them and the jurors are more likely to remember what was heard first. You want them to remember that even the opponent's witness had something positive to say about your case. Subjects upon which you must cross examine, but for which your cross is weak, should be buried in the middle. In defending a personal injury case, for example, where liability is contested vigorously and there is a smaller quarrel over the amount of damage sustained by the paraplegic plaintiff, cross examination on the amount of care that will be required belongs in the middle of your cross examination. As with direct examination, end on a strong point that will make the re-direct examination difficult to begin.

Cross examination is not an attempt to tell a story. To be sure, there is some advantage in an order of inquiry that does not follow an easily discernible pattern. If the pattern is clear, it will be clear to the witness. Witness confusion is an asset for the cross examiner. After you have identified the areas of inquiry and the probable order, prepare the specific questions that you intend to ask. Check the questions to make sure that they are in the proper form to elicit safe answers. Check the order, again, so that you are comfortable with the shape of the examination and satisfied that it will end on a high note. After you have reviewed the questions, know the pattern, and are satisfied that the cross examination is a useful one, throw the questions away. Discarding the word for word questions is as important as any step in the preparation process. Cross examination places a premium both on preparation and on flexibility. If you are locked into specific questions (and you will be if you keep them) you will not have the flexibility to cross examine the actual testimony in court, adapting for the additions, omissions, and unique emphasis. If you have cross examination questions in front of you, you will not hear the direct examination as well as you should and you will certainly miss the nuance of answers on cross examination. No matter what you decide to bring to the courtroom, your number one priority has to be to listen to the witness' answers and be able to respond to them. Even if your better judgment is that you do not have the skills or information to respond to what you hear, the preparation is what starts to separate good cross examiners from the mediocre ones. Place the list of areas for cross examination, the abstract of the prior testimony, the index, and your indexed impeachment materials in your trial notebook under the individual witness tab. It should contain all that you know about the case and the witness. Your memory has stored the questions you wish to ask and it will produce them when it is time to use them on cross examination.

Direct examination never produces exactly what you expect of it, and so cross examination never proceeds exactly as you planned it. The last, and most important step in preparation for cross examination, is to listen to and to watch the direct examination. Do not think about the cross that you have planned, your mind will dredge it up, word for word, if you need it. Do not write down everything the witness says on direct. You will not have time to read your complete notes. You have already identified the areas of cross examination, and you cannot write down everything and still watch and listen at the same time. You must listen to what is said, and watch how it is said. The witness will not say all of the things the witness said before, in the same way, or in the same manner. You will cross examine only the "what" and "how" that is said in court, so view it carefully. Remember that you need not and should not cross examine on everything the witness said on direct. Don't get caught in the tit-for-tat time game. Just because the witness testified on direct for four hours doesn't mean your cross examination should take the remainder of the day. A short and sweet fifteen minute cross examination might make the point that the witness didn't have much to offer during four hours of direct examination.

In listening to the words of the witness, listen for three kinds of testimony that frequently occur. Every once in a while a witness will say something unexpectedly during direct examination that helps you more than it helps the direct examiner. When that unexpected bonbon falls in your lap, be sure you catch it. Write down the exact words the witness used. If your pre-prepared abstract sheet works for you, write the bonbon down near where that subject is covered in the abstract. The "I don't believe the witness really said that" bonbon might be something that helps you substantively or, though substantively neutral, gives you a natural opening into cross examination or impeachment. Don't miss this gift by not listening carefully to the direct!

Impeachable matter is the second thing that you must listen for with great care. If the witness says something contrary to a prior statement, write it down word for word on the right hand side of the abstract sheet, near the area that it contradicts. During direct examination you should not try to make a judgment about whether the inconsistency is critical. Just write it down word for word. You can make the usefulness judgment after the direct is completed, and before beginning the cross examination.

The third area of interest of concern is for what is not said on direct. Sometimes your opponent will forget to elicit important information from a witness during direct examination. This is particularly true when the witness has a number of subjects to cover. Pay close attention to what is covered, and what is not. If a matter of interest in the case is not covered on direct, do not ask anything on cross that will allow the lawyer to go back and pick it up on rebuttal. If the matter is not covered by the time the direct examination is over, note it on your abstract sheet with a large note to yourself to stay far away from the subject during cross examination.

While the witness testifies on direct examination, you must watch both the witness and the jurors. You must judge how the testimony was given and how the witness was received by the jurors. If you do not watch what is going on, you cannot know what kind of a relationship exists between the witness and the jurors at the end of the direct examination. You need to understand that relationship so that you know what attitude to adopt on cross examination. Your attitude on cross will reflect your personality, but it must reflect it in a manner appropriate to the relationship between the jurors and the witness. In addition, you need to make careful note of juror reaction to specific points in the direct examination. If you do not know what was important to the jurors, you cannot make the final adjustment in your list of cross examination goals that will allow you to match the questions that the jurors have in their minds with the questions you will ask on cross examination.

Although each direct examination calls for a specific cross examination, there are some areas of and rules for cross examination that recur regularly. No case or witness presents all of them, but most of them show up at one time or another. If there is nothing to cross examine from the direct examination, don't cross examine. This is often the hardest cross examination to make. We all believe there is an admission of relevance and correctness when testimony on direct goes unchallenged on cross. None of us wants to make that admission. We get up and cross examine, even if we do not know where we are going, or why we are going there. The problem with doing a cross examination when you do not have a cross examination goal is that you will unduly emphasize the testimony of the witness. Such a cross examination usually sounds like a rerun of the direct examination the only difference being the sneer on the cross examiner's face intended to tell the jurors the lawyer does not believe the witness. Nothing sells so well as repetition, particularly repetition in an interrogation that is ostensibly hostile to the witness. If you have no good questions to ask on cross examination, a disdainful, "I have no questions for this witness, your honor," is better than asking questions that allow the jurors to hear the direct again and pick up any parts they may have missed the first time.

Most areas of cross examination recur because killing cross examinations almost never occur. The number of times that a witness testifies on direct that the light was red, and on cross that it was green, is less than one. The number of times that a witness admits to a series of facts that will form the foundation for a closing argument that the witness is clearly lying or mistaken is more than one, but not much more. More often than not, the best that you will do on cross examination is to change the emphasis or the effect of the direct examination. You will often chip away, but you will rarely knock down. If you try for the unlikely knock down, you will probably miss the opportunity to chip away.

The touchstone for chipping away, for changing emphasis and diminishing effect, is the realization that life is grey while most testimony is black and white. Witnesses are not usually content to tell things as they are. They usually tell things as they are, plus a little added for how it would be best for them to be. This is not the conscious lie, nor even the big mistake. It is a matter of human nature when a person is put under oath and placed in a courtroom. Each witness wants to be precise and knowledgeable as can be. The result is that facts that are eighty percent favorable to the other side are presented as ninety-five percent favorable. If, for example, weather condition matters and there was a very light rain on the day in question, it is likely to be described by the witness for one side as a mist and by a witness for the other side as a rain shower. The plaintiff's witness is likely to describe a roadway that was barely damp, while the defendant's witness will talk about the slick wet roadbed. If a witness is a very close friend of one of the parties, the witness might claim to be "a friend" or characterize the relationship merely as "we work together." Witnesses who view accidents from half a block away looking through a screened window are likely to say that they had a "clear view" of the accident. The cross examination that aims at correcting the emphasis and chipping away at the foundations for the direct testimony will be more useful than the attempt for a "kill." There are two important reasons: (1) the kill is difficult to execute by the best of cross examiners, and (2) witnesses rarely put themselves in a position to be killed, because they rarely tell lies or make mistakes that are so obvious that a cross examiner will have the tools to point them out.

The two common areas of cross examination are "what" the witness said and "who" the witness is.

If you attack "what" the witness said you must attack the witness' ability to observe what happened or attack the witness s' ability to recall what was observed. Interrogation challenging what was said can take as many different shapes as there are situations about which to inquire. Common examples of inability to observe range from the identification witness that saw the person in strong backlight for only five seconds, to the person who claims to have heard a conversation in the next room while the television set was playing. Attacks on ability to recall are often more subtle, but just as important.

The individual who claims to recall the appearance of one person in a crowd, or one of a hundred people seen over the last three months is vulnerable to an attack on recall ability. Likewise, the witness who recalls minute details of something unremarkable when it happened last year is vulnerable. The most common use of the attack on one's ability to recall comes during impeachment, when the witness testifies to facts at trial that were omitted in a writing made almost contemporaneously with the event reported.

If you attack "who" the witness is, you are demonstrating to the jurors that there is a reason to suspect the witness' direct testimony because of the witness' identity. A most obvious example occurs when the witness is the defendant's spouse:

Q: You are married to the defendant, Mrs. Peel?

A: Yes.

Q: How long have you been married?

A: Ten years.

Q: You're in love with your husband, aren't you?

A: Yes, of course.

Many witnesses have a relationship to the parties, or a stake in the result, that must be explored on cross examination, but don't be heavy handed about it. While you might get away with a question such as, "You don't want your husband to go to jail, do you?" it is dangerous. The question argues with the witness by implying that she would lie to keep her husband out of jail. You are likely to get the following answer:

"No, but I would rather he go to jail than for me to tell a lie after having sworn before God to tell the truth."

Even more dangerous than either the "love your husband" question or the "go to jail" question, is the following:

Q: If your husband goes to jail, there will not be anybody to make money so you and the kids can eat, isn't that right?

If you ask that question, you deserve the result you get when the wife breaks into tears, and admits you are right. The problem with the question, however, is not the answer. The problem is that the jury will hate you for asking it. The lady is not on trial. Even if she were lying to keep her husband out of jail to feed the kids, isn't that forgivable? What is unforgivable is for you to embarrass the poor lady by pointing out something that everybody knows, and everybody but you, understands. The jurors will not believe her, but they will forgive her. They may not forgive you.

A more subtle attack on "who" is testifying is the examination of the bias inherent in the position in life occupied by the witness. While the attack on relationship tries to show the jurors that the witness may have a reason to shade the truth, the attack on bias inherent in the position in life tries to show that the witness may have trouble recognizing the truth that happened. Although this phenomenon can exist because of relationship (the lover who believes the average looking object of affection to be a "10") it is more common to find perception bias due to life experience. A medical doctor's description of the bloody scene of an accident, for example, is likely to differ from that of someone without medical training and experience. The perception of a seventy-five year old that "the car was speeding down the road in front of me," may differ drastically from a teenager's perception of the same vehicle's speed.

The most unfortunate attack on "who" is testifying is the use of a prior criminal record. Fed.R.Evid. 609, adopted in virtually every jurisdiction, maintains the belief that a witness convicted of the felony of possessing of a small amount of an illegal drug is less likely to tell the truth than a witness who was kicked out of a card club for cheating. If the opponent's witness has a criminal record that falls within Fed.R.Evid. 609, you must use it to impeach the witness' credibility. It may not seem fair to you, but you are not paid for making that judgment. The legislature or the Supreme Court of the jurisdiction was paid for that wisdom and you must take advantage of it unless you believe there will be juror backlash due to the remote nature of the crime and the otherwise pleasant personality of the witness.

There is another area for cross examination that does not fit neatly into attacking "who" is testifying or "what" they are testifying about. This type of cross examination seeks to make a theater demonstration, rather than attack a particular witness or challenge particular testimony. This tool is probably beyond anything that you should do in a first trial, but an awareness of the possibility will sharpen your cross examination eye.

There are certain witnesses and situations that are too well rehearsed or staged. The successful cross examination shows the staging or the rehearsal to the jurors. A common example is the two law enforcement partners that made a DUI arrest six months before trial. At the time of trial, neither one remembers the incident for the hundred others that have occurred in the interim, but both have read the report they wrote at the time. Occasionally they will come into court and attempt to look extra credible by testifying from "memory" rather than using the report to refresh recollection. If you have invoked the rule to exclude witnesses, there may be profit in cross examining each witness with the exact same questions about details of the activity of the defendant when arrested. You are likely to find that each policeman makes the exact same response. The car pulled over and parked "three feet" from the curb—not two or four, but three. The man "staggered" as he got out of the door—not stumbled, unsteady, or unsure, but staggered. He "reeked" of alcohol—not smelled, or stunk, or had the odor of, but reeked. If done with the proper skill, and assuming that the defendant will testify clearly to contrary facts, you might persuade the jurors that the police had no recollection of what happened and that the exact duplication of the testimony suggests that they rehearsed together. The pat preparation cross examination is among the most subtle. Do not try it in your first trial, but listen to see if your opponent's witnesses sound overly prepared. Fed.R.Evid. 612 allows the court to let you see the documents from which the witnesses prepared, even if they would not be otherwise available to you.

Another common staging problem involves the witness who appears on the witness stand to be something very different from what the witness' background suggests. The classic example is the drug culture, marijuana possession defendant that shows up in court with a three piece Brooks Brothers suit and hair cut just above the ears. You are not likely to get a shot at him if he is just a prop at the counsel table. But if he takes the stand to testify, you will have a rare opportunity.

Q: When you met Agent Kelly in the bar, you were wearing an old ripped pair of blue jeans, weren't you?

A: Yes.

Q: Your hair was down below your shoulders the night he arrested you, isn't that right?

A: Yes.

Q: You hadn't shaved for a week or more when you first met Agent Kelly, isn't that true, Mr. Thomas?

A: Yes.

Q: When you met him, you introduced yourself
    as "el Dopo," didn't you?

A: Yes.

A more subtle example of the same phenomenon
is the workman who is describing how he laid sewer
pipe, in terms that would sound pompous for a
college professor. The best cross examination may
be the one that encourages the pomposity. In both
of these situations if you have a video-taped deposition, photos or other tapes of the witness in their
"original" pre-trial state, it can make for a great
"before and after". You may be able to capture the
angry or sarcastic witness, or the witness who
couldn't remember anything but who has been
cleaned up for trial. Whatever the circumstance it
can be worth the effort if you have a way to let the
jurors compare the "before and after".

Every party to a lawsuit has some evidence that it
would prefer to forget about. In some cases, cross
examination can demonstrate that the other party
is trying to hide something. Jurors like to have all
the facts before them and the suggestion that one
side is hiding something does not sit well. The
advantage to bringing out the matter on cross examination is not the information itself, but rather,
the jurors' belief that the other side did not want to
produce it and may have even more it is hiding. In
some cases, the point can be made very subtly by
asking about evidence the other side does not really
care about, but neglected to offer because it did not
seem to be meaningful. If raised properly on cross

examination, the evidence can appear more meaningful than it is, just because the other side did not
raise it and you did. Like the pat preparation and
inconsistent appearance situations, the implication
that the other side is hiding something must be
done with a light and subtle hand. In some circumstances the lawyer may be outraged during the
cross examination, but the outrage must be justified. Outrage will work only when the other side
has failed to produce a piece of testimony that is
particularly relevant. When, for example, the direct
examiner does not disclose the defendant's prior
criminal record during direct examination and the
priors are similar to the crime charged.

Q: Mr. Culprit, did you tell the jurors the truth
on direct examination?

A: Yes.

Q: And you told them the whole truth, did you?

A: Yes.

Q: You told them everything that you thought
they ought to know?

A: Yes.

Q: I do not remember hearing you tell the jury
about being twice convicted before of burglary and armed robbery; didn't you think that
was something the jurors might want to
know?

A: (Probably silence.)

Q: You were twice before convicted of burglary
     and armed robbery, weren't you, Mr. Cul-
     prit?

A: (Wait until the witness says) Yes.

If the jurors are outraged by the failure of the
witness to tell about the convictions, you can be
outraged by the failure and maybe even engage in
some mild sarcasm or disdain. On the other hand, if
the evidence is only ambivalent, you cannot press
the idea that the other side is hiding something.
You can make the same point more subtly. Given no
other consideration, most of us believe that the
person who brings something up does so because it
is helpful to that person's position. Conversely, if
someone does not bring something up, and an opponent does, we assume, without more, that the first
person did not raise it because it hurt. A common
example is the physical measurements at an accident scene. More often than not, the physical measurements are ambivalent, and will support either
side. Often, there is much better evidence of liability and the ambiguous measurements may be ignored by the plaintiff. Under the right circumstances, and with a closing argument to be made
based on the measurements, the defense might
make some mileage by cross examining on the
measurements with the appropriate witness. There
is never any suggestion that the other side is hiding
something; it is not needed. The closing argument
that uses the measurements, combined with the
fact that they were brought out on cross examination of the plaintiff's witness rather than on direct,

will tell the jurors that the measurements must help the defense and, therefore, the argument based on them must be right.

The last of the "theater" cross examination examples is perhaps the most subtle, and therefore, the most dangerous. Many witnesses are just plain unpleasant. For whatever reason, some witnesses are so belligerent, or squirmy, or subject to sweating and hand wringing, or some other unpleasant characteristic, that the jurors just do not like them. Your opponent, however, may have no choice but to put such a witness on the stand. Your cross examination of the witness may not be aimed at any particular substantive goal, but may exist merely to give the jurors more exposure to the witness' most unpleasant characteristics. Of course, if you guess wrong about how the jurors are reacting to the witness, you lose. If you cannot ask the right questions on cross examination to highlight the unpleasant characteristic, you allow the witness to tell the direct testimony to the jurors a second time. You might save this subtle cross examination for a trial other than your first.

The last area for cross examination is different because it is not aimed at diminishing the opponent's evidence pile, but rather, at adding to your own. Not all cross examination must be confrontational. Some witnesses called by the other side will be friendly to your client. Others, although not particularly friendly, may have information helpful to your case. Many beginning lawyers become so wound up in the adversarial cross examination that they forget to put in their own case through cross examination when the opportunity presents itself. Even if the matter is not covered on direct examination, you can ask about it on cross. If the court is strict on the scope of direct rule, offer to take the witness on direct, as permitted by Fed.R.Evid. 611 for the limited matter that the witness can offer for your case. Cross examination where the witness has something substantive to offer for your case is not uncommon. In some cases the witness will be a little hostile, and you will lead in order to control the answer:

Q: When you saw the red Ford it was not going more than ten miles per hour was it?

A: No, it wasn't.

In other situations, the witness will be essentially neutral and you can go for the persuasive benefit of having the witness tell the jurors how fast the red Ford was going, rather than having them hear it from the lawyer, who, after all, was not there:

Q: How fast was the red Ford going when you saw it?

A: Not more than ten miles per hour.

Another example of allowing the witness to testify freely on cross examination is the situation in which the witness' testimony can be defeated by other testimony, or by some rule of common sense. When such a witness has testified on direct, and you have another witness, other evidence, or irrefutable logic to defeat the assertion, the best thing

that you can do with cross examination is to have
the witness repeat and highlight the assertion to be
destroyed. You do not attack the witness; you encourage. The whole purpose of repeating the direct
testimony, usually a terrible idea, is to enhance the
theater of the later destruction of the witness. It
follows that you must have the evidence to defeat
the assertion, and that the evidence you have will
be naturally more persuasive to the jurors. The only
reason you have the witness repeat the testimony is
to nail down its exact contours, and to highlight it
for the jurors so that in closing argument you can
say:

> "Remember on cross examination that I asked
> Mr. Phillip only one question. I asked him if the
> reason he could see the man in the car was
> because there was a big full moon that night. You
> will remember that he said, 'that's right.' As I
> recall he even went to some lengths to describe
> how the moon looked and that the sky was clear,
> with just a 'wisp or two of cloud' occasionally
> crossing it. Remember Mr. Oliver from the Na-
> tional Weather Bureau who testified that there
> was a new moon on the night Mr. Phillip claims
> to have seen my client in the car, and that it was
> heavily overcast besides."

You can make the same argument from Phillip's
direct testimony about the moon, among all the
other facts he relates on direct, but it will not have
as much impact as when you set it up by repetition
on cross examination. This particular version of
"the bigger they are, the harder they fall," only
works when you have the witness dead-to-rights. Be

careful about having the witness repeat something that seems to you to be improbable on the assumption that it will seem improbable to the jurors as well. It rarely works that way. Never set the witness' testimony up tall before the jurors on cross examination unless you are certain that you can knock it down.

There are additional cross examination goals and types of cross examination. The possibilities for cross examination are endless, and this listing of possibilities is like any other list, it is useful only as a stimulus to think about your specific cross examination. It is the thinking not the list that will make a successful cross examination.

When the direct examination is concluded, it is time for you to execute the goals you have established for cross examination. Many of the rules and techniques for executing the cross examination have already been discussed within the context of maintaining control and executing a "safe" cross examination so that the worst you get is a tie. The general admonitions not to explore too many areas on cross, even if they are available, not to try for too big a victory, and not to argue with the witness are the foundation for executing the cross examination. Adherence to the safety-control rules means that a well executed cross examination is one in which the lawyer "testifies" or "puts words in the witness' mouth" through declarative questions, and the witness just agrees or disagrees. You should not vary that technique without a reason.

There are instances when you will have a reason and will not want to lead on cross examination. A number of them such as the pat preparation exceptions have been alluded to already. Although most of those exceptions to the leading rule are for cross examiners of great experience and skill, there are times when you will not want to lead during your first cross examination.

The reason will always be related to the fact that you do not have a need to control the answer by the form of the question. Usually, it will be because you can identify a specific device, other than the leading question, that provides the control that you need. In some instances it will be that the witness just testified to the matter on direct, and there is no reason that the witness would want to change the statement on cross. Control may be lessened when the testimony relates to a prior out-of-court statement that the witness is unlikely to repudiate or to a matter where irrefutable extrinsic evidence exists. Most often, control is forsaken because the question does not ask about something in controversy.

Before you decide that you have found a reason not to ask leading questions on cross examination, be sure that it does not involve something in controversy. You may have a prior out-of-court statement by the witness, but that does not necessarily mean the witness will not repudiate it. If the matter is in controversy, the chance that the witness will repudiate the prior statement in one way or another is great. Similarly, if it is something that the witness just said during direct, even if it is in controversy, there is a chance that, after reflection, it will be repudiated on cross. Be very hesitant about making the judgment that you have a reason not to lead on cross. Unless you believe that value will be added to your case by allowing the witness to testify without leading, continue to lead. It is the failure of experience that makes the beginner's judgment suspect, and accounts for the safety-control rules in the first place. Once you let go of the leash it may be hard to get the witness back on it. It might be better to work on softening the tone of your leading in your first few trials than letting the witness take the spotlight.

One reason to avoid leading continually during a cross examination is that it is boring to the jurors. Although there are times when a pattern of leading questions is useful to mesmerize a witness, the pattern over an entire cross examination is likely to put the jurors to sleep. Vary your cross examination with non-leading questions that call for a specific response. This technique has the advantage of changing the pace and the tone, while still allowing the examiner to maintain a fair amount of control. "What color was the car?" does not invite the witness to explain or narrate, but does allow the witness to say something other than "yes" or "no." Be certain, however, to revert to leading questions when the answer matters. When the answer matters, put it in the leading question and the let the witness agree:

Q: Where were you standing when the accident happened?

A: On the sidewalk near the corner.

Q: What were you doing?

A: Waiting to cross the street.

Q: You were standing right here (pointing to diagram) next to a large elm tree, weren't you?

A: Yes.

Q: Was there anybody else standing with you on the sidewalk?

A: No.

Q: There were other people around the intersection and in the area, weren't there?

A: Yes.

Q: How long were you standing there before you heard the accident?

A: I'm not sure.

Q: It wasn't more than a few seconds was it?

A: No.

Q: How long did you stay after you heard the accident?

A: Not very long.

Q: Do you have any idea?

A: No, except that I left as soon as I could tell that nobody was hurt.

Q: You saw the police officer arrive, didn't you?

A: Yes.

Notice that on every issue that matters to the cross examiner, the question to the witness is leading, declares the answer, and only leaves it to the witness to agree. The questions that help show the whole picture, but are not critical are asked in an open form to give the examination some variety.

Occasionally, you will have a question to ask for its own sake; and you do not care what the answer is. It is usually a question of accusation, which is a risky and argumentative approach to cross examination under most circumstances. Such a question is usually the last question in a cross examination, and the examiner is almost back in his chair by the time the witness gets an opportunity to respond. This kind of a question, if used sparingly, is an exception to the rule that you do not make points on cross, you make them in closing. The classic example of this kind of a question is the prosecutor's accusation at the end of the cross examination of the murder defendant who testified in his own behalf:

Q: And then you killed her, didn't you?

The response, of course, is irrelevant. In the right circumstances, that final question need not be leading for the theater to be effective. If, for example, the cross examiner has asked leading questions that suggest the defendant's motive for murder, the prosecutor might finish by asking the non-leading, "Why did you kill her?, and sitting down before the defendant can begin the denial. Before you decide to ask an accusatorial question for its own sake, be certain that you have the foundation for it in the rest of the cross, the timing to make that kind of drama work, and the chutzpah to pull it off.

Attitude and timing are the foundation for executing the theater of cross examination. Because the real force of cross examination is in the theater of defeat, rather than in the substance of the answers, failures of attitude and timing can make a cross examination that looks perfect in transcript, fail miserably in the courtroom.

Attitude in cross examination gets perilously close to style, a subject beyond the scope of this primer. Nevertheless, there are some rules that are so universal and some corresponding mistakes that are so common that you should learn the rules and avoid the mistakes.

Cross is what you do, not what you are. There are times when the cross examiner's righteous indignation is appropriate. There are even times when the cross examiner can demonstrate a small amount of disdain for the witness, but both situations are so rare that the beginner should not be concerned with them. If the situation arises, the lawyer's indignation or disdain will probably add nothing to that of the jurors' because the cause of the reaction will be obvious. The great danger is that many beginners believe that unless they appear tough and mean and sneering and doubting they cannot cross examine. It is almost always the wrong posture and it almost always gets the cross examiner into hot water. The jurors do not empathize with the lawyer; they empathize with the witness: "There but for the grace of God, go I." It is alright to defeat the witness on cross examination, but it is rarely alright to be mean about it. If possible, your attitude during cross examination ought to reflect that you think the witness is mistaken, rather than that you think the witness is a liar. You should not use the word lie in a courtroom, lying connotes perjury and judges are quick to admonish lawyers about accusing a witness of lying under oath. Similarly, it is better for your attitude to reflect that the witness is wrong rather than foolish. Even with the most unlikable, lying, unreasonable, s.o.b., be careful to avoid overkill. You do not need to beat up a witness so badly that the witness gains the sympathy of the jurors—even if the witness deserves the beating. It is good to be unfair during cross examination by asking questions that naturally deny the witness an opportunity to explain, but it is never useful to appear to be unfair.

The witness expects the cross examiner to be an enemy. After all, witnesses have seen as many courtroom movies and TV shows as lawyers have. Many lawyers go out of their way to begin a cross examination by trying to disarm the witness' apprehension. Whether this is useful for your personality or will make the particular witness less wary, is a matter you must answer for yourself at the time. If, however, you decide to proceed in that fashion, do it with the questions. A smiling face and a soothing voice will not disarm a witness to whom you have asked a confrontational cross examination question.

Beginning the cross examination by asking the witness about matters the witness testified to, and with which you have no quarrel, may lessen the witness' apprehension. This exercise is a combination of attitude and timing. If you are going to spar with the witness eventually, the timing of the questions, easy ones first, tough ones second, will be more effective than the soothing demeanor approach. Among other things, if you begin with an overly cordial or soothing demeanor, it is difficult to change it without looking like a phony to the jurors.

The major timing error for beginning cross examiners is the desire to bring the hammer down on the witness too early. Knowing that the witness has left an opening on direct examination, the lawyer cannot wait to jump into the breach and hammer the witness with the omission, the contradiction, or whatever it is the lawyer discovered. The problem is that the jurors do not know all about the case. They do not know that there is an omission, or a contradiction, or whatever it is the lawyer discovered. When the lawyer jumps right in with the hammer, the jurors do not understand what happened. Worse, when the lawyer jumps in early with the hammer, it is likely to be the lawyer's thumb that gets hit when the witness understands what is happening and moves.

Proper timing of cross examination requires that the lawyer clamp down the witness' position before hammering. If the witness' position is not tightly clamped down, the witness will wiggle out of the way when the lawyer begins to swing the hammer.

When the witness wiggles, the lawyer misses. Take as an example, the witness who identifies the defendant as the person sitting in the car at night, and who, in addition, testifies that the moon was full. You, the cross examiner, have your expert ready to show that there was a new moon that night. You think the witness saw a car, saw somebody in it, and has become convinced that the defendant the prosecutor charged with the crime is the person the witness saw—a case of honest self-delusion. Your final questions to the witness are going to be:

Q: You were able to see the man in the car clearly because of the moon, is that right?

A: That's right.

Q: There was no other light source, was there?

A: No.

The chances are that if you ask the witness, "You were able to see the man in the car clearly because of the moon, is that right?" at the beginning of the cross examination you will not get the "that's right" answer. The question signals where you are going and the witness will see the hammer coming. Being committed to the person in the car was the defendant and surmising from the question that the moon might not have been so bright, it's time to hedge:

A: Well, the moon made it a little easier.

What answer are you likely to get if now you ask about another light source?

If you decide that the direct testimony about the full moon was not significant enough for the jurors to conclude that it was by the light of the moon alone that the witness saw the defendant, you must try to clamp that testimony down on cross:

Q: Mr. Peepers, what time was it when you saw the car on the street?

A: About 11:00 p. m.

Q: Where were you when you saw the car?

A: Standing on the porch in the front of my house.

Q: You never left the porch, did you?

A: No.

Q: The car was parked to the east of your porch as I understand it?

A: That's right.

Q: Were you on the east end of your porch as you saw the car?

A: Yes.

Q: During the time that you were able to see the car, did it move?

A: No.

Q: Did the car have its lights on?

A: No.

Q: How about the lights inside the car?

A: No. They weren't on, either.

Q: None of the houses on the street had their porch lights on, did they?

A: No.

Q: Did you see anybody else out on the street or sidewalk while the car was there?

A: No.

Q: Were you out on the porch reading?

A: Yes.

Q: Does your porch have an overhead light?

A: No. I had the lamp on next to the chair I was sitting in.

Q: That is a screen porch, is that right, Mr. Peepers?

A: Yes.

Q: Your house is near the middle of the block, isn't it?

A: Yes.

Q: The car was parked in front of the house that is right in the middle of the block, wasn't it?

A: Yes.

Q: Are there street lights in your neighborhood, Mr. Peepers?

A: Yes. They have one at each intersection.

Q: Those are suspended over the middle of the intersection to allow traffic to see at the intersection, aren't they?

A: I think so. (Never settle for an answer that leaves an out.)

Q: They are in the middle of the intersection aren't they?

Q: Those lights aren't much help for seeing things in the middle of the block, are they?

A: Not really, they are there to light up the intersection.

Q: Those lights didn't really throw enough light into the middle of the block to allow you to see the man in the car, did they?

A: I saw him clear as could be. There was a full moon.

Q: Oh. Well, the lights would not have helped without the moon, would they?

A: No.

Q: You were able to see the man in the car clearly because of the moon, is that right?

A: That's right.

Q: There was no other light source, was there?

A: No.

Although it takes some time, the care to pin down the witness' physical position, the alternate light sources, and the position of the vehicle will pay dividends. If you start with the question about the moon, you will find that every house on the block had lights on, the dome light in the car was on, there are street lights every twenty feet, there was no counter-light on in the porch, and, by the way,

"I think the moon was bright." Before you say to yourself, "I do not have to worry about clamping the witness down piece by piece before the witness knows where I am going, because the witness would not lie," consider the witness' choices. The witness is convinced that the defendant is the person in the car, and it is an honest, although erroneous, conclusion. The witness has already sworn under oath that the defendant was in the car. If you stood up and said to the witness, "I can prove that the moon was just new, and clouded over that night," would you expect the witness to respond: "Oh, I must not have been able to see the person's face?" A more likely response, consistent with the witness' honesty, but also consistent with the mistake, is: "I sure did see his face clear as I can see it now; must have been the dome light in the car, or the porch light from the house next door. I wasn't really paying attention to why there was light, I just noticed a person sitting out there alone in a parked car in my neighborhood."

"You were able to see the man in the car clearly because of the moon, is that right?" is as likely to alert the witness as much as if you had stood up and said: "There was no moon." It is the warning that starts the man's rationalization process. If you start the examination without the warning and clamp down the testimony piece by piece it will not alert the witness, even though it is clear to you where you are going. If you have some doubt, go back and reread the interrogation, and say to yourself as you read the first question about time, and subsequent questions, that you have not been warned yet that lighting is the issue. The honest witness will not have the rationalization system plugged into the lighting problem until half way through the examination—if then—and will still be comfortable with the moon as the lighting that allowed the identification. By the time you get to the reason for sufficient lighting, the witness will be locked into the moon because other sources have been eliminated. Remember, locking the witness in is not difficult so long as the witness does not receive a subtle alert. Timing is the difference between success and failure.

The most common timing rule among cross examiners is the rule that you should finish with a flourish. A cross examination that ends with a good answer from the witness is deadly for the cross examiner. Even if you did substantive damage on cross, you will be perceived as "dying in the dust" if the witness makes a good answer on the last question. A cross examination that ends with a nothing question and a nothing answer is not much better for the lawyer. The last question is the last shot. Make sure the witness is "dying in the dust," at least on the last question.

Failure to understand the importance of timing and attitude must account for one of the most common mistakes made by beginning lawyers. They cannot resist nit-picking. Given two major areas of witness vulnerability and fifteen small mistakes, the beginning cross examiner will use up seventeen minutes, one minute for each area or mistake. The equal treatment of the major areas and the nits to be picked tells the jurors the major areas are not major. The nit-picking makes the entire cross examination seem "picky." The nit-picking ruins the rhythm, destroys the emphasis, and resurrects an otherwise losing witness.

In the identification example, assume the arrest was at 10:45 (not 11:00) and that the witness has made an earlier statement that says the house next door is really one down from the middle of the block (not the middle); and the street lights are on the far corner and reach out from a one piece pole (not suspended over the middle of the intersection). Should you cross examine on the differences between the answers to your clamp down examination and the earlier statement? Just because the testimony is wrong in many particulars does not mean it should be subject to cross examination. The only time that you can afford to pick at a witness is when there is nothing else that you can do with the witness, and the accumulation of the nits picked might raise a doubt in the jurors' mind about the witness' ability to observe. The occasion almost never occurs. Do not diminish the theater of a good cross examination by nit-picking.

Impeachment by Prior Inconsistent Statement

The importance of timing, pace, clamping down the witness' testimony first, and all of the other theater propositions about cross examination are exemplified by the technique of impeachment with a prior inconsistent statement. No cross examination is more dramatic, more confrontational, or more important. If you can successfully impeach a witness' direct testimony with a prior inconsistent statement, you are as close to a "killing" cross examination as you are likely to get. It is a cross examination in which the jurors can see the witness fall down and "die in the dust."

The first requirement for a successful impeachment by prior statement is testimony on direct examination that can be impeached. Although that may seem definitional, many beginning lawyers, armed with a prior statement that contains an error try to point out that error even though the witness does not repeat it testifying on direct. The only statement that can be impeached is a statement that the witness makes from the witness stand. This is why listening is such an important skill. If the witness doesn't say it on direct, there is nothing to impeach. Further, if the statement is not made on direct examination, it cannot usually be elicited on cross examination, and then impeached.

The second requirement for a successful impeachment is an impeaching vehicle that can be offered into evidence if the substance of it is denied by the witness. This is usually a deposition, a signed statement, a report, or some other similar writing. It can, however, be an oral conversation so long as there is a witness that heard the conversation and can repeat it if necessary. Before beginning an impeachment, it is important to review the evidence lore with respect to collateral matters. There is a big difference between statements or facts upon which you can cross examine and facts and statements you can use to impeach a witness. If a fact or statement is considered "collateral" you may ask a cross examination question, but you will be stuck with the answer you get from the witness, even if you have contrary extrinsic evidence.

If you have a statement on direct that is contrary to a statement in an impeaching vehicle, and it is about something that matters in the lawsuit (not collateral,) you are on the threshold of the most dramatic presentation in a lawsuit. Be sure your statement fits both criteria. It must be inconsistent; not sort of or kind of. The impeachment does not work unless the jurors believe that what the witness said on direct examination is inconsistent with what is said in the impeaching vehicle. It also has to be about something that matters in the lawsuit. Impeachment on personal or collateral matters looks like bullying to the juror. Don't use the full scale impeachment if you just need to correct someone's testimony.

The power and importance of impeachment is in the drama. The substance of the impeachment, if you get it in, may be of interest to an appellate court someday, but it is the theater of the impeachment that matters with the jurors. It is the ultimate shoot out. If the jurors cannot see the witness clearly die in the dust, you have wasted your time and thrown away a great opportunity.

You must start the impeachment by doing something that is usually the cross examiner's worst mistake; you must have the witness repeat the part of the direct examination you intend to impeach. You cannot have a successful impeachment unless just before the hammer hits, the witness appears to the jurors to be really driving home, again, the best part of the direct examination. If the witness was quite definite on direct examination, you may be able to elicit the story by asking the kind of question that you would ask on direct. On the other hand, if you are not at all sure that the witness will repeat the testimony, you will have to lead. The in court identification of a criminal defendant is the kind of statement that, if impeachable, can be left to the witness to repeat on cross. A misstatement on direct in a description of what the man was wearing at the time of the robbery may require the cross examiner to lead to insure that the same testimony that was heard on direct is set up on cross to be impeached.

Assume that a witness testifies to seeing your client robbing the store, that the robber was about six feet tall, had short brown hair, was wearing blue jeans and a green sweatshirt, jogging shoes, and had a three or four day growth of hair on his face. Further, that the witness got a good look at the robber as he ran past and out the door. His face was round, he wore glasses, his eyes were small and blue, and he had a small scar on his cheek. The description fits your client, and the clothing is like clothing he owns. Your client appears in court clean shaven and in a suit. You wish to impeach the witness' detailed description by contrasting it with an equally detailed description the witness made in a statement that places the scar on the chin, and talks about the beginnings of a moustache.

Not only must you first clamp down the testimony to be impeached, you must be certain that there is an inconsistency. Lead the witness:

Q: Mr. Sawem, it sounds as if you got quite a good look at the man that was robbing the store?

A: I sure did.

Q: When he ran past you, he looked right at you, didn't he?

A: Yes.

Q: And you looked right at him?

A: Yes sir.

Q: Did you get a very good look at him?

A: Yes.

Q: He had glasses on, didn't he?

A: Yes.

Q: You could, nevertheless, see that his eyes were small, couldn't you?

A: Yes.

Q: Did you say that they were blue?

A: Yes.

Q: He had a three or four day growth of beard, didn't he?

A: Yes. (If you get a no, and he goes back to moustache, it is time to bail out to another area of cross examination.)

Q: I take it that it was a dark beard covering most of his face?

A: Not all of it.

Q: Did it cover the lower portion of the cheeks, the chin, and just above and below the lips?

A: Yes.

Q: As I recall your testimony on direct, you said that he had a small, thin scar on his cheek. I gather you could see that above his beard line?

A: Oh yes.

Q: He did have a small, thin, scar?

A: Yes.

Q: It was on his cheek?

A: Yes.

Q: You could see it clearly above the beard line?

A: Yes.

Q: I gather it was just an inch or so below the left eye?

A: No, it was an inch or so below the right eye.

Of course, none of this testimony takes place unless the defendant has a small, thin scar about an inch below the right eye. Notice that the witness looks very good to the jury. He has again identified the man in the store in great detail, and the characteristics are close to those of the defendant. In addition, he even tripped up the lawyer trying to fool him on which eye the scar was under. If this were the end of the cross examination, your client would go directly to jail. If you are going to successfully impeach the witness' very complete description of your client by attacking the two errors out of eleven observations, you must set the witness up sure and tall, overemphasizing the importance of a couple of details which, if not impeached, will send the defendant directly to jail. If the witness does not look very good to the jurors at this point, the distance he falls when impeached will not be enough to make the witness a loser.

Because the witness feels like he is doing well, repeating everything that he said on direct examination without any problem from the cross examiner, you can afford to heighten the drama, and make it appear as if the identification hinges on the scar:

Q: You are absolutely sure that the man you saw in the store had a small, thin scar on his left—I'm sorry—on his right cheek just an inch or so under the eye?

The answer must be yes because it was yes on direct, yes on cross, and most importantly, because your defendant has that small thin scar on his right cheek. After you get the yes, give the witness one last chance to recant:

Q: You have no hesitancy at all about the scar?

A: No.

Q: You are sure you saw it just above the three or four day growth of beard that you testified you saw on the man as he looked right at you?

A: That's right.

Q: I take it that you are equally certain about the three or four day beard on the man's cheek, because it was right below the scar?

A: Yes.

You have now heightened the drama as much as you can afford. The testimony to be impeached could not be clearer. The jurors could not be more convinced that the defendant is guilty because he is the man with the scar that the witness saw.

The next step in the impeachment is most important, and usually the most difficult. You must accredit the impeaching vehicle. If you do not, and you attempt to bring the hammer down immediately, you will bloody your own finger, again. Timing is critical. If you ask, "Didn't you say earlier that the man you saw in the store had a moustache and a scar on his chin?", the answer is going to be "no." When you confront the witness with the impeaching vehicle, unaccredited, the witness will explain to you why it does not represent what he said.

Q: You told the police that he had a moustache and a scar on his chin, didn't you?

A: If that's what the paper says, it's wrong. That's not what I said and that statement isn't in my handwriting.

Q: Did you sign the statement you made to the police?

A: Sure, but I was told to sign what the man had typed, and I did—I never got an opportunity to read it.

You avoid this kind of disaster by accrediting the impeaching vehicle before you swing the hammer by asking about the contrary earlier statement. In fact, if you anticipate the inconsistency, as you might in this case, given the position of your client's scar, you might accredit the impeaching vehicle before letting the witness repeat the direct examination testimony that will be impeached. It is safer. If you cannot accredit the impeaching vehicle, you can abort the impeachment without the strong repetition of the direct examination. The usual order, however, is to set up the testimony to be impeached and then accredit the impeaching vehicle. It focuses the jurors' attention on the importance of the impeaching vehicle just before you use it as a hammer with which to hit the witness.

If you have a strong impeaching vehicle, you must proceed to show the jurors why the impeaching vehicle is entitled to more credit than the in-court testimony that they have just heard from the witness on direct and again on cross. If, on the other hand, your impeaching vehicle is not strong, you might well decide at the outset to forego the impeachment. A conversation with a friend, overheard by another friend, is not very strong; the impeaching testimony of the overhearing friend will not be worth much. The friend might have heard wrong or remembered wrong. The witness might have been in a passing conversation and not been particularly concerned about the accuracy of what was said. If, on the other hand, the impeaching vehicle is a statement that the witness gave under oath to the police, knowing that the police were going to radio the description out to other police officers so that they could apprehend the robber when they spotted him, the impeaching vehicle may be entitled to more weight than the in-court testimony. Both are under oath. The first statement is not only closer in time to the event, it was for the purpose of finding a dangerous man who was loose on the streets. You must lead through the accrediting of the impeaching vehicle, and not proceed to the hammer questions until the witness has acknowledged the importance of the impeaching vehicle:

Q: Mr. Sawem, you spoke to the first police officer on the scene, didn't you?

A: Yes.

Q: The officer asked if you got a look at the man who robbed the store?

A: Yes.

Q: You gave as complete a description as you could, isn't that right?

A: Yes, sir.

Q: Did the officer go to the squad car and radio the description you gave out to other officers?

A: The officer took me out to the car, and had me stand there while the description went out over the radio.

Q: You knew when the officer first talked to you that your description would be used to try and catch the man who robbed the store?

A: Yes, I sure did.

Q: You went back to the police station with the officer didn't you?

A: Yes.

Q: Did the officer have you repeat everything you saw to a stenographer who took it all down?

A: Yes.

Q: You told the stenographer the same thing that you told the officer, didn't you?

A: Yes.

Q: Before taking your statement, did the stenographer put you under oath?

A: No sir.

Q: Did you tell the truth in that statement?

A: Of course.

Q: You came back to the station the next day to sign a typed copy of the statement, didn't you?

A: Yes.

Q: You had to travel quite a distance from your home to the police station just to sign that statement, didn't you?

A: Yes. Sure did.

Q: When you got to the station you were given the statement, weren't you?

A: Yes.

Q: It was the same officer you talked to the night before in the store, isn't that right?

A: Yes.

Q: You were told by the officer to read the statement and check it over, weren't you?

A: Yes.

Q: Of course, you did as you were asked?

A: Yes.

Q: After you read the statement over carefully, you notified the officer, didn't you?

A: Yes.

Q: Did the officer have you take an oath and then sign the statement?

A: Yes.

Q: And this was done before someone who notarized the statement, wasn't it?

A: Yes.

The next step depends upon whether you want to confront the witness with the statement, or impeach without allowing the witness to look at it. Fed.R.Evid. 613 has changed the long standing rule that you could not hammer a witness with a statement until the witness first had an opportunity to look at it—presumably so the witness could duck. The rule allows you to impeach the witness without showing the document to the witness.

If the document contains a flat contradiction, as this one appears to, you might wish to ignore the advantage that Fed.R.Evid. 613 provides. Although it is easier to impeach a witness who is not looking at the impeaching vehicle, it does not seem quite as fair to the jurors, especially if it comes out of a deposition the size of a phone book. Further, there is more drama in the hammering if you can do it while the witness is forced to look at the document with which you are hammering. When the contradiction is flat, there is nothing the witness can do by looking at the document. The jurors will realize you are not "taking advantage" of the witness.

When the impeachment is by an omission in the document, or by a difference in context in the document, then there is good reason to take advantage of Fed.R.Evid. 613, and impeach the witness before the witness has an opportunity to review the document and explain why there is an omission, or why your view of the context is wrong.

If you decide to confront the witness with the document, it is the last step in the accrediting of the impeaching vehicle:

Q: Mr. Sawem, I am handing you a document that purports to be a statement. Is that your signature on the bottom? (In some jurisdictions you must mark the document you refer to even if you have no intention of offering it. If you are not required to have it marked, don't. Save the marking for the time when you must offer it.)

A: Yes.

Q: Is that document the statement that you gave to the stenographer, read over the next day, and then signed under oath?

A: Yes.

Q: Does it say the same thing now that it said when you signed it?

A: Yes.

Q: And when you signed it, it said the same thing that you said to the stenographer the night before?

A: Yes.

Q: You told the stenographer the same thing that you told the officer on the scene, didn't you?

A: Yes.

Q: So this statement contains the same description of the man who looked at you as you gave to the officer to radio out to other officers, doesn't it?

A: Yes, it must. (Do not allow room to wiggle, clamp the witness down.)

Q: It does contain the same description as you gave the officer, doesn't it?

A: Yes.

The testimony to be impeached is now before the jurors, and you have just given them reason to think that the original statement was made under conditions in which it was unlikely the witness would lie or be mistaken. It is time to swing the hammer.

The impeaching question will be based on the impeaching vehicle. Regardless of your choice under Fed.R.Evid. 613, to let the witness see the impeaching vehicle as you swing the hammer, or to keep it to yourself, you may eventually have to confront the witness with the impeaching statement. Nothing kills the high drama of a good impeachment faster than a thirty second pause while the lawyer gropes through the impeaching vehicle looking for the impeaching words. You cannot successfully swing the hammer unless you know where it is. Although you can often have it ready before you begin cross examination that is not always the case. You must have an impeaching vehicle such as a deposition well indexed. Similarly, you should have the contradictory statement, impeaching letter, or any other smaller document close at hand so that impeachment takes place on schedule.

The hammer question must be effective, or the work of setting up the testimony and accrediting the impeaching vehicle will go for naught. There are many different approaches to swinging the hammer, all of which depend upon the particular sense of drama of the impeaching lawyer. Some experienced cross examiners, with unique styles and heightened sense of what is going on about them, can break most of the rules for swinging the last blow with the hammer and still make the impeachment work. Beginners cannot. In fact, most cross examiners cannot.

As you are poised to swing the hammer on the witness, maintain a reasonable attitude. If you smirk, or show any characteristics of "going for the kill," you are likely to anger the jurors. Generally, the lawyer who kills the witness with regret does better than the lawyer who kills with glee. Just get to the killing, don't brag about it.

The safest way to insure a good clean impeachment is to use the exact words of the impeaching vehicle in the hammer question. How easy it will be to do depends upon the strength of the impeachment. Obviously, it is easier to impeach with a flat contradiction than it is to impeach by an omission. Similarly, an omission of something important in a statement is an easier impeachment than one that depends upon interpretation and context of a statement. The more general the impeaching language, the more difficult it is to impeach. To be sure, the initial decision to impeach will be influenced by how sharply drawn is the contradiction. The fuzzier the contradiction, the more critical the impeachment must be before it justifies the risk that the final hammer blow will not hit squarely on the mark. Here there is a flat contradiction on the scar and the three day growth. There is not, however, a flat contradiction on the real issue of impeachment, the identification. The statement contains many physical characteristics that are correct and there is other evidence that the apparel portion of the identification was accurate. Nevertheless, the contradiction is obvious enough so that you can quote the impeaching vehicle exactly. The last question in accrediting the impeaching vehicle established that the witness made the same identification to the officer as he made in the statement that he has been shown. (Note: In this case, showing the statement to the witness for identification was important. If, however, the witness still had the statement in front of him while answering the last accrediting question, you might not get the same answer. You might get an argument.)

Q: (The last accrediting question): It does contain the same description as you gave the officer, doesn't it?

A: Yes.

Q: In the statement that you gave to the police you said the man had a scar on his chin and the beginnings of a moustache, didn't you?

If he did not know he was going to get hammered with the statement before—and you might be surprised at how often that happens when lawyers do not properly prepare their witnesses—he knows now. You may get the witness to answer the ham-

mer question, "Yes," or, "If that's what it says, I
guess so." It is much more likely, however, that the
witness will begin to wiggle and look for someplace
to go. Here are some answers you might get:

A: No, that is not what I told them.

or

A: If that is what the statement says, it is
     wrong. I told them that he had a scar on his
     right cheek.

or

A: I don't think so. I was pretty excited at the
     time, but I am sure that I told them the man
     had a scar on his cheek. In any event, he did.

There are a number of variations on the same
theme, but all constitute an attempt to avoid admitting the contradiction.

Now, you must use the document to hammer
another blow. There are two schools of thought on
how you ought to use the document. Many lawyers
believe that nothing plays so well as the witness
having to choke on his own words as he reads them.
Others believe that if the lawyer reads the impeaching language, the lawyer is free to give it the
emphasis that will provide the most drama and the
greatest effect on the jurors. There are local customs that restrict one or the other in various jurisdictions. If there is no such restriction, you should
make your judgment based on your own sense of
what will work. There are, however, some guides to
follow. The better the witness, the more likely you

are to seriously lose control if you let the witness read the impeaching language. On the other hand, the flatter the contradiction, the more likely that the witness cannot take control with the reading, and is likely to choke on the words. In this case, the safe way is to ask the court's permission to approach the witness, show him the document and do the reading yourself while he looks at the document. (Remember if you are going to read from a document, Fed.R.Evid. 1002 requires that it be produced into evidence.)

Q: Mr. Sawem, I'm handing you the document that you told us was the statement that you signed under oath, and that contained the same information that you gave to the officer on the scene. It has your signature on it, doesn't it?

A: Yes.

Q: That statement you made describes the man as having—I'm reading from right here (pointing), Mr. Sawem—"the beginnings of a moustache. Below that, on his chin, there was a small scar." That is what the statement says, isn't it Mr. Sawem?

A: Well, I . . .

Q: Excuse me, Mr. Sawem, is that what the statement says?

A: Yes.

Q: It says he had the beginnings of a moustache and a scar below it on his chin, isn't that right?

A: Yes.

It is now possible to display the impeaching vehicle to the jurors by using a document camera as you have the witness look or read. In later trials, you may even play the excerpt from the taped deposition so that the jurors can see and hear what the witness said earlier. Obviously you only want to go to such dramatic lengths if the witness and the statement warrant.

How many blows you can deliver with the hammer and how argumentative you can be depend upon the same factors as the judgment about whether you or the witness should read the impeaching language. The flatter the contradiction and the less skilled the witness the more that you can hammer, subject always to the danger that too much beating on a witness will create sympathy for the witness with the jurors. In this case, if you go further, the witness might get up out of the dust and beat you:

Q: So the description you gave the officer and that you repeated for the stenographer was different from the one that you told to the jurors here today.

A: Not really. It was the same man. He had the same look, the same glasses, the same eyes, the same hair. He even had the same expression on his face.

Q: Mr. Sawem, you told the police that the man who robbed the store had a scar on his chin, didn't you?

A: That's what it says there, but I don't think I
did. If I did, it was because I was excited.
Because that man there (indicating the defendant) is the man that ran by me in the
store after robbing the place.

Any question that poses to the witness the argument that you will make to the jury is going to give
the witness an opportunity to do something like the
example above. There is nothing that you can do to
stop the witness. The witness is cornered, everybody in the courtroom knows it, and nobody is
going to let you stop him from making his explanation because you invited it by striking gratuitous
blows with your hammer.

Every impeachment blow must be delivered with
precision to avoid allowing the witness to explain.
Assume that the statement to the police does not
say anything about facial hair of any kind, and does
not mention scars. When there is an omission in the
impeaching vehicle, there is a temptation to hand
the statement to the witness and say:

"Will you read for the ladies and gentlemen of
the jury where in this statement it says anything
about the man having a three day growth or a
small thin scar on his right cheek, just below the
eye?"

The problem with approaching the impeachment by
omission this way is that you hand control over to
the witness. When he begins an explanation, it will
be difficult for you to regain the control:

A: Do you want me to read in here where I described the defendant over there to the police? (Witness begins to read description that generally fits defendant.)

It is more precise to ask about the specific omission than to ask the witness to read something—even if the something is the specific omission. The question that allowed the witness to argue asked the witness to read; whereas, a question that asks about the omission gets a better result:

Q: This statement does not mention a three day growth does it? (If witness does not answer, let the jurors watch him read the statement, and give him all the time he needs. When he is finished, if he begins to form any word but "No," repeat the question and wait until the witness says, "No.")

Q: This statement does not mention a scar on the man's face, does it, Mr. Sawem?

A: No.

The hardest part of the impeachment for most lawyers is the sitting down part. Nothing is as heady as the successful impeachment. Nothing is as important as sitting down when it is finished. Chances are that the impeachment will be the end of the examination. It is hard to imagine a better ending. Once a witness is "dying in the dust," two bad things can happen if you try to hit the witness again: (1) the jurors will take pity on the witness and hate the bully, and (2) the witness will grab the hammer from your hand and beat you over the head with it. The problem is that the lawyer has a hard time exercising the judgment to stop doing the best thing the lawyer has done all day. The last important step in impeachment is to realize the usefulness of this paraphrase of that simple wisdom from a great baseball catcher, Yogi Berra: "It's over, when it's over."

Rehabilitating the Witness

The direct examiner has an opportunity to conduct a redirect examination to rehabilitate the witness. Most of the time there is no reason to conduct a redirect examination. Redirect is not an opportunity to repeat everything that was said on direct and it not an opportunity to give the direct examiner the last word, just for the sake of having the last word. Redirect is for rehabilitation.

The first rule for the redirect examiner is: "If it ain't broke, don't fix it." Most cross examinations end in a draw, with the witness' credibility intact, and the pile of evidence in about the same state as it was after the direct. The minute that you begin a redirect, you send a signal to the jurors that you believe some repair is needed for the witness' credibility or the substance of the testimony. If the jurors were not aware of a problem, your redirect is likely to start them wondering. Use your attitude to convey to the jurors that nothing happened to hurt you on cross. During the cross, if you were calm and neutral, your confident announcement of no redirect might be enough to make them wonder whether the cross examination accomplished anything.

The second rule for the redirect examiner is: "If you can't fix it, don't try." There will be times when the witness is in bad need of rehabilitation and there is no way to do it. The last thing you want to do is get up for redirect, fumble around accomplishing nothing, and then give the cross examiner a legitimate chance to take a couple more swings. The best thing to do with a witness that has "died in the dust" beyond resurrection, is to get the body off the stage quickly.

If you have a witness that has been wounded, but you have something to fix it with, you should proceed directly to the fixing. Redirect, like direct, requires preparation. If the prosecutor in the identification case has done the proper preparation the contradiction between what the witness says about a scar on the cheek and what the statement says about a scar on the chin and the moustache on the upper lip will be painfully apparent. Since the prosecutor cannot change the testimony, cannot change the scar, cannot change the statement, and cannot afford to drop the case while waiting around for a perfect one, the redirect will be prepared.

If there is a logical explanation for the difference between the statement and the testimony, the purpose of redirect is to get that reason before the jury. The best redirect question is usually some version of, "how come?" In some jurisdictions there is a custom that allows leading questions on redirect.

Although there is no clear rule reason for allowing the lawyer to lead the witness, the custom may be an unhappy admission that the lawyer did not prepare the witness well. All of the reasons for not leading on direct examination are extra-applicable on redirect. If the witness has really been wounded, only the witness can persuade the jurors that the wound drew no blood. Rehabilitation is not limited to impeachment by prior inconsistent statement. There may be any number of cross examination events that justify asking rehabilitative questions of a witness. The impeachment example, however, provides the most urgent need. As in the identification case, it may be that there is no particularly good explanation for the inconsistent statement. The rehabilitation, therefore, must focus on the validity of the identification in general, even if there was a small mistake or two. This approach shows the jurors that the identification as a whole has not been impeached:

Q: Mr. Sawem, how long were you in the store while the robber was in the store?

A: At least two or three minutes, maybe more.

Q: How far away from the robber were you when he was at the cash register?

A: About ten or fifteen feet.

Q: What was between you and the robber?

A: Nothing.

Q: Which way was the robber facing when he was at the cash register?

A: He was facing the back of the store. I could
      see the right side of him.

Q: What happened after he took the money?

A: He ran right by me and out the door.

Q: Did he go directly from the cash register to
      the door?

A: Yes.

Q: How close did he come to where you were
      standing?

A: He turned from the cash register and ran
      right toward me. He got within a couple of
      feet of me, brushed right past me, turned his
      head toward me as he went past, and then
      went out the door.

Q: Is the man that was in the store, that ran
      right toward you, and that looked at you as
      he ran out of the store in the courtroom?

A: Yes.

Q: Where is he?

A: Right there. (Pointing resolutely at the de-
      fendant.)

Q: Mr. Sawem, are you absolutely sure that the
      man you just pointed to, the defendant, is the
      man you saw in the store?

A: Yes. That's him.

If the impeachment had been by omission, the
redirect examiner might have added, or substituted,
an explanation of why the statement did not say
anything about a scar or facial hair:

Q: Did you tell the officer about the scar and the three day growth on the man who robbed the store?

A: I'm not sure if I did or not. Things happened so fast. I tried to tell the officer the things that I thought would help catch the guy. The scar was so small and at night the fact that he was not shaven would not help if he wasn't in the light. I might not have mentioned them to the officer, but I really can't say for sure.

Q: Why did you mention the scar and the three day growth here in court?

A: Well, you asked me to describe the man, and I wanted to be as complete as I could. I have had a lot of time to think about the face, and I am not likely to forget it. I thought I was supposed to tell you everything that I could remember.

Q: Does the description that you gave on direct examination fit anybody in this courtroom?

A: Yes. Except for the three day growth that is gone now, it fits that man over there. (Pointing resolutely to the defendant.)

If redirect is necessary to rehabilitate, make it as short and to the point as possible. The longer you go on rehabilitation, the more trouble you must have had to begin with. Know whether your jurisdiction allows for re-cross after your redirect. You certainly don't want to reopen the same can of worms if your opponent can cross again.

CHAPTER 10

THE LAWYER'S PART: EVIDENCE ADVOCACY

The lawyer's part during the presentation of evidence is best played if the lawyer has no lines to speak. The lawyer who makes no objections never looks to be hiding something. The lawyer who offers evidence without having to speak in justification of the attempt never looks to be trying to get away with something. Unfortunately, the lawyer rarely presents a play so well written that there is no need for the lawyer's part. There is always some evidence offered by the opponent that is so damaging and inadmissible that keeping it out is worth the jurors' perception that the lawyer is hiding something. There is always evidence so important, but questionably admissible, that getting it admitted is worth making a losing argument in front of the jury.

If you start with the premise that the lawyer should never speak any evidence lines in front of the jury, you will make judgments about evidence questions from the proper perspective. The general rules are as follows:

(1) Do not object unless the evidence is really damaging and you are likely to keep it out.

380

(2) Do not make an evidence argument in front of the jury.

(3) Do not lose an evidence argument in front of the jury.

The best technique for keeping the lawyer's lines to zero, without sacrificing the ability to deal with the evidence, is to handle as many of the evidence problems as possible before taking a single step onto the courtroom stage. There are two different pretrial opportunities to deal with evidentiary matters:

(1) Pretrial conferences and (2) motions *in limine*. Each method allows the lawyer to raise an objection to, or make an offer of, evidence and argue about it without a juror ever knowing anything about it.

The pretrial conference, if held in your jurisdiction, provides an excellent opportunity for extensive discussion of evidentiary problems, complete briefing by the lawyers, and leisurely decision making by the court. Unfortunately, it is impossible for a lawyer to anticipate all of the evidentiary issues before the trial, and without hearing the preceding evidence it is difficult for the judge to rule on admissibility. This is particularly true for matters of relevancy and hearsay, where the remainder of the evidence and the context of the offer may be determinative. Pretrial evidence rulings are most often about diagrams, models, and other physical evidence that is admitted by stipulation, or for which all the relevant evidence is ascertainable before the case is presented. If there are questions about major evidence, the pretrial conference may provide a forum for decision. If a trial is likely to turn on the statement of a deceased, for example, and there is a dead man's statute objection, the court is in a position to rule on admissibility before hearing other evidence and after reviewing the legal arguments of counsel. If you are presenting deposition testimony and need to resolve issues about the admissibility of certain testimony, or have to edit a taped deposition, this is the time. On the other hand, a hearsay objection that involves the excited utterance exception cannot be fully considered until the court hears the testimony about the circumstances of the utterance. It can be determined before trial if depositions have been taken and you can anticipate opposing counsel's proposed use of the evidence.

A motion *in limine* differs from evidentiary motions made at a pretrial conference in two important respects. The *in limine* motion, literally "at the threshold," is made as close to the beginning of the trial as the local rules and propriety will allow. The motion is properly made only if it is based upon the assertion that in addition to being inadmissible, the proposed evidence is such that the attempt to offer it in the presence of the jury will create incurable prejudice. In most jurisdictions, the motion *in limine* can be made at anytime. In some jurisdictions, local rules purport to prohibit motions *in limine* if they are not made by some specified day before trial, usually three or four. The reasons for the rule are instructive about the benefits and the dangers of the motion *in limine.*

The motion is made at the height of inconvenience for the court and opposing counsel. If raised the morning of trial, the judge must consider it while a jury panel is sitting and waiting and while valuable trial time is ticking away. Further, the judge does not have the benefit of the opponent's prepared response and is required to make a ruling on the spot. The opponent is forced to stop thinking about the opening statement, consider an evidence problem that might not be on the lawyer's radar screen and make a lucid argument before the judge rules. The judge will, despite the inconvenience, and maybe the anger, rule on the motion *in limine* because, if properly raised it is worse to put off the ruling until the matter arises at trial. The pressure on the court to hear the motion *in limine,* even in the face of a rule that requires the motion to be made earlier is the realization that it may be more time consuming and inconvenient in the long run to delay hearing it. The foundation for the motion *in limine* is the suggestion that if the evidence is offered at trial and not admitted, the offer itself will necessitate a mistrial. Even judges that do not appreciate motions *in limine* like them a lot more than the prospect of retrying a case because the jury was unduly prejudiced by an avoidable question or other offer of evidence. The mistrial possibility is what substantively differentiates the motion *in limine* from other pretrial evidentiary motions. To prevail on the motion *in limine* you must prevail upon the prejudicial nature of the offer and persuade the court that the evidence is inadmissible.

It should be obvious that the motion *in limine* is not a proper tool for just any evidentiary matter concerning an answer that might hurt a little if it comes before the jury. Measure the propriety of raising the motion by comparing the prejudice from the improper offer against the inconvenience to the court in hearing a last-minute motion that the opponent does not have time to consider. Consider whether it must be heard before voir dire or opening statement. One of two situations can occur. The testimony you believe is inadmissible might be so bad that the jury really shouldn't hear about it in opening statement or voir dire. Second, if the evidence is bad, but you are uncertain about keeping it out for the whole trial, you may need to raise it with jurors during voir dire to test their attitudes. If you have a matter that ought to be raised *in limine,* you must be sufficiently prepared to reduce the inconvenience to court, counsel, and the waiting jury. The motion should be prepared in writing, along with a short brief (no more than a page) with the main point and any evidentiary authority. Although the court may not read the motion, believing that it is more efficient to listen to your argument, do not ignore the value of the written motion. It is something that you can give to the opponent the minute you hit the courthouse, thereby reducing the court's irritation for the failure of notice without adding substantially to the opponent's ability to respond. It demonstrates to the court that you are serious about the matter, serving as a symbol that the matter cannot be brushed off without substantial risk of irreparable error. It also provides a concise outline from which to make your oral argument to the court when you, the court, and your opponent should be occupied with other matters. Your brief and presentation must demonstrate the factual prejudice that will result from the offer and the legal authority for the exclusion. You should lead off with the factual demonstration of incurable prejudice because that is what forces the court to make an immediate ruling and because it is likely to be the strongest argument. In addition, you may get partial relief from the court even if it is not persuaded that the evidence is, in fact, inadmissible.

A classic example of the subject for a motion *in limine* is an 8 x 10 color photograph of the blood and gore of an instantaneous death. The plaintiff wants it in for its revulsion value. The defendant wants it out for the same reason. Without a pain and suffering issue, and if the picture does not relate to causation or identity, the plaintiff may have difficulty admitting the picture. If the jurors see the picture during the plaintiff's opening statement, or during an attempt to lay the foundation for its admission, it will not matter that the picture is later excluded. Even if the picture has some probative value, the court is likely to prohibit the opponent from using the picture during opening statement and may require the defendant to approach the bench to warn the court and counsel before attempting to deal with the picture in any fashion. Prior to ruling the court will be required to weigh the probative value against the prejudicial effect of the photograph.

Expected oral testimony can also be the subject of a motion *in limine.* If you consider the possibility that a question which raises plaintiff's collateral sources of support, defendant's insurance, or a similar prohibited area is likely, the matter should be handled *in limine.* By considering it before trial the court can set up a protective procedure that will ensure that the matter does not sneak out before the jury. You should not be forced to object, in front of the jury to exclude evidence that both parties know is inadmissible.

Fed.R.Evid. 103(c) encourages the court, "to the extent practicable," to have evidentiary matters considered so that the process of offer and objection does not bring inadmissible matter to the jurors' attention. It provides evidentiary authority for the motion *in limine* whenever the motion is made. In some jurisdictions there are "standing" motions *in limine,* to govern matters such as insurance, other sensitive issues, or impermissible argument. You may find them on the court's website if one exists. If not, ask beforehand. Some judges have the lawyers try to reach agreement on all items first. Be prepared for a judge to grant all motions and leave it to the lawyers to follow through with approaching the bench and attempting to get the evidence introduced at the proper point during trial.

In many instances the motion *in limine* does not resolve the evidentiary issue. Fed.R.Evid 103(a) says that once the court has made a "definitive ruling on the record" counsel need not raise the matter again to protect the record, but safety concerns suggest that a lawyer who succeeds in excluding evidence *in limine* not rely at trial on the definitiveness of the court's pretrial ruling. Should the opponent attempt to offer the evidence, approach the bench and renew the objection. If you are the lawyer who has lost an *in limine* motion to admit evidence, when the time at trial to offer the evidence arrives, be sure to approach the bench and make your offer of proof—even if the *in limine* ruling excluding the evidence purported to be "definitive." There are two important reasons for rearguing the matter. The *in limine* ruling, despite court and counsels' understanding that it was "definitive," might not seem that way to an appellate court. In that event, the issue is lost for appeal. Of more practical importance, given the rarity with which trial evidentiary rulings are reversed on appeal, the judge's mind might be changed by your offer of proof in the context of the trial that was not available when the matter was decided *in limine*.

Most evidentiary advocacy occurs in the courtroom in front of the jurors because most offers of and objections to evidence cannot be handled in pretrial conferences or by motions *in limine*. Never enter a trial courtroom without your pocket-sized copy of the rules of evidence. Because you are in front of the jurors, you must consider two often conflicting objectives: prevailing on the evidence issue and presenting the best play for the jurors. You might, for example, believe that you can keep some harmful evidence out; but you might be concerned that the situation will make your objection look too unreasonable to the jurors. On the other hand, you may be offering a mildly useful piece of evidence, but be concerned about interrupting the interrogation for the long bench conference that will be needed to get the one mildly useful piece admitted. There is, unfortunately, no easy answer other than experience to the problem of knowing when to push an offer or an objection. A balancing of the effect of the evidence against interference with the presentation of the play provides a useful perspective from which to make a judgment.

Most lawyers believe that the attempt to exclude evidence from jury consideration provides the greatest risk to the advocate. It endangers the presumption of credibility and is more troublesome than defending an offer of proof. Likewise objections give jurors the opportunity to get guidance from the judge about your credibility. Throughout the trial the most influential source for the jurors, the judge, remains neutral and quiet except when an objection is lodged. Most jurors pay close attention to any real or perceived signals they believe are being sent by the way the judge treats the lawyers during objections.

Every objection to evidence begins with communication to the judge that the lawyer objects to the evidence. Objections are usually made just after the

offer, but before the receipt, of evidence. Questions
are objected to after they are completed, in order to
avoid the court's admonition, "Let counsel finish
the question!" The objection must, however, be
made before the witness has an opportunity to blurt
out the answer. No amount of "strike that from the
record," nor admonition to the jurors to disregard
can pull the information back out of the jurors'
heads. An objection can properly be made in the
middle of a question only when the question itself
contains the inadmissible evidence. Even in that
instance the court may admonish the objector to
allow the lawyer to finish the question. If the question is certain to contain the inadmissible material,
ask to approach the bench and explain to the court
that you interrupted only because you anticipate
that the damage will be done from the question, not
the answer. If the judge is knowledgeable, you will
get a ruling on the objection. Objection to physical
evidence is usually not made until the opponent
formally offers the matter into evidence. If, however, the material needs to be handled carefully to
avoid exposure to the jury before admission, it is
proper to object as soon as you see the proposed
evidence. The objection will not be to the offer, but
to the method of offer. It will be made at the bench.
Objections during trial should be made at the time
that something is objectionable. The objection could
focus on the evidence itself or the method of its
introduction. An objection in the middle of a question or before an offer of physical evidence is proper
if the inadmissible activity takes place then.

Objections to evidence must be made with precise assurance. Every objection begins with, "Objection, your honor," and is followed by the specific ground of objection, "hearsay." Make the objection from a standing position and in a voice that is loud enough to be heard by the judge and to dissuade the witness from answering the question. The objection that is made apologetically is usually not heard by the court, does not stop the witness from blurting out the answer, and makes the jurors think that the lawyer is either inept or does not believe that the objection is valid. Stand to show respect to the court and to gain control of the courtroom. Speak positively to solidify the control. The specific ground is stated because Fed.R.Evid. 103 requires the specific ground in order to preserve the point for appeal. More important, it shows the court and the jury that you know what you are doing. A side benefit is that it is impossible to say something inappropriate while stating a specific evidentiary rule of exclusion.

If you know that something is objectionable, and you are not sure of the evidentiary rule of exclusion, stand up anyway and make a firm objection, the tone of which says that the question is obviously objectionable. The court may know the reason and sustain the objection even though you do not know why. The court may ask you why the question is objectionable. If that happens, at least you will have gained another twenty seconds to think about it. If the twenty seconds have not brought the specific ground to mind, you might consider requesting a bench conference. So long as you are a beginning lawyer, you may ask the court for help when you get to the bench:

> Your honor, this evidence is very damaging to my client's cause, and it is very unfair in this context. I know that the rules of evidence reflect basic fairness and that this is unfair. Unfortunately, I cannot remember the exact grounds that exclude this evidence. I hope that the court can tell from the context of the question and the trial why this evidence is inadmissible.

You do not want to take this kind of drastic action with every garden variety objection. On the other hand, the worst that can happen is that the judge will tell you that you must try your own lawsuit. (This is one of the reasons for the rule: Never enter a trial courtroom without your pocket version of the evidence rules.)

No matter where you are in the courtroom, at counsel table or at the bench, everything that is said about evidence must be said to the judge. The court is the only one that can rule on evidence. Beginning lawyers often follow an objection with a colloquy between the lawyers—often in front of the jury. Don't do it! It not only looks bad to the jurors and wastes time; it makes judges angry and will gain you an admonishment in front of the jurors. Talk about evidence to the judge.

Once you have made your objection and stated your grounds, wait for the court's ruling. If the court does not rule, but invites a response from the offeror, you must determine whether a bench or

sidebar conference is necessary in order to avoid
having the evidence suggested to the jurors by the
nature of the offeror's response. If a sidebar seems
unnecessary and the offeror responds, look to the
judge to see if a rejoinder from you is appropriate. If
you believe that the court may have been persuaded
by the offeror's response, and the court does not
invite a rejoinder from you, you may want to ask
the court, "May I respond, your honor?"

Any evidence conversation that goes past the
stating of a specific ground for exclusion, a response
in terms of an exception to the rule of exclusion,
and a rejoinder on the inapplicability of the exception will probably require a bench or sidebar conference. The Fed.R.Evid. 103(c) suggestion that evidence discussion be outside the hearing of the jury
has encouraged bench conferences as the major tool
for handling objections at trial. In some courts, a
bench conference occurs at almost every objection,
in others, rarely. Try to determine your judge's
practice so that you know just how much the jurors
will hear. As an advocate, it is important to understand that while the bench conference keeps the
conversation from the jurors' ears, it nevertheless,
takes place in front of the jury. The jurors know
that somebody objected to evidence and that it is
important enough to take time out from the trial to
discuss. Presumably, they have inferred that it is
"hot" enough so that they cannot even be allowed
to hear it discussed, let alone see or hear the actual
evidence. In any event, it will be boring for the
jurors to sit and twiddle their thumbs while the

lawyers are huddled at the bench around the court reporter. At worst, it will increase the jurors' awareness of the evidence or cause them to speculate about the evidence in a fashion more damaging than the evidence itself. The bench conference can provide important audio shelter for sensitive matters, but because it emphasizes the process, be sure that you ask for it only when the potential danger justifies it.

If you do not want the discussion or the objection to be made in front of the jury, ask the court "May we approach the bench, your honor?" Unless you have abused the privilege, the court is likely to nod, or in some other way, assent. When you go to the bench, remember that the jurors are waiting and are either very curious or very bored. If you are presenting your case, it is in your best interest to keep the bench conference short. If the other side is presenting its case and you do not want the return from a long bench conference to highlight the proposed testimony, it is in your best interest to keep the bench conference short. In addition to being short, a bench conference must be on the record if you wish to preserve the point for appeal. Some courtrooms are designed so that bench conferences take place around the court reporter. Most courtrooms, however, are designed so that the court reporter must move to get to the bench conference. Do not start without the court reporter. If you do, there is no record for review. Court reporters hate bench conferences because everybody talks at once, at everybody, and in a whisper that cannot be distinguished from a mumble. When you get to the bench, and the court reporter is in position, tell the court succinctly why you asked for the conference. Speak with enough volume so that the court and the court reporter can hear you, but softly enough so that the jurors cannot hear you (even if you want them to). Speak slowly so that the court reporter can transcribe it, but speak with enough speed so that the bench conference does not take all day. If the matter is going to be long and involved, and you did not have the foresight to try to handle it *in limine,* ask the court for an in-chambers hearing. The in-chambers hearing avoids the possibility that the jurors will overhear the conference, and it gives them a recess, diminishing the negative aspects of the bench conference.

Evidence objections, whether they are heard in open court, at the bench, or in chambers, are usually decided in favor of the best evidence advocate. Almost all evidentiary problems are addressed to the discretion of the court as a matter of law. Because few cases are reversed for error in exclusion of evidence, and even fewer for error in admission, virtually all evidence matters are within the discretion of the court. Most beginning lawyers, unfortunately, approach evidence advocacy with the impression that every evidence problem has a "correct" solution, and that every judge will eventually see that solution. The result is that they do not make reasoned evidence arguments. The belief that if you are right the judge will rule for you and if you are wrong the judge will rule for your opponent is as misguided as the assumption that the truth alone will prevail in a lawsuit. Judges do not get paid for knowing the evidence rules; they get paid for knowing enough about evidence so that they can decide between two acceptable evidence positions argued by counsel. Just like any other decision maker, the judge is subject to influence by authority, logic, and passion. Although the method of persuasion is different from the method used with the jury, a judge rules in favor of the party that persuades. Any evidence problem that requires more than the citation of a rule and an exception, goes to the best evidence advocate.

There are some rules of evidence advocacy that are almost universal. Never say "... and it will prejudice my case" in front of a jury. If the evidence gets in, it does not need your endorsement as good evidence for the other side. Further, never say "prejudice my case" to a judge at the bench unless you are prepared to follow it immediately with a detailed factual recital of the prejudice and explanation of the effect upon the jury. "Prejudice" and "irrelevant" are buzz words that turn off judges' ears. They hear them so often from lawyers who do not have anything intelligent to say that they have grown immune to accepting them standing alone. Precise factual demonstration of the contextual problem is the key to winning any evidence argument that deals with "prejudice," "relevance," or any other objection that addresses the inadmissibility of evidence because of its context. If you merely label it as "prejudicial" or "not relevant," the judge will not listen and you will not win. The classic example is the Fed.R.Evid. 403 balance. Any lawyer who approaches the bench and tells the court that the prejudicial effect of evidence outweighs its probative value, without detailing the prejudicial effect and demonstrating why it is more important than the described probative value, receives the ruling the lawyer deserves—overruled.

Never withdraw a question, offer of evidence, or an objection. Even if it suddenly appears that you might be wrong and even if you think of nothing to say, do not withdraw. Neither the jury nor the judge will think more of you for the withdrawal. At best, it is a needless admission of defeat. At worst, you will withdraw evidence that would have been admitted or an objection that would have been sustained. Assuming that you have not offered the evidence or made the objection for an unethical reason, give it a chance once you have started. In the first place, your flash of intuition that the evidence is inadmissible or the objection unsupportable might be wrong. Secondly, the judge might get it wrong. Give the judge an opportunity to rule in your favor. The worst thing that can happen when you say nothing is that the court will rule for the other side. That is no worse than withdrawing the evidence or objection yourself.

Try to avoid long and involved responsive arguments. The judge will give you a good clue by word or action when ready to decide the matter. Once the judge has made a ruling, do not argue further unless you have new matter that the judge did not have an opportunity to consider before the ruling. "New matter" does not mean an old idea stated more succinctly. "New matter" means a new idea. The only thing worse than continuing the discussion after the judge rules against you, is continuing the discussion after the judge rules for you. For reasons that are never clear, beginning lawyers want to say more even after they have won. The danger, of course, is that you will say something that persuades the judge to change the ruling. The benefit, of course, is non-existent.

Never allow the court to avoid ruling on your objection. Trial judges are not fond of being reversed. Rulings cause reversals when they are wrong. Non-rulings never cause reversal. If a judge can get a lawyer to withdraw an objection, there is nothing to be reversed. If the judge can avoid ruling on an objection, there is not much to be reversed. If you do not hear a "sustained" or "overruled," ask the judge for a ruling. Do it politely, but insist upon a ruling. Don't be fooled by "move along counsel" or other such admonitions; they are not rulings.

Most judges will not only be happy to make a ruling, but if asked, will explain the ruling. Do not be afraid to ask the assistance of the court. If you have, for example, tried to lay a foundation for a piece of evidence, and the "foundation" objection is continually sustained, consider asking the judge what you must do to complete the foundation. You should go to the bench to ask and you ought to be sure you have done everything you can think of. If you think the foundation is there and the judge does not, ask the judge what is missing; you'll probably get an answer. You cannot afford to ask a judge to explain every ruling, but when it really counts and when you really do not understand, ask. Listen to your opponent's objections and the judge's responses or rulings for clues as to how you can correct your error.

Never conduct evidence advocacy in a fashion that will cause a judge to lose face in front of the jury. Some judges will rule quickly on objections, without giving the offeror an opportunity to respond. If you feel compelled to make a showing and attempt to reverse the ruling, be sure that you give the court an opportunity to reverse itself gracefully: "If I may, your honor, I agree with the court that the conversation might normally be hearsay, but I believe that in this instance there may be an applicable exception, may we approach the bench?" When you get to the bench, show the judge the law and explain why your anticipated response fits within that law.

The same basic courtesy is important when you lose an evidence issue. After the court has made a ruling, some lawyers say "Thank you, your honor," whether they have won or lost. The "thank you" has a couple of advantages. It is very difficult to look pained or say something that you will regret upon losing an evidence point while your mouth is saying "thank you." Secondly, it may confuse the jurors as to who prevailed on the evidence point. Some judges do not like the "thank you," because it appears as if the lawyer is thanking the judge for a favor, or trying to give the jury the impression that the judge is on the lawyer's side of the case. If you decide to use "thank you, your honor" as the end of every evidence ruling, be sure you do it after every ruling, whether you win or lose or whether you are in front of the jury or in chambers. The court will very quickly recognize that the "thank you" is an acknowledgement that the court has given you a fair hearing on the evidence issue, that you expect nothing more than a fair hearing, and that you appreciate having received one.

Two special evidence advocacy techniques require the lawyer to do something more in offering and objecting to evidence than just making or meeting an objection. Voir dire of the witness and the offer of proof are extended techniques for dealing with evidence. Voir dire of a witness is usually a technique for exclusion. Offer of proof is usually a technique for admission.

If your opponent is attempting to offer evidence through a witness, and you believe that the witness does not have the proper foundation to admit the testimony, it is proper to ask the court for permission to voir dire the witness. Typically, the request to voir dire the witness comes when an expert witness is presented and the witness is getting to the point in the testimony where the opinion will be given. If you believe that the opinion is demonstrably outside of the witness' expertise, you should interrupt the interrogation and ask the court: "Excuse me, your honor, may I voir dire the witness for the purpose of making an objection." In some jurisdictions the phrase, voir dire, has been lost and the request is simply, "May I inquire for the purpose of laying a foundation for an objection." Regardless of the phraseology, the court will allow you to interrupt the direct examination and conduct your cross-examination limited to the legitimate purpose of voir dire, to test the foundation. The voir dire need not be limited to an expert witness. A witness may be about to testify to something for which you suspect the witness has no firsthand knowledge. While the normal course is to make an objection that the witness has no firsthand knowledge or that the question calls for a response based upon hearsay, it is proper to ask to voir dire the witness rather than make an affirmation to the court of your own belief about the source of the information. If, for example, the witness was in the vicinity of an important event, is asked about what happened, and is about to respond with what somebody else said without acknowledging that the information is secondhand voir dire is an effective tool:

Q: Mr. Sheffey, you were at the corner of Fifth and Izard at 5:00 p.m. weren't you?

A: Yes.

Q: At the time of the collision you were looking away from the intersection towards a friend walking toward you on Fifth, isn't that right?

A: Yes.

Q: You did not see the collision did you?

A: No.

Q: Anything that you could tell us about what you think happened would be something that someone else told you they thought happened, isn't that right?

A: Yes.

Although you are likely to get the same ruling as you would have had you explained at sidebar that you thought the witness was about to testify to hearsay, the objection and assertion approach might get you a "let's wait and see what he says," response from the judge. The voir dire approach allows you to control what the witness says, and lessens the chance that the witness will blurt out a response that is based upon hearsay, before it is apparent to the court. No amount of striking and admonishing by the court can bring you back to even. Voir dire allows you to protect yourself.

In addition, voir dire can be a valuable tool of persuasion. If for example, your attack on an expert witness is going to aim at the questionable nature of the expert's field of expertise, such as personality description from handwriting analysis, the foundational challenge in the middle of the direct examination may be very effective. If the court ultimately allows the opinion, the challenge to the weight of it through voir dire may be more effective than through the use of cross-examination after the expert's opinion is before the jurors. Even in *Daubert* jurisdictions, where major challenges to an expert's core qualifications must be raised by motion to the judge, voir dire is still a useful tool for insuring that the expert's opinion falls within the expert's qualifications. Your opponent might try to stretch the expert's area of acceptable expertise or the "science" of the expert in general. An emergency room doctor, for example, is perfectly qualified to discuss aspects of care rendered while the patient was in an emergency room, but would not be qualified to render an opinion on whether the cardiologist followed the standard of care in the Coronary Care Unit. Identification techniques that were once "accepted" without question in many courts have come under scientific attack since *Daubert*. Hair, fiber, and handwriting analysis, once considered almost the equivalent of fingerprint identification, have been excluded in some courts. In those courts where they are still permitted as methods for excluding possibilities, experts are not allowed to claim they are identifiers. (Indeed, even fingerprints are being challenged in some quarters.) Voir dire presents an option for making those challenges and limitations in the middle of the opponent's direct examination of the expert. Whether that is better than waiting for cross-examination to challenge or limit the "science" is a matter of feel at trial. Voir dire gives you the flexibility to choose whichever persuasive approach you prefer. It is important to keep voir dire limited to the purpose for which the judge allowed you to interrupt. If you abuse the privilege, and attempt to put your entire cross-examination in the middle of your opponent's direct, the court is likely to sit you down with an admonition that will not put you in the best light with the jurors.

The offer of proof is a tool for gaining the admission of evidence and protecting the record when the offer is rejected. It should be used when the court sustains an objection to anything that you want to put before the jury such as a witness, a particular question, or a piece of physical evidence. Not every refusal to allow evidence justifies an offer. It is a somewhat cumbersome procedure and should be saved for the times when the evidence is critical to your presentation or when you believe that the ruling is a likely foundation for appellate reversal.

After an objection has been sustained or any ruling has been made that prohibits you from presenting something, it is proper to ask to approach the bench. If for some reason the court does not grant permission, tell the court that it is for the purpose of making an offer of proof. There are two customary methods for making the offer. The most common involves a recitation of the proof by the lawyer. Some situations, however, merit presentation of the offer through the witness.

If the offer is to be made by the lawyer, it should be made at the bench in the presence of the judge and the court reporter. If they are missing, there is no offer (judges will frequently tell lawyers they can make the offer during a recess, that's why you need to make sure the judge is present to rule and the court reporter is there to make the record). The offer of proof begins with the lawyer identifying the question or other presenting vehicle to which objection was sustained. Generally, a brief recitation of the lawyer's position on the law follows the identification of the challenged ruling. Next, the evidence that would have been produced, but for the ruling, is set forth in detail. It is important to include all of the critical points of the evidence that would follow, in addition to any further evidence for which the excluded evidence provides a foundation in fact or law. Finish with a brief description of why the testimony is important to the case.

The complete recitation of the proposed evidence and its importance to the case accomplishes two goals. It forces the court to give additional thought to the ruling in the context of knowing the evidence and its importance; and it provides the reviewing court with some idea of the weight of the error, if the exclusion is error. Your first goal is to persuade the trial court to allow the evidence. That is why the offer needs to occur while you still have the ability to call or recall the witness. Evidentiary matters rarely provide grounds for reversal, but it is critical that the reviewing court know exactly what prejudice was suffered by the exclusion. If the reviewing court is forced to speculate because the lawyer did not make an adequate offer of proof, the trial court will be upheld.

Do not underestimate the effect of the offer on the trial court. Not every sustained objection is followed by an offer of proof, but the offer tells the trial court that this particular evidentiary problem is important. This is something that the court was probably not aware of when it made its initial ruling. An effective offer not only gives the court time to reconsider the matter in light of the knowledge that the lawyer is very serious about the issue, but it provides a foundation upon which the court can change its mind without losing face. The offer also provides the court with a more pointed reminder of the possibility of reversal.

The offer of proof at the bench ought to be conducted quickly. If the matter is too extensive for bench treatment, consider asking for an in-chambers hearing. Unless you are certain that the court will not change the ruling, and that you will remember to make the offer later, do not allow the court to forestall the offer by suggesting that it can be done in chambers during the next break. Insist that the presentation of your case depends upon the admission of the evidence, and that you believe the court ought to hear the offer now in the event that the offer persuades the court to change the ruling.

If the evidence is of the kind that is critical to the case, consider making the offer of proof by eliciting the testimony outside the hearing of the jury. All of the reasons for conducting an offer of proof are more sharply served when the actual testimony is presented to the court. The procedure takes time, however, and ought to be reserved for only the most important issues. Usually the offer will take place in the courtroom, with the jurors being excused to the jury room. In some jurisdictions, the matter is concluded in chambers. If the testimony is presented in chambers, be sure that the court reporter is there, that the witness is sworn, and that in all other respects the offer is conducted exactly as if it were during the trial in the courtroom. When you are opposing an offer of proof, make sure you point out any defects in the testimony being offered. Your job is to make the judge feel comfortable with the original ruling and to demonstrate that the testimony does not warrant a reversal.

The lawyer's part has some lines that do not deal with evidence, and that should never be spoken in front of the jurors. Motions for directed verdict at the end of the plaintiff's case and at the conclusion of the evidence, settling of instructions, and objections to instructions are matters that the lawyer must attend to in shaping the case and preserving the record. Unless you have some reason to believe that it will help you if the jurors know the court denied your motion for directed verdict—an impossibility—be sure that these lines from the lawyer's part are spoken at the bench or in chambers.

The lawyer's part is a very small part as far as the jurors are concerned. There is little that the lawyer can do in saying the lines of the lawyer's part that will positively influence the jurors, although there is much the lawyer can do in delivering those same lines that can hurt the case with the jurors. The lawyer's part, in the main, is directed at the court and the opposing counsel. The way that the lawyer's part is played can have a great effect on the outcome of the case because of the influence it can have on the court's rulings and the opponent's activities.

The lawyer's part must be played to the court and opposing counsel with precision, authority, persuasion, logic, and with a constant awareness of ethics.

There is very little "how to do it" value in ethics and a full discussion of the subject of trial ethics is beyond the scope of this primer. Every lawyer should understand, however, that in the long run there is no aspect of the lawyer's part at trial that is more important than ethics. How both the court and counsel approach you and your case will depend in large part upon their view of your ethics. While ethical lawyers receive no accolades from judges and lawyers, unethical lawyers enter the courtroom with a suspicious judge and an opponent prepared to defend by striking the first decisive blow. Your first trial is not likely to be your last. You will win or lose that trial because of your case and your talent. Your reputation as an honorable trial advocate must be built and rebuilt with every case. A reputation as a cheat, on the other hand, can be created in one trial, and will live with you forever. It is never worth the price of a single case. The minute you cheat, you tell the opponent that the gloves are off. Chances are that lawyer has been punching longer and has learned more tricks than you have. If your duty to yourself will not control your conduct, remember that the other lawyer may "whup" you. Remember, most lawyers now practice in firms and you will have not just made an enemy of that lawyer but every lawyer in their firm and all of their friends! That's a lot of enemies waiting to pounce on your every misstep or to deny you the extension you so desperately need.

The adversary system depends upon the honor of lawyers.

CHAPTER 11

LAST SCENE: THE CLOSING ARGUMENT

Just before the judge instructs the jury on the law, and in a few fortunate jurisdictions, just after the judge has instructed the jury, the lawyers make closing arguments. Even though we know jurors start making tentative decisions early, a close case often turns on the success of the last act. Of course we would love to begin the closing argument knowing that all the jurors are in our corner, but it rarely happens that way. Because dramatists unreasonably emphasize the closing argument and many beginning lawyers believe that a great closing can rescue an awful case, we start this discussion of closing arguments with a reminder that good evidence is more important than a good closing argument. While there is little doubt that a better case will generally prevail over a better closing argument, many cases that go to trial are close on either liability or damages and are prepared and presented well. In those cases the closing argument that most influences the jurors' discussion of their perceptions is likely to carry the day.

The lawyer's approach to the closing argument given at the end of the trial is different from the approach to the first draft of the closing, constructed as the early guide to the case. Although the closing argument actually delivered builds on the initial draft's analysis, the lawyer's concern in creating the closing argument is for the persuasive form it will take. The first draft closing argument and the notes generated during preparation and trial will provide all the substantive ideas for the argument. Your closing argument has been rumbling around in your head (and heart) since you first took on the case. Even if you had no real choice in this particular case your close is why you chose to become a prosecutor, plaintiff or defense lawyer. Now is the time to pull together all of the inferences you hoped the jury "got" as the evidence developed. All the arguing that you wanted to do in your opening statement you can do now. If you have prepared your case and followed the suggestions in the way you have tried the case, worry less about what to tell the jury and work on how best to tell it. It is time to motivate those jurors to take immediate action to answer the judge's charge to the jury in your client's favor.

There are few universally useful techniques for closing argument, but no area of trial advocacy is burdened with more "standard" suggestions. Closing argument is pure persuasion, and every good advocate has an idea about and a personal faith in a particular method of persuasion. You know you can persuade. You have either decided to take Trial Advocacy in law school because you can imagine yourself a trial lawyer or you are in practice and have persuaded someone into being a client. Lead from your strength whatever it is and don't worry about being anyone other than your most persuasive self in the courtroom. Your personal style will be better than any attempt at emulating someone else or following some cookbook recipe for instant closing argument. Closing argument is the uniquely personal part of the play for the trial lawyer. The success of the closing will depend more upon how effectively the advocate's personality is projected towards the jurors than upon any other single factor. Because most of the "standard" suggestions are a successful trial lawyer's attempt to universalize what works best for that lawyer's particular method of communicating to the jurors, they are unlikely to help the beginning lawyer. "Always thank the jurors for their attention," is a typical example of the "standard" suggestion that no beginning lawyer can afford to uncritically insert into a closing argument. For some lawyers, it is natural, projects true gratitude, and endears them to the jurors. For others, it is plugged in, projects nothing, and is considered condescending or phony by the jurors. At this point in the trial the jurors have probably gotten to know you, so be yourself. If you are passionate, now is the time to show some emotion. If you are quiet, show some intensity in the way you are most comfortable. It is useful to read about closing arguments and see what others have done, but, do not use an idea or someone's "standard" suggestion unless you understand the persuasive reason for the suggestion and can articulate why it will work for you.

Closing argument is a distinct and specific part of the trial and your advocacy should be as well. The jurors are focused on their decision task that has been looming ahead since voir dire began. They are about to deliberate and answer very specific questions. What is the easiest and best help you can give them? Give them the answers. You know the specific questions the judge will submit to the jury in the verdict form. The central structure of your argument works around the judge's charge to the jury. Organize the discussion of your theory and theme around the answers to the questions. Put the critical questions or definitions up on paper or the whiteboard so that you can write down the answer as you are telling the jurors why the evidence supports that finding. Using the charge as your argument outline also makes it easy to engage the jurors without using notes. Take a few minutes before you begin your close to organize your big exhibits or demonstrative evidence and use them to supplement your argument. Lining up your props makes it easy to focus on the jury and to talk to them without written notes because your props are your notes. Structure your argument and answers to the critical charge questions in the way that best helps you. You do not have to follow the questions in order and neither do the jurors. If you are the defendant and causation is the heart of your case, start there and encourage the jurors to do the same when they retire to the jury room. Use the language of the charge where it really helps you. Since it is the court's charge, not yours, you can use the imprimatur of the judge on issues like the burden of proof, sympathy, or circumstantial evidence. This is not an invitation to read key phrases to the jurors, but to persuade them with vivid and concrete examples or analogies. Re-reading the definition of the burden of proof does not make it any more understandable to jurors trying to decide whether to convict a defendant. Find an analogy; think of concrete examples. Maybe it is that nagging feeling as you lay in bed at night wondering, "Did I lock the front door?" or the uneasiness in your stomach before you signed for a mortgage to explain reasonable doubt; or the story of Robinson Crusoe discovering footprints on the sand of his deserted island to explain circumstantial evidence. Whatever your key definitions or instructions, find specific ways to help your jurors understand how they apply to the case. Make sure you cover all of the key elements of the case such as damages and liability. Don't assume that the jurors know how you want them to answer the questions. Tell them!

This is not the time to adopt the "summation" approach to closing argument. No fact or law should be presented to the jury in closing argument unless you have and state an argument that the fact or law supports. The closing is not a summary, it is an argument. To be effective, it must be organized and constructed on points of logic and conclusion, rather than on facts or law presented. Once the argumentative structure is in place, the lawyer selects the facts and law to be rehearsed in the closing as support for the arguments presented.

Who are you talking to on the jury? At this point you have jurors that are for you, maybe some against you and maybe some undecided. As you persuade, be conscious of giving the jurors who are already with you ammunition to use when they get to the jury room. If you have not persuaded those undecided or against you by the time you sit down, it is your favorable jurors who will take up your mantle in the jury room. They will have to complete the work you started, so give them all the help you can. Your job is to give the jurors a logical and emotional reason to find for your client. The logical we get, the emotional seems harder. Everyone in the courtroom "knows" that the decision cannot be based on sympathy, yet every human also "knows" that every decision in some way starts in the "gut." We don't buy cars, or houses only on the paper. Few of us left for college or law school without looking at pictures of the campus. We have jury trials precisely because the case could not be decided on motions. Motivating jurors to "want" to find for your client does not mean manufacturing false emotional ploys. In fact emotional deception is the easiest to detect and has the most adverse consequences. Great actors enable us to feel our emotions through them, instead of us watching them "act." While you have to show some emotion to get some, it is not your outrage that will fuel the jurors but their own. You need empathy not sympathy. Point out specific, concrete, vivid images of the evidence to illustrate your points—the mother with a back injury that will never let her pick up a young child again; the father whose injury means he will not be able to walk his daughter down the aisle; the hard working small business person who is locking the doors to a business for the last time. The jury has seen the witnesses and heard them testify. The emotional groundwork has been laid, so the closing does not need to be heavy handed. Even when you are a defendant, embrace the emotions rather than ignoring them or trying to run away from them. Genuinely acknowledge how sad the situation might be, but diffuse it and refocus the jury back to the real issues in the case.

For most young lawyers the primary concern is less about what to say, but the pressure of how to say it. Some of the concern about picking the perfect phrase, making the right gesture, and following the formula for a successful argument is the result of the misapprehension that the jurors must like the lawyer's performance. Closing argument is not the showpiece of the lawyer's part. The lawyer is not center stage, the client's case is. The distinction is not merely semantic. If the jurors believe, at the end of your closing argument, that you have done a magnificent job, you have not accomplished much. If, on the other hand, the jurors believe that any lawyer could win with a case as good as the one your client gave you, then you have done something. The jurors' impressions must be about the case, not the lawyer. The only impression about the lawyer that should be left with the jurors is that the lawyer believes in the client's cause. As with most things in trial, the lawyer can only accomplish that indirectly. It is both unethical and unpersuasive for the lawyer to make an explicit statement of belief in the client's cause. It is, however, imperative that the lawyer's manner of presentation clearly demonstrate belief in the propriety of the argument that the lawyer presents for the client.

Closing argument answers the question: Why? Evidence presents the "what" to the jury, the court tells the jury "how" to deal with the evidence according to law, and the lawyer tells the jury "why" the lawyer's client should win. The theme of your client's cause ought to be the centerpiece for your closing argument. Whether you wish to think of it as the backbone, the keel, the center, or whatever image strikes your fancy, the theme ought to run from the beginning to the end of the closing argument. It serves as the reference point to which you return after every argumentative excursion about a particular piece of evidence or point of law. If you started your case with your theme and used it to construct each direct and cross-examination, it should flow easily during your closing argument. In our trade secret case for example, our theme of theft was used in voir dire to identify jurors who might have personal experience with having something of value, even an idea stolen from them. In opening: "The most valuable property XYZ Corp had wasn't its furniture or equipment, it was an idea." Now in close: "Copy Corp didn't just steal something out of a safe. They didn't steal something like a stereo that could be easily replaced. They stole what mattered most to XYZ; they stole their ideas, their dreams. Every child in kindergarten knows that we cannot take something that doesn't belong to us, theft is theft, stealing is stealing."

The entire tone of the closing should be positive because the argument tells the jurors "why" your client should prevail. This is a most difficult task for beginning lawyers who, if not beguiled into making the closing a summation, are tempted to argue with the opponent by telling the jurors why the opponent should not win. Even in the "no defense" criminal defense, where the prosecution has the entire burden of proof beyond a reasonable doubt the closing argument ought to begin with and be framed in the positive terms of the defense case. Consider how useless it is to begin a concentrated attack on the failure of the government's proof without having first persuaded the jury that the most important issue in the case is the vindication of the system of justice and the maintenance of a strict standard of proof engaged to guarantee individual freedom. In civil cases, whether you or your opponent has the burden of proof, you should always tell your story first, and argue with your opponent's second. If you are motivating jurors to take action, answer questions favorably and equip your jurors with ammunition, a negative attack is not going to be very useful. Consider that one of the oldest tactics of the accomplished trial advocate is to get the other side to talk about what is wrong with the advocate's case, rather than what is good about its own. The party with rebuttal has even more reason and more opportunity to avoid starting the initial argument by talking about the other side's case.

The positive approach is best even when knocking the other side's case. If you are making a major attack on the opponent's occurrence witness, couch it in terms of the credibility of your own occurrence witness. If you discuss the unbelievable witness as a contrast to your believable witness or physical facts, you make the argumentative point without running the risk that you will appear to the jurors to be picking on the unbelievable witness. After all, the reason that you point out the failings of another's witness is usually so that the jurors will believe yours. The positive approach of selling your witness' credentials and contrasting them with those of the opponent's incredible witness adds weight to your witness while subtracting weight from the opponent's. The former is as important as the latter. The same approach works for discussing your opponent's theory of the case. Knock it by the unfavorable comparison to your case. Demonstrate its weaknesses in the context of the strength of your own theory. If your theory of defense is failure to yield, and the plaintiff's theory of recovery is failure to maintain a lookout, discuss the inapplicability of the plaintiff's theory in the context of failure to yield, rather than attacking the theory without first setting out your explanation of the occurrence.

There isn't much "law" of closing argument, but there are a few rules to remember. The party carrying the burden of proof at the end of the case goes first and has the rebuttal, last word. (A change should only have occurred if a motion for directed verdict was granted, disposing of claims.) You must "fully open" which requires at least touching on the major issues in the case, such as both liability and damages. Of course you will want to save ample time to rebut the defendant's close and save your best ammunition for the very last words the jury will hear from you. The defendant needs to anticipate the rebuttal and may even make specific reference to the fact that, "Mr. Goldberg will get the last word with you. I won't be able to respond, but when he starts tugging on your heart strings ask yourself: What does the evidence really show? What would Ms. McCormack have to say about that?" The "Golden Rule" prohibits lawyers from asking jurors to put themselves in the place of one party or the other. In many jurisdictions you cannot tell the jurors the effect of their answers to the charge; i.e., "if you put 51% or more on this line, Mrs. Injured won't get anything." As is true for opening statement, you should try not to object to your opponent's closing argument unless absolutely necessary and unless you will win the objection. Be forewarned that most objections that counsel is "misrepresenting" the evidence get met with non-rulings from the judge such as: "The jury will remember the evidence".

When you deliver the closing argument, remember that the jurors are as tired at the end of the play as you are at the end of this book. Knowing that the end is near heightens the impatience. Deliver your closing argument from the intensity with which you tried the case, make your points, consider thanking the jurors for their attention, and then sit down when it is finished.

†